The Story of
FINSTALL

The Story of FINSTALL

The 1640s to the 1940s

Jennie McGregor-Smith

BREWIN BOOKS

Published in 2018 by Brewin Books

Brewin Books
56 Alcester Road,
Studley,
Warwickshire,
B80 7LG
www.brewinbooks.com

© Jennie McGregor-Smith 2018

The author has asserted her rights in accordance with the Copyright, Designs and Patents Act 1988 to be identified as the author of this work.

All rights reserved. No part of this publication may be reproduced, stored in a retrieval system, or transmitted in any form or by any means, electronic, mechanical, photocopying, recording or otherwise, without the prior permission in writing of the publisher and the copyright owners, or as expressly permitted by law, or under terms agreed with the appropriate reprographics rights organization. Enquiries concerning reproduction outside the terms stated here should be sent to the publishers at the UK address printed on this page.

The publisher makes no representation, express or implied, with regard to the accuracy of the information contained in this book and cannot accept any legal responsibility for any errors or omissions that may be made.

A CIP catalogue record for this book is available from the British Library.

ISBN: 978-1-85858-588-8

Printed and bound in Great Britain
by Page Bros Ltd.

Contents

Acknowledgements vii
Introduction ix
  1. Finstall Heath 1
  2. The Civil War 6
  3. The Early Days of Finstall Farm 11
  4. The Brettell Family in Finstall House 16
  5. The Ellins Family and Rigby Hall 23
  6. The Albrights, Finstall Farm and the Village Hall 28
  7. Finstall Heath and The Cross 41
  8. Finstall Park Estate from the 1850s 51
  9. The Oakalls and Hopgardens Farm 61
10. Grimley Hall 70
11. The Stud Farm and Penmanor 76
12. Pikes Pool: Fishing Pond or Waterworks? 82
13. Rigby Hall after the Ellins 88
14. Dusthouse Lane: Finch End to the Dusthouse 96
15. Slideslow and Caspidge Farms .112
16. Finstall Vale: Fairways and Scotch House 123
17. Walnut Lane 131
18. Finstall Hill 136
19. Back Lane or Finstall Road 146
20. The Tutnall and Vigo Connections 150
21. Wartime in Finstall 156
22. "Our Village in the 1920s" 165
Appendix: Abstract of Title 177
Bibliography 180
Index 182

For Graham and Heather,
who grew up in Finstall,

and John who lived in
Finstall for 53 years.

Acknowledgements

Much of the information has come from The Hive at Worcester, Birmingham Library Archives and a little from Stratford-upon-Avon Shakespeare Trust archives. I've not given the reference numbers for these files as they would fill the book! *The Bromsgrove Rousler* magazine has been very helpful, having printed numerous articles that relate to Finstall. Several other books were invaluable, including Alan White's *A Hundred Years in Tardebigge* and Margaret Dickens' *A Thousand Years in Tardebigge*. The ability nowadays to search old newspapers online has been extremely useful, and there have been many websites that added information. Other books are listed in the Bibliography.

I am most grateful for generous financial support from the Bromsgrove Society.

Kate Shaw did much proof reading, as did Joyce Egremont, Sonia French and John McGregor-Smith, and all need special thanks.

Many people have spent time with me and I am very grateful, and apologise for not being able to include everything I was told. Please forgive me if I have left off someone who has helped. The people I am most grateful to are: Michelle Atkins, Alan Baker, Peter Baker, Doreen Baylis, Rev. Wyn Beynon, Neville Billington, Tony Blake, Mary Brettell in Australia, Jackie Cater, Jane & Terry Critchley, Margaret & Paul Evans, Jill Findon, Marie Forsyth, Andy Frisby, Paul Glover, Alan Greatwood, Graham Hall, Neville Hancock, Emma Hancox, Jean & Philip Harper, Andrew Harris, Patricia Hinton, Topsy Hobbs who started me off with Finstall stories, Emily Horton, Matthew Horton, Julian Hunt, Peter Kooner, Institute of Mechanical Engineers, Chris Milton, David Myers, Rob Oldaker, Steve Orr-Cooper, Jim Page, Christopher Pancheri, John & Pamela Phillips, Peter Poole, Stephen Price, Sylvia & Bob Richardson, Fran Rogers, Rosemarie Ryan, Mike Sharpe, Isabel Singleton, John Suffield, Pat Tansell, Murray Thomson in Canada, Nikki Thorpe of Bromsgrove School, Jenny Townshend, V&A Images, Dave Webb, Karron Weston, Ann Wheeler, Robin Whittaker, Zilla Wildridge and J & J Wilson.

* * * *

Population: In Finstall parish in 1848 there were thought to be 120 families. In the 1881 census there were 997 people, and in 1951 there were 2,946. These are very much guesstimates, but give you some idea of how the area grew. The railway and wagon works and easier travel brought a lot of people to live in Finstall and Aston Fields, while house building after WWII really changed the place.

Illustrations: Reproduction of old postcards and the author's own images have not been credited. Many photographs have been generously lent by people to whom I am most grateful. Images from the following have been indicated by initials as shown below:

BA   Birmingham Archives
BC   Brotherton Collection, Bromsgrove
WRO Worcestershire Record Office

Wages: The yearly wages of labourers were about £18 in the 18th century; in 1914 weekly wages were roughly 16s 9d, though they went up during the war to 36s. By August 1920 the minimum wage was about 46s 7d per week.

Money: Before 1971 money was divided into: pounds (£), shillings (s. or /-) and pence (d.). One shilling = 5p; a florin = 2 shillings = 10p; a guinea = £1.1.0 = one pound and 10p.

Measurements: Acres, Roods, Perches. An acre originally was as much as a team of oxen could plough in a day. The length of the acre (the furrow-long, or furlong) was as far as the team can plough without needing a breather. The width was the number of furrows that could be ploughed before the oxen had to be put out to pasture for the day. At least as early as the 8th century an acre was a piece of land 40 perches long by 4 perches. A rood is a quarter of an acre, a perch is $30¼$ square yards. There are 2.47 acres in a hectare.

Introduction

This book, though concentrating on what we know as Finstall, also includes parts of Bromsgrove, Burcot, Tutnall and Tardebigge when land ownership crossed the boundaries, but equally *doesn't* include one or two areas which might well be regarded, either now or in the past, as Finstall. Because my previous book *From Bromsgrove to Aston Fields* covers the growth of Aston Fields and its wagon works, railway, school and church, there is little about these subjects in this book, neither have I even mentioned the canal, which of course was fully covered by Alan White's important book. Neither have I gone much further back than the Civil War, nor gone much further forward than WWII.

Throughout the book I use names and words according to how they were spelled at the time in the original – i.e. Lickhaye, or Casbridge/Caspidge, or Featherston/Fetherstone. In 1255 Lickey was written as 'la Lecheye', and meant 'cleared forest'. Some things were extremely confusing. Finstall Farm was the name of three different farms at different times; several buildings changed their names, as did Finstall Hall/Park/House; people moved about from one cottage to another. And during the time of Ellins, Brettells, Brooks, Smallwood, and Albright, they were forever buying and selling bits of land to and from each other, making it very confusing for this writer.

I was interested in the number of Quakers and industrialists who came into the village, most of them moving from Birmingham. I have been shocked by some of the things I've read, such as the 13 year old boy who was committed to Worcester gaol for a month, and afterwards sent to a reformatory for *five years*, for stealing 3lbs of cheese and 2lb of bread (1878); or George Taylor who was drunk in Finstall, and fined 2s 6d plus 8 shillings costs, or seven days hard labour. You would have had to be very well off in 1881 to be able to afford to pay that fine.

Irene Brake's description of the village in the 1920s makes a good ending; her friends and neighbours really come alive, and I hope you enjoy her writing.

Finally, please forgive the inevitable mistakes.

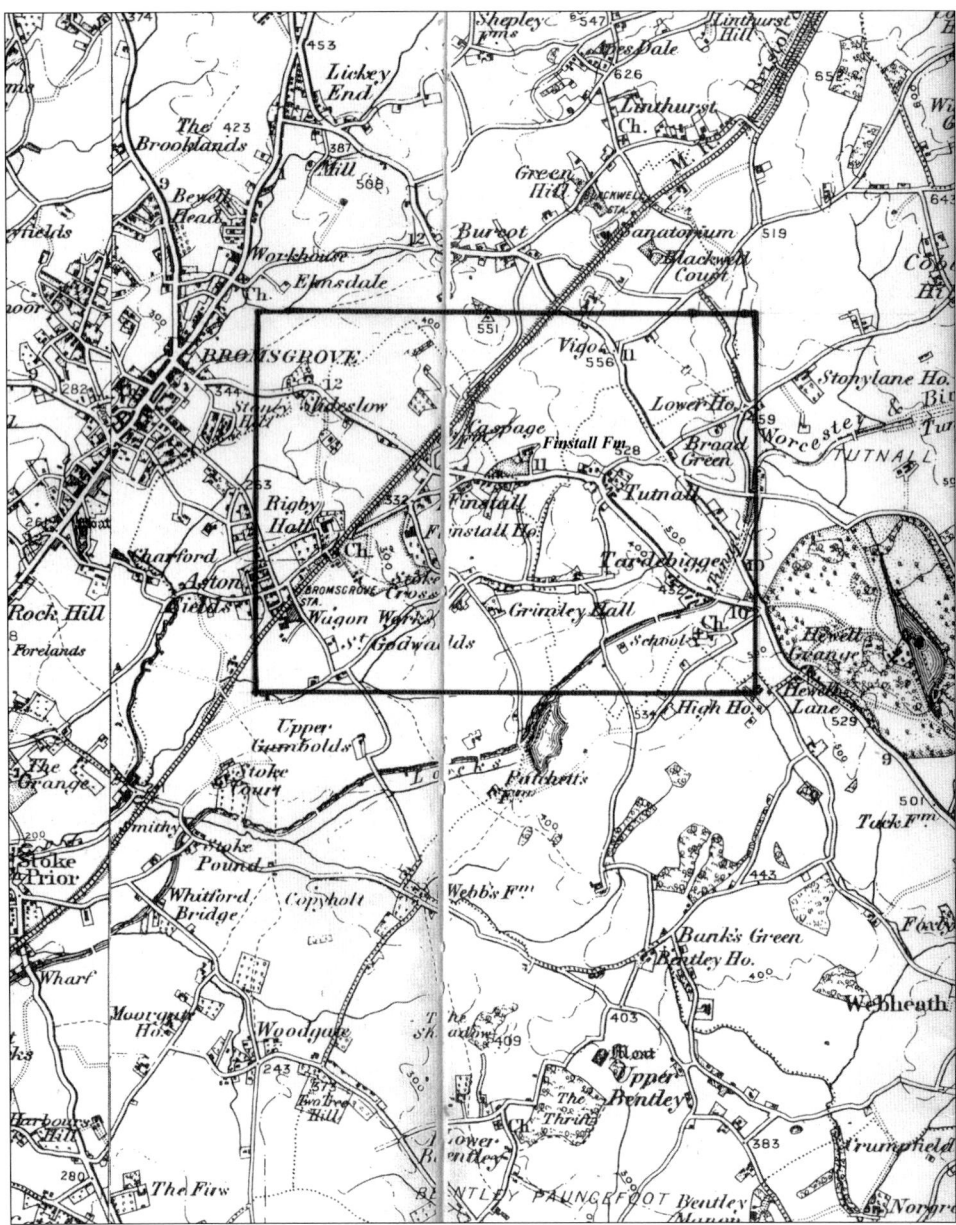

From a map published in 1895, to show the area covered in this book.

Chapter One

Finstall Heath

Finstall was named as Finstall Heath on early maps, which gives an indication of what it was like. The Episcopal Register of 1295 calls it Vinstalstude 'a place for heaping wood', 'fin' meaning a heap of wood, 'staell' meaning place. This seems logical, but later, and more unlikely, historians suggest that 'fina' meant a woodpecker, or that the Anglo-Saxon 'finc' was a finch.

Finstall Heath was thought to be within Feckenham Forest, which in 1629 during the reign of Charles I had been officially disafforested. Much of the Forest area was already denuded of trees, primarily because of the salt pans at Droitwich, which needed wood for boiling and evaporating the brine from the salt springs. Humphreys described it as 'a territory of waste lands, moors and heaths, and open commons with bogs and marshlands besides, and throughout the area there were numerous woods in which the game harboured.'[1]

The Domesday Survey of 1086 tells us that the manor of Bromsgrove owned thirteen salt pans and three salinarii (boilers of the salt), which rendered annually 300 mittas or measures of salt, for which three hundred cartloads of wood were required. Leland, in the 1530s, said this wood came from Worcester, Bremis-grove, Alchirch and Alcester, while Cox's Worcestershire in 1720 says the fuel needed was 'antiently wood but now they use Pit-coal', and that they now clarify 'their brine with White of Eggs'.

The iron industry that was building up to the north east of Bromsgrove, in what would become Birmingham and the Black Country, would also have helped to speed up destruction of the forest, though the Lickey hills remained forested at least until the 1680s. In 1665 Dud Dudley[2] described the destruction of timber in the north of the county for providing wood for the preparation of charcoal and manufacture of iron. He said:

> Within ten miles of Dudley Castle there be neer 20,000 Smiths of all sorts, and many Iron works at that time, within that Circle decayed for want of Wood (yet formerly a mighty Woodland Country).

Thus many Finstall trees would also have been cut down over the years and sent towards

---

1   J. Humphreys, *Studies in Worcester History*, 1938, Cornish Brothers, Birmingham.
2   Quotation from *Metallum Martis*, Dud Dudley, in R.C. Gaut's *History of Worcestershire Agriculture and Rural Evolution*, 1939, which provides splendid background on the county from earliest times until the 20th century.

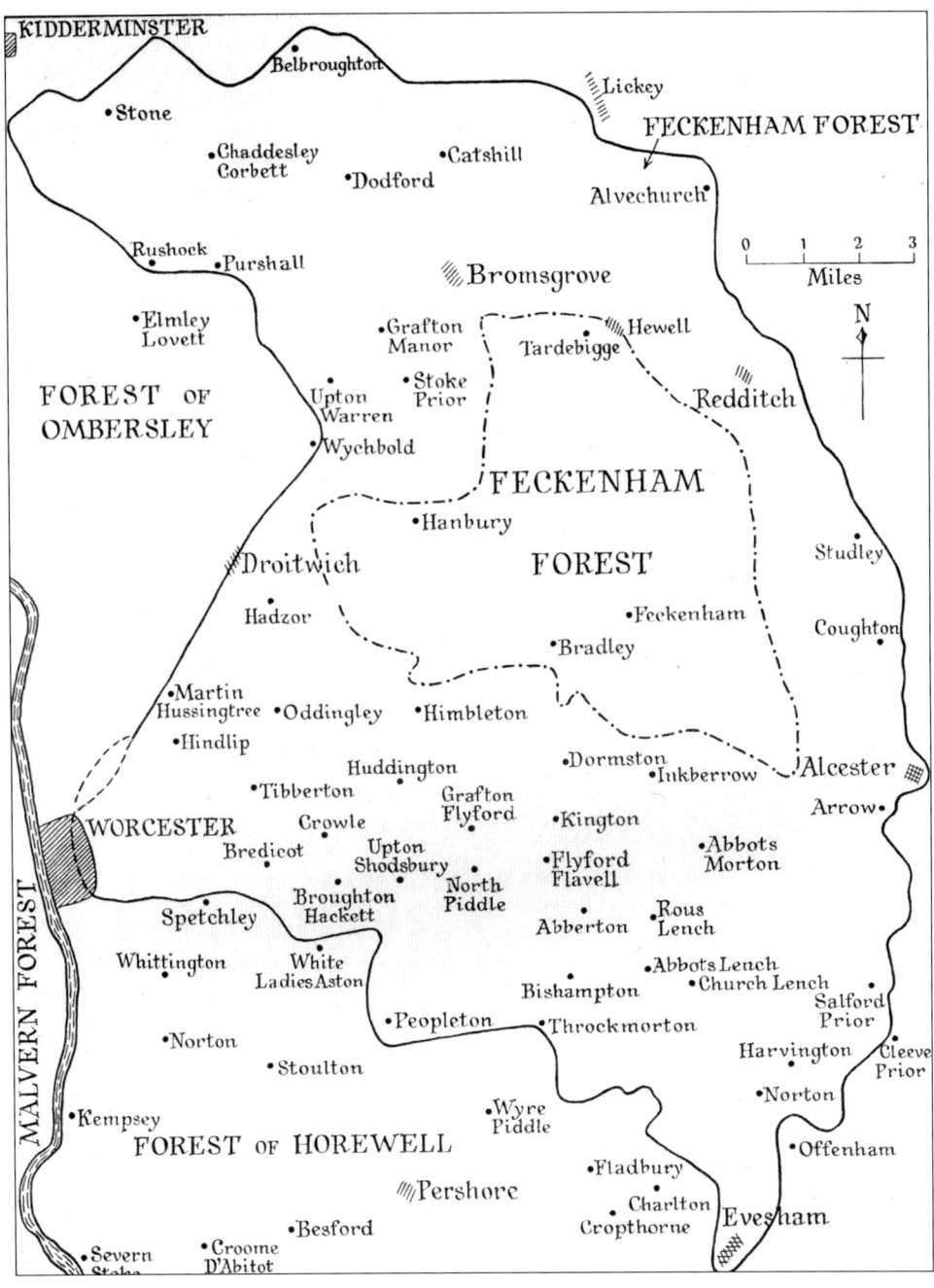

Feckenham Forest as drawn for John Humphreys of Bromsgrove (1850-1936), who not only became Professor of Dentistry at Birmingham University but became a respected historian and naturalist.

1. Finstall Heath

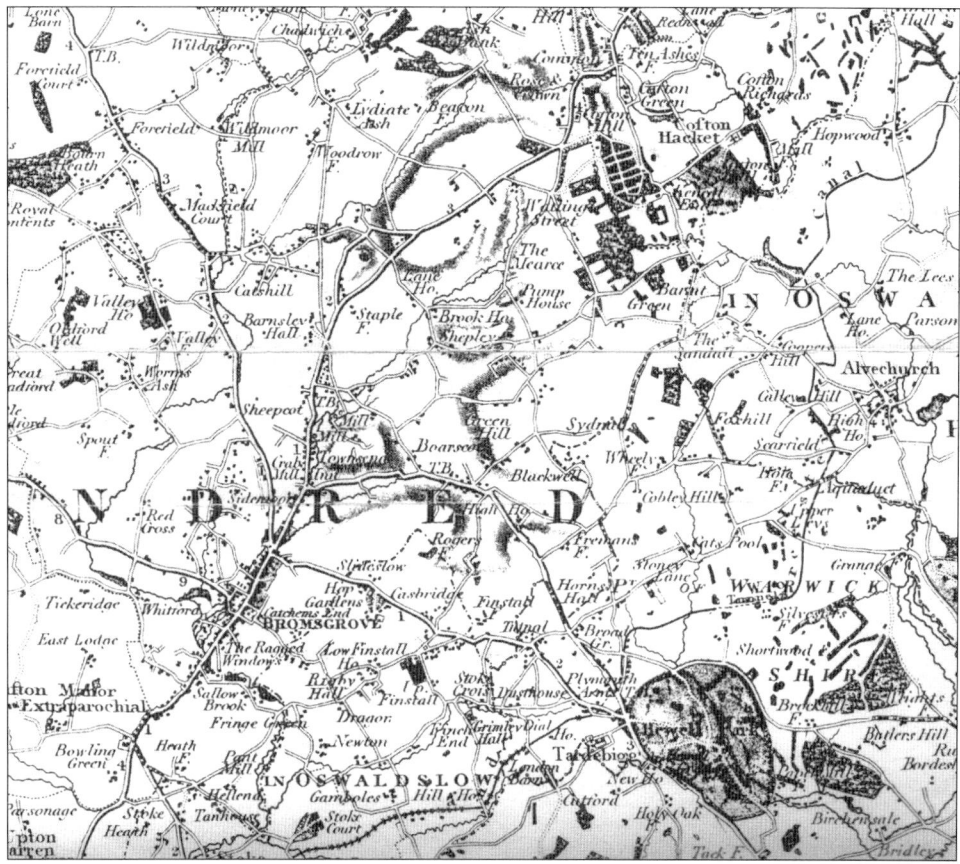

1822 map surveyed after the canal was built but before the railway. Finstall is marked above the site of Finstall Farm, Finstall House is marked as Up. Finstall, and Rigby Hall is shown. The Rose & Crown on the Lickey hills is at the top, just right of centre. (Bromsgrove Library)

the Birmingham plateau, and to Droitwich. The wagons on their return journey from Droitwich brought the much needed salt. This had huge value because it was used when tanning leather, and also in butchery, for at Michaelmas meat was laid down in casks of brine for the winter, there always being a shortage of cattle feed during the cold months. The result for Feckenham Forest was loss of trees, leaving waste lands, heathland, bogs and marshlands with occasional spots of woodland left to protect the game.

After the Commonwealth the forest laws fell into disuse, and the land largely passed into the possession of Worcestershire yeomen and smallholders. This borderland was gradually taken into cultivation with small fields and enclosed crofts, while local people, before the Enclosure Act of 1772, were using common lands for grazing, and – for a fee – allowing their pigs into the remaining woodland to forage for acorns and beechnuts.

Finstall was at the north of the Stoke (Prior) manor, belonging, when surveyed in 1086 for the Domesday book, to the Church in Worcester. Stoke then had a total population of 13 villagers, these being 7 smallholders, 4 slaves, 1 female slave and 1 priest.[3] Stoke manor remained in the possession of the priory until 1540, when it was granted to the Dean and Chapter of Worcester who kept it until 1650 when Parliamentary Commissioners sold it. At the Restoration it was recovered by the church, who kept it until 1859 when it was taken over by the Ecclesiastical Commissioners. Thus those we might call 'owners' of land were in fact 'copyholders' or leaseholders, who paid an annual tithe to the priory, a tithe which included rents from their own tenants. As early as the 13th century there had been an active market even in small fields or closes, when peasants paid entry fines to the priory but also paid the previous tenant.[4] Gradually most landowners bought their copyhold, but the system did not completely die out until 1926.

At the time this story begins in the 17th century Finstall had no centre and was an area that just had a very few small farms with adjacent hovels for workers, and a few trackways between them. Bromsgrove was only two miles away and provided necessities such as clothing and footwear from its markets and shops. By the 17th century the hillier area in the north of the village already had several quarries, with local sandstone being used for the houses in the parish.

Harvesting in 1909. (Jane & Terry Critchley)

The soil in the north of the village, though sandy, is heavy, being a fertile clay-loam soil with good drainage (though it is suggested that the word Slideslow meant 'slough' or 'mire'[5]), while the more southern flatter land is Keuper marl with higher acidity.

The very few cottages – rather than hovels – in Finstall at the end of the 17th century were probably built with stone or locally made bricks within a wooden frame – whichever was cheaper at the time – with a tiled roof or thatch. Many of the brick cottages now in Finstall have stone in part of their buildings. The poorest people would have just one room, labourers would have two or three rooms, with small windows because of the cost of glass. There may have been an attached stable, as can be seen in the photograph of the Heydon's house in Heydon Road, Chapter 16. Food would be cooked in the living room, and there would be no kitchens, bathrooms or lavatories. Food and human waste would

---

3   Slaves could be bought and sold by the lord, the lord in this case being the church in Worcester.

4   Dyer, Christopher, *Bromsgrove: a small town in Worcestershire in the Middle Ages*, Worcestershire Historical Society, 2000.

5   Ekwall, E, *Concise Oxford Dictionary of Place Names*, 1936.

1. Finstall Heath

Cutting a meadow in 1900. (Jane & Terry Critchley)

go on the midden outside the house. Most dwellings large or small would have needed a well, and kept fowl near the house, and maybe had a small close or field for growing hops for their home-made ale. There would be a vegetable garden and the wealthier would have a pigstye. If they were lucky enough to have more land they might have a pair of oxen and a couple of sheep, and also grow their own beans, wheat, oats and barley. Ploughing was usually done with the oxen or horses, and because of the cost of such animals they often would belong to the local big house, used by all the tenants.

When reading this book visualise all the roadways to be narrow mud tracks, the broadest only wide enough for one horse and cart and used mainly by farmers to reach their fields. Many of these tracks are still in existence as footpaths. Apart from a need to go to Bromsgrove for market days and Stoke chapel (at Aston Fields), Tardebigge church or St John's in Bromsgrove on Sundays, there was little need for travel for the occupants. It was however a government requirement that rural parishes must keep in good repair any roads commonly used by 'foreigners' (i.e. the road, later a toll road, from Bromsgrove to Alcester), and each householder was obliged to work on the roadways for four consecutive days a year under an unpaid Surveyor of Highways.

This book now opens at the beginning of the Civil War, in 1642.

Chapter Two
The Civil War

When the battle of Powick Bridge at Worcester happened on 23 September 1642 there was a man from Finstall in the Royalist army, commanding a troop of Prince Maurice's Horse. He was Captain William Sheldon, who owned a large area of the north of Finstall and whose family owned land in Burcot. This battle was the first Worcestershire skirmish of the Civil War and appears to have been a fine muddle, with both sides being surprised by the other, though the Parliamentarians ended up fleeing, many drowning in the River Teme. Prince Maurice himself was wounded.

The Civil War, which had begun over the previous few months, affected not only the conscripted men but whole areas of the countryside. King Charles I expected that landowners should not only join his army themselves but should take some of their tenants with them to fight, thus leaving their families and crops to look after themselves. In 1645 the King's army marched through Inkberrow, Droitwich and Bromsgrove on the way to Naseby. The 1,000 man Scottish army marched down to Alcester then back up to Droitwich on its way to attack Worcester. By 1651 the King demanded a huge £3,000 in taxation from Worcestershire county, and there was one period when he insisted that to feed his troops the county must provide 50lb [22 kilos] of bread and 50lb of cheese <u>daily</u> to the camps at Worcester and Evesham. Bromsgrove town had also been ordered to store 10 barrels of gunpowder and 776lbs [350 kilos] of match[6], probably kept in the church for safety.

Powick Bridge, near Worcester, where the first major cavalry engagement of the English Civil War, led by Prince Rupert, was fought on 23 September 1642.

As the men moved through the countryside they commandeered horses and carts – which the army was always short of – as well as stealing sheep, pigs, chickens and grain for food – even sometimes marching across fields thus destroying crops. There would also be some lone travellers who had escaped the armies, desperate to return to their homes,

---
6   Match were lengths of cord soaked in saltpetre used to ignite the charges of muskets.

2. THE CIVIL WAR

on their journey asking for alms from the poor families struggling to keep going without their main breadwinner. So Finstall people, none of them well off, would have suffered. The nine years of civil war, ending with the battle of Worcester in 1651, had repercussions for everyone. Historians think that, proportionately, more people were killed in the civil wars than in WWI.

William Sheldon, gent.,[7] one of just eleven Royalists in the county, was owner of land that ranged in the north from Burcot, southwards to the lands of Finstall Heath and Tardebigge, included four farms and other fields, probably adding up to about 75 acres. His six tenants – Elizabeth Hill, Jane Richardson, William Bell and Francis Knight – would have paid him an annual tithe, and it was his responsibility to pay some £75 each year to the Manor via the Sheriff. With the success of Parliament in the war the Royalist landowners were fined and threatened with the loss of their estates. Sheldon had to pay £96 – 10% of the value of his estates – to the Lord of the Manor of Bromsgrove.

Sheldon was in trouble with Parliament in 1650.[8] Despite valuing his estate in Bromsgrove (Finstall) at £40 a year, and his estate at Tardebigge at £2 (in the family since Bordesley Abbey closed), it was found that the true value was £80 and also that he had concealed from them that he owned land at Astwood near Feckenham. There was also an extraordinary report 'that Edw. Bagshaw of Norton Pinckney [Gloucestershire] had 2 or 3 great trunks of money and treasure, value £7,000 or £8,000 belonging to Wm Sheldon, Papist delinquent'. There were arguments, the Committee hearing that 'Sheldon was in arms with the Scots at Worcester in 1651, and [had]

Prince Maurice, younger brother of Prince Rupert, King Charles' nephew and commander of the Royalist cavalry.

---

7   William was one of the Sheldon family who were part of the congregation of St John's church Bromsgrove, who were probably part of the Sheldon family of Beoley. Little is known about William Sheldon, except that his family – Edward, Samuel, Renne, Benjamin – all lived in Burcot during the 17th century. Despite the various difficulties caused by the family being Royalists and Catholic he still attended St John's church in Bromsgrove, for his name is on the donors' board for providing an annual sum to be given to the poor at Christmas and Easter, and he and other family members were governors of Bromsgrove School. He married Susanna, daughter of John Barnsley of Barnsley Hall during the 1650s, whose brother Henry lived in Burcot at King's Tottenhill. Their son William was born in 1653.

At this time William's father still attended St John's, for Edward Sheldon of Burcot, a former churchwarden, in 1667 bequeathed to his two sons 'the seats or sittings which I now have and usully doo sitt in in the p'sh Church'. (From *Fairly Mounted on a Hill, Bromsgrove's Church and its people*, Simon Henderson, 2015, and 'From Bromsgrove to the Baltic and Beyond', Jenny Townshend and Jean Walker, *The Rousler* No.9, 1994)

8   Committee for the Advance of Money: Part 3, 1650-55 British History on Line.

encouraged men to take arms with the Scots' King against Parliament', while Sheldon complained through his counsel that the correct court procedures were not being followed. Parliament was defeated by this, and ordered that he should be 'discharged, the seizure of his estate taken off, and his securities returned'.

Despite this result Sheldon refused to pay his 'grievous fine', resulting in him becoming outlawed – a penalty imposed upon people who evaded justice when sued for debts. He was brought before the Sheriff of Worcestershire at an inquisition on 17 April 1665 at the Rose and Crown at Lickhaye, and was 'seized of the ... messuages, and tenements' – which were all his property in Finstall.

Four years later a certain Thomas Chetle, gent., who was owed money by Sheldon, offered to pay a fine of a guinea to the Exchequer for the Sheldon properties which he could then hold at a yearly rent of ten shillings and sixpence. Part of the agreement also was that he and his tenants were granted hedgebote, firebote, ploughbote, gatebote and cartbote[9]. One wonders what Chetle had done to achieve this tremendous bargain. Sheldon, who now thought he was relieved of any more payments, found in 1681 that he had 'alienated his lands held of the Lord of the Manor by which there happeneth to the Lord a heriot according to the custom which is not yet seized, and that Mr Wm. Bell is tenant to the Lord for the same (lands)'.[10]

Thomas Chetle, gent., was a Catholic – a Popish recusant – and was fined £12 for refusing to attend the parish church.[11] There were only six other recusants living in Stoke Prior, including Francis Knight who was the tenant at The Hopyard, which Chetle now owned[12]. The respected Chetle family's home was at the Wallhouse near Feckenham (worth about £150 per annum), and they were connected by marriage to the Packington

---

9 Hedgebote was an allowance of wood for repairing hedges or fences, firebote was the right to take from the land a reasonable amount of wood for maintaining fires in his house and in those of his servants, and ploughbote, gatebote and cartbote were allowance of wood sufficient for ploughs, harrows, carts, and other instruments of husbandry. Other similar grants were pannage (the right to turn swine into woodlands to eat acorns and beechmast) and stallage (the right to set up stalls at fairs and markets). Murrage was a toll on horses and vehicles coming laden into a town, which raised funds to wall-in such places for defence.

10 i.e. because Sheldon had been forced to transfer ownership of his lands to another person he had to pay a heriot – a tribute in cash or kind – to the Lord of the Manor, which he clearly had not done. See Chapter 3 for more on William Bell.

11 A Popish recusant was one who remained loyal to the pope and the Catholic church and who refused to attend Church of England services.

12 Bromsgrove had 25 recusants, Tardebigge 37, Hanbury 2 and Rushock 5. Other local recusants in 1676 included Mr Adys of the Durrance, Upton Warren, John Arden of Upton Warren, gent., Francis Knight of Bromsgrove, victualler, Thomas Smith of Bromsgrove, Yeoman. From *Religious Census for Worcestershire with the Names of the Roman Catholics, Nonjurers and others who refus'd to take the oaths to his late Majesty King George*, by Commissioners and Trustees for the Forfeited Estates, Charles Cosin, John Cosin.

2. The Civil War

and Vernon families. Their properties also included extensive buildings in Worcester, in Herefordshire and Gloucestershire. Earlier the Chetle family were clothiers in Worcester (now most of them Parliamentarians), and latterly included a law enforcement officer – a Sheriff. He was another Thomas, who was not necessarily popular with everyone, as the following quotation shows: 'Hanna Bromfield of Upton Warren, Worcestershire, declared in 1696 that:

> "King William is a son of a whore, and if ever King James comes in I'll be one that shall help to put down Justice Chettle's house or set it on fire, but I'll have it down." Aflame with both local and national grievances, she had to answer for her words at the Worcestershire Quarter Sessions.'[13]

It seems that Chetle was no better able to manage his finances than Sheldon, and in 1689 there was a Parliamentary bill 'to enable Thomas Chettle Esquire to sell Lands to pay his debts and make Provision for his Wife and Children'.[14] In 1715 Chetle was returned as a Jacobite non-juror who refused to swear an oath of allegiance to William and Mary, who came to the throne in 1689.

A cavalier soldier.

A group of roundhead soldiers.

The complications of the times seem extraordinary to us; how did the ordinary person – or even the more educated gentlefolk – keep up with what was expected of them? Did they have enough education to be able to read any publications about the different ways of serving God, Royalty and Parliament? Many must have just followed what their Minister told them in church, and kept their heads down, but some such as William Sheldon and Thomas Chetle stuck to their principles and suffered for them, sometimes just financially but other times with imprisonment or even death. Sometimes other Catholics 'protected themselves' by attending Protestant church services, crossing their fingers behind their backs instead of making their usual sign of the cross in the sight of everyone.

First Sheldon and then Chetle became owners of a large amount of Finstall and Tutnall lands, but then their names die out from all local

---

13 *Dangerous Talk: Scandalous, Seditious, and Treasonable Speech*, David Cressy, OUP, 2010.

14 *Journals of the House of Commons*, Volume 10.

lists. But they seem to be among the first of the many investors who in later more peaceful times bought up farms and cottages, building up estates for the benefit of their children, though they did not always live in these properties. Messrs Brettell, Ellins, Smallwood, Everitt, Albright and Boultbee Brooks were all men who later found Finstall a place where they wanted to live and who contributed to the Finstall we know today. Their stories come as this history of Finstall progresses.

Chapter Three
The Early Days of Finstall Farm

While William Sheldon and Thomas Chetle were spending time arguing at the Manor Court at Lickhaye the land they owned continued to be worked by tenants. Much of the area round what they then called Finstall House, but since then has been Finstall Farm, included across the Turnpike Lane [now Pikes Pool Lane] 'a great fishpool lying near Burcot and two other pools called the "pink pools"' was worked by Jane Richardson. Other local lands owned by Sheldon were tenanted by John Wilkes, who worked Oldhill; some fourteen acres including Withy Meadow and Hernes Grounds worked by William Bell of Bittell; The Hopyard, 1½ acres occupied by Francis Knight; and nineteen acres occupied by Elizabeth Hill. It was unusual for women to be tenants unless they were widowed, but as it had been a requirement for Royalists like Captain Sheldon to bring men from their properties to fight, it is quite possible that husbands were marched off to war and never returned.

After Chetle started selling his property he found a buyer for Finstall Farm in William Bell, who agreed to the rent of 54 shillings and 6 pence paid to the Manor of Bromsgrove. William Bell was related to Thomas Bell, Clerk Vicar of Tardebigge church, and decided in 1714 to lease the farm to Thomas in 'consideration of five shillings to him in hand paid by the said Thomas Bell'. To put it as written on the lease:

> The said William Bell hath granted bargained and sold and doth hereby grant bargain and sell unto Thomas Bell that messuage and tenement and farm called Finstall Farm ... now in the possession of Thomas Carpenter (meaning Carpenter was the tenant farmer).

But not only that:

> also all that messuage, tenement and farm and all lands meadows leasows pastures and grounds thereunto belonging ... to the Hollow Tree farm ... now in the tenure of said Thomas Carpenter and Walter Albort [Albutt] as his undertenant ... and also all that other messuage or tenement and all lands and tenements and heredimentss thereunto belonging situate lying and being in parish of Bromsgrove and late in tenure of ... Carpenter widow and all pooles, ponds, watercourses ...

For all this land Thomas Bell Esq held 'for a year paying one peppercorn at the feast of Saint John the Baptist'.[15]

---

15 ER 3/209, Shakespeare Birthplace Trust, Stratford-upon-Avon.

Thomas Bell, AM[16] was vicar of Tardebigge for 39 years, between 1705 and 1744, and was there under the patronage of Other Lewis[17], Lord Plymouth of nearby Hewell Grange. Sad words in the parish burial register read that three of Bell's children were buried at Tardebigge between December 1736 and January 1737, the dates so close presumably because the poor children had caught a highly infectious disease like measles. He wrote in the register that Mr Thomas, Miss Anna Elizabeth and Miss Mary were buried, and specified that they had all been wrapped in wool. This was because Charles II had made an edict that woollen fabric should always be used for this purpose in order to encourage the wool trade. Any disobedience was punished by a fine of £5, the money going to the poor of the parish, and within eight days of a burial a Justice of the Peace, the mayor or a clergyman must sign an affidavit that the burial complied with the Act. Earlier, in 1570, there was an Elizabethan law saying that all should wear woollen caps on Sundays and holidays. 'In 1596 the jury of Lady Windsor's Court Baron at Tardebigge prayed her, on behalf of themselves and residents, to allow them to compound for not wearing such caps on Sundays.' This request was granted on payment of a fine of one penny yearly from each family.

The Bell family had been living in the area since 1595, when George Bell bought land to the south-east of the Hewell Estate, near Tack Farm – this the family sold early in the 19th century. Property was bought in Tutnall and included Hennefields and a 'dole' of meadow, about an acre, in Puddle Meadowe which was near the Puddle Lodge to the Hewell Estate (now demolished), and they also had land at Webheath – including Tinsey Field, Hopgarden Meadow – and at Bittell near Alvechurch where William lived in 1714. In 1716 the four daughters of newly widowed Jane Sheldon surrendered all her lands in Tardebigge to the use of William Bell, who was admitted as tenant, taking the place of Isaac Parkes. William and Henrietta Maria Bell had a son John, who was buried at Tardebigge in 1726, and there used to be an 18th century brass to the family in the church. The family also rented Old Hill Farm at Tutnall with about fourteen acres, which was later renamed Tutnall Hall.

Joseph Steedman had taken over the working of Finstall Farm, and over the next 100 years the tenants included William Griffin, Ann Sherwood and Edward King as undertenants, as well as Thomas Gardner. It must be remembered that the railway line later cut across Finstall Farm land, and it was in 1820 that Mr Farmer Parkes of Astwood in Dodderhill bought the land and the Birmingham and Gloucester Railway Company negotiated to buy the land for the railway line from him.

But the Bells and the Parkes weren't the only people restlessly buying and selling property. John Ashmore, the wealthy Bromsgrove carrier[18] who was living at the Broom

---

16 AM (Artium magister), Master of Arts.
17 Other was a Plymouth family Christian name, explaining the naming of Other Road, Redditch.
18 John Ashmore the Bromsgrove Carrier, Julian Hunt, *Bromsgrove Rousler*, December 2012.

3. The Early Days of Finstall Farm

House (later known as Ford House), together with his sons Benjamin and John junior, had begun to encroach even further into the countryside from Bromsgrove – they already owned land along the Bromsgrove Alcester toll road, and Benjamin occupied Bumper's Hill and Stoke Heath. By 1825 Benjamin owned Finstall Farm, the blacksmith's shop at Finstall Heath, and had bought The Maltshovel at Vigo from Thomas Sanders. By 1832 bachelor Benjamin was owner of the house, land and buildings of Hollow Tree Farm, the year the Reform Act came to pass, which enabled him to vote for the first time. John's grandson, John III, had been left 'Hill Croft [10 acres] and one piece of meadow ground called Caspidge [9 acres]', thus linking the Ashmore lands to the 159 acres of Finstall Farm with its Pikes Pool and Pinke Pooles.

However it seems that the Ashmores were buying much of their property by taking out mortgages. At these times many people borrowed the required large sums on security of their property from wealthy people who lived locally, such as the Sanders family in Bromsgrove. Others investing their money in loans to the less well off included Thomas Brettell and Henry Ellins. Should the mortgagor not repay the money on the agreed date then the mortgagee could appropriate the land, which is probably the case with Miss Sanders below.

For in 1841 Miss Mary Sanders was admitted to Finstall Farm, with undertenants William Connard and Michael Ashmore, an act covered by John Ashmore's will which was signed by him with his mark: X.

The Maltshovel at Vigo was a small alehouse, on land now owned by John Bonnaker, whose farm reached both sides of the Burcot Alcester road, down to Finstall Farm's northern border. Bonnaker married Sarah Connard (see previous paragraph), and their daughter married John Ashmore III, their son John IV marrying his cousin, Martha Connard.[19]

Finstall Farm came on the market following the death of its tenant Benjamin Ashmore, its auction in December 1845 offering in *Berrows Journal*:

> a substantially-built HOUSE, which at a little expense may be converted into a most genteel residence; ... sundry Closes of superior Arable, Meadow, and Pasture LAND .... The Meadow Land is of superior quality, and may be irrigated at pleasure. ... The Auctioneer calls the attention of Capitalists, Manufacturers, and others to this Property. ... The House stands upon a pleasing eminence, and the lands ... are eligibly situated for Villas and Residences, commanding extensive and picturesque Views of the surrounding country, and within about Half a Mile of the Bromsgrove Station.

But it didn't sell. Despite being on offer privately the next year, it wasn't until 1853 when 'by direction of the mortgagees' there was another auction of the 'Farm House, excellent Pasture, Pool of Water, etc.', when it was bought by Mr Richard William Johnson of

---

19 The Connards: A Lost Bromsgrove Family, Mike Sharp, *Bromsgrove Rousler*, December 2013.

Foxlydiate House, who the same year bought and gave to his wife Sarah nine acres of Caspidge land 'whereon a messuage formerly stood, and 2 closes near adjoining Finstall Heath called Hill Croft, 10 acres'.

Mr Johnson had come to the area about 1848 because of his role with Bromsgrove Railway Carriage and Wagon Company – for the railway running alongside and through Finstall Farm land at the beginning of the Lickey Incline was opened in 1840 – and for a couple of years he was a member of the Institute of Mechanical Engineers which had been formed on the Bromsgrove railway in 1847.[20] In 1858 he and Mr William Stapleford of Oldbury patented 'improvements connected with the break levers of railway wagons', a patent which was prolonged in 1865. Johnson was sufficiently well thought of in Bromsgrove to have been invited to take the oath as a Justice of the Peace in 1852, and in 1866 was a director of the Bromsgrove and Droitwich Water company which proposed to take water from Pikes Pool to Droitwich. He was, of course, owner of Pikes Pool.[21]

Foxlydiate House, briefly home of R.W. Johnson who bought Finstall Farm in 1853.

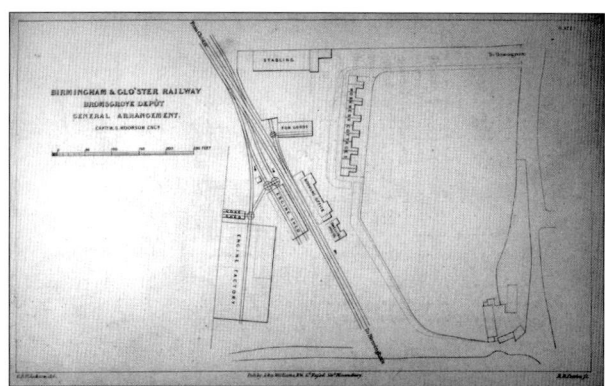

The layout of the Birmingham and Gloucester Railway wagonworks at Aston Fields. (Warwick Sheffield)

During the Johnson ownership of Finstall Farm Thomas Gardner was the tenant, a man also well known in Bromsgrove, whose father had been tenant at Finch End. He was the sort of man who involved himself in local activities, including serving on the Bromsgrove Highways Board, in order to superintend repairs to roads. He was appointed a local Constable, met the Local Board monthly, was involved in the town's discussions about the purchase of a new fire engine, and was a supporter of the Conservative party.

---

20 For the story of the founding of the Institution of Mechanical Engineers see *Flint and Steel*, Neville Billington, 1996.

21 See later chapter on Pikes Pool.

3. The Early Days of Finstall Farm

Gardner lost his wife in 1853 at the young age of 37, though he was remarried three years later to Agnes Gower of Dormstone, east of Worcester – a place connected in earlier times with the Sheldons and Gardners. His son, also Thomas, died in his twelfth year in 1859, and daughter Jane also died too young, aged 31, at Bentley House in 1878. These were times when smallpox, measles and typhoid fever were in the area, and probably every year there were deaths from these highly infectious diseases.

However Thomas Gardner, the pillar of society, was still living in the Bailiff's house at Finstall Farm, with undertenants to support him, when RW Johnson decided to sell the farm from his new home Bricklehampton Hall near Pershore.

Finstall Farm was put up for sale in 1871 by an auction house in Birmingham. The publicity shows the kind of buyer they were looking for, as part of the sales promotion was that:

> The situation of the property for diversified and beautiful scenery is scarcely to be surpassed in the county of Worcester. From the summit of the estate, which nearly all slopes to the south-west, can be seen distinctly the Abberley, Clent, and Malvern Hills, and a great range of country extending into the far distance.

and once again there was emphasis on the purchase being very desirable 'for the ultimate object of dividing into Lots for Villa residences'.

However no-one bought at this auction. The story of what happened next, which changed Finstall for ever, is in another chapter.

Chapter Four

The Brettell Family in Finstall House[22]

The Brettell family of Staffordshire, living there since at least 1550, extended their lands far and wide, often by marrying the right girl. Their money came from glassmaking, coal mining, nailmaking and careful purchase of, or inheritance of, farming land. They were living in Stourbridge, the Lye and Audnam, Kingswinford, Amblecote, Clent, Romsley and Chaddesley Corbett, and were sufficiently important to have a glassmaking area between Stourbridge and Dudley named after them, through which still runs the mile long road known as Brettell Lane (A461).

Thomas Brettell began his working life as a farmer's boy, became a farming bailiff, and afterwards became a successful attorney. In 1748 he cannily married Sarah Henzey of Broseley in Shropshire, who was of the extremely wealthy Hungarian glass manufacturing family.[23] However, the Henzeys too were canny, for in the marriage settlement Thomas Brettell had to agree to spend £400 within five years of his marriage on property in the counties of Worcestershire, Staffordshire or Shropshire. This he proceeded to do and Sarah's life continued to be a comfortable one.

Thus it was natural that Thomas Brettell, of Summerhill House in Old Swinford, should add Finstall House to his collection – but he didn't pay for it. Henry Knight Clark of Romsley, Thomas's grandfather, left the property to him in his will. The farm's tenant, William Edwards, continued to work

Summerhill House, Old Swinford, Stourbridge, home of Thomas Brettell who was the first Brettell owner of Finstall House, and of his son Thomas.

---

22 I am most grateful to Mary Brettell of Brisbane, Australia for her help and information about the Brettells.

23 Marriage between the Brettells and Henzeys was not unusual. In 1617 John Brettell married Mary Henzey in Oldswinford. Joshua Henzey married Joan Brettell who was born in 1589 and died in 1671. Richard Brettell of Romsley Hill, Halesowen, married Anne, daughter of Philip Clarke of Romsley, who had two sons John and Thomas. John married Anne, only daughter and heiress of Paul Henzey; Thomas and Sarah Henzey's story is above.

An equally advantageous match was that of Richard, son of Thomas Brettell, who married Mary, daughter of Michael Grazebrook, proprietor of the Audnam glassworks. Their son Richard married his cousin Matilda, another daughter of Michael Grazebrook.

4. The Brettell Family in Finstall House

the farm until 1755. During this time Thomas agreed that he, Thomas, should sow clover and grass seed, while Edwards must 'preserve these crops from being eaten by sheep, goose or pigs and preserve the same from Candlemass ... and suffer him to plant crabtree stocks and other young trees'.

In 1763 one Joseph Shelton surrendered to 'Thos Brettell a messuage, barn and five closes situated in Finstall' as a result of non-payment of mortgage. In 1770 two of those five closes – the six acres of Comb Close and Comb Meadow – were sold by Brettell to James Mackmillan. In 1771 for £4,000 Brettell purchased a parcel of land, 'two closes known as Point of Size 7 acres, the lane leading from Stoke Cross towards Webb's Farm and part of Sheltwood Farm, land belonging to Whitfield Esq. in the holding of Widow Page, and another coppice or woodground belonging to Smith of Worcester'.

When the Brettells arrived at Finstall Farm (Finstall House) the old farmhouse was soon rebuilt in fashionable Georgian style, though Thomas continued to give his main address as Stourbridge – maybe they thought of Finstall as being their holiday home. The first son, Thomas, continued living in Summerhill House which, built in 1756, is an imposing mansion with a grand façade (now a Harvester restaurant). He was obviously educated and interested in literature, religion and history, for he contributed to various publications, and he acted as attorney for Viscount Dudley and Ward. Richard, the second son, was the farmer in charge of Finstall land, while their third son Joseph married Ann Holden and set up a solicitor's practice in Bromsgrove, living with his seven children at Steps House, St John Street. Suzannah, the only daughter, married John Fidkin of Brockencote, near Chaddesley Corbett. The fourth son was Ananias, named for one of the French glassmakers who came from Lorraine and started the Stourbridge glassworks in about 1630.

Ananias was a student at Worcester College[24], Oxford, matriculating in 1771 aged 15, and achieving his BA in 1775 and MA in 1778. He was ordained in Hereford Cathedral in 1779, and went on to be Rector of Stoke Bliss church, near Tenbury Wells, though in 1813 he still gave his address as Finstall House. When his father died in 1796 he was treated in a slightly different way in the will, for in addition to his quarter of the property left to the four brothers he was given 'a close at Cross Brook, then a hopyard and 10 acres of Grimley Hill and he shall for ever hold and enjoy the little house at Cross Brook'. However, the Rev. Ananias Brettell decided in 1813 to pass on to his brothers his one fourth share which had been 'the Grimley House estate, an estate in Stourbridge and ... three houses in Rye Market, Stourbridge'. He also gave up his share of an annuity arising out of 'forges, mills, messuages and lands in Linley, Salop' (just 2¼ miles from

---

24 Worcester College's re-foundation in 1714 was the gift of Sir Thomas Cookes of Bentley, whose money had also given Bromsgrove School similar benefit. The 18th century buildings of Worcester College were designed by Nicholas Hawksmoor, James Wyatt and Henry Keene; the Chapel was refurbished in 1864 by William Burges.

Broseley where his mother had lived), and his share in money owing to Thomas Brettell from 'mortgages of the tolls of the Stourbridge and Halesowen turnpike road'.[25] And in his own will of 1820 he left to various relations 'Lands called the Rose and Crown on the Lickey'. Most of the rest of his property he left to the children of his siblings, his nephews and nieces. He also specified that he should be buried in Finstall chapel-of-ease which his father had paid to be rebuilt in 1772.

This small rectangular brick building was very simple, sited where a very early chapel had been from 1275. It had large pointed plain glass windows, a gallery for the choir, accommodation for 130 worshippers including benches and seats for the poor of the parish, and most important for Mr Brettell, a vault beneath the chancel for the use of his family's burials. Later there were three memorials to the Brettell family, now in the porch of St Godwald's church down the road. St Godwald's was built in 1883, designer John Cotton, with stone donated by Mr Featherstone of Finstall. It was necessary because the expansion of Aston Fields meant that the chapel was too small and therefore not worth the restoration that was sorely needed at that time. The chapel continued to be used for memorial services, until the building was closed for safety reasons in the 1960s; it soon collapsed, but though traces of the chapel are few, the graveyard is still in use today and the whole grassy area is covered in snowdrops and daffodils in spring.

Finstall chapel, rebuilt in 1772 on 13th century foundations by Richard Brettell. There is a small bell turret on the roof, which was moved to St Godwald's church when the chapel was demolished. A painting by John Cotton in 1910. (Bromsgrove Library)

The 1790 will of Thomas Brettell was not unusual,[26] apart from the exception above for Ananias, leaving almost everything to his wife then his family, though his codicil of 1791 offers the ability for son-in-law John Fidkin to spend on 'a Barn and other houses as appurtuant to the Mansion house at Brockencote' and money could be spent on purchase of land adjoining Brockencote house. He had previously arranged that Sarah if widowed should move to Brockencote to be near Susannah.

By the time the Brettell family left Finstall they had added much land to the original farmland they had inherited. Thomas Brettell left not only Finstall House but also land at Brockencote, land at Erdington, Birmingham, an estate in Stourbridge including 3

---

25 http://www.exploringsurreyspast.org.uk/GetRecord/SHCOL_4363

26 Other Brettell wills could come up with some interesting features. In 1770 a Janns Brettell of Shropshire left his estate to a daughter, but another daughter, Mary, was left but 'one shilling and no more as she has behaved undutiful towards me'.

houses in Rye Market, and forges, mills, messuages and lands in Linley, Salop (which must have been connected to his wife's family) and received tolls from the Stourbridge and Halesowen Turnpike road.

At Finstall he had bought Tack Farm (which became the home farm), Hill Farm, Gambolds Farm, Crossbrook Farm, Stone House Farm, Grimley House and its farmland, a little house at Crossbrook and a hopyard and 10 acres of Grimley Hill. Several closes were in Aston End ('with outbuildings, gardens, orchards and New Orchard, Brandland Meadow, 2 closes pasture called Ancotts, 2 other closes called Pease Closes, 3 other closes called Bovehills and pasture Crysome Orchard with the appurtenances') and Broad Close. 'Two closes known by name Point of Size 7 acres, lane leading from Stoke Cross towards Webb's Farm and part of Sheltwood Farm and land belonging to Whitfield Esq in the holding of Widow Page and another coppice or wood ground belonging to Smith of Worcester'

The doorway of the chapel just before demolition. (M. Dowty, 1968)

(bought from Ann Lilly's estate in 1771). Also 'two closes there adjoining called Hither Charpidge and Middle Charpidge'. Soon Finch End Farm and Dusthouse Farm were added to the collection.

Their father having died, his sons continued the family habit. In order to expand the garden grounds round Finstall House they arranged a land swap with Thomas Horton, who owned 3 acres 1 rood 28 perches known as Shaw's Close, that ran almost up to their house. This would make a good sized garden, so the Brettell brothers surrendered in exchange the Coit, Upper Oakalls Close and part of Russey on Oakalls Meadow – a total of 3 acres 5 roods 28 perches. Everyone was happy.

> Sacred to the Memory
> Of THOMAS BRETTELL who caused this Chapel to be rebuilt in the Year 1772
> and died the 19th day of January 1792.
> Of SARAH his Wife who died the 18th day of July 1801
> Of SUSANNA the Wife of their Eldest Son THOMAS who died the 1st day of August 1778
> Of RICHARD their second Son who died the 2nd day of November 1799
> Of SUSANNA their Daughter the Wife of JOHN FIDKIN who died the 21st day of June 1807
> Of THOMAS Son of their Son RICHARD aged six Months
> Of SARAH an Infant Daughter of their Son JOSEPH who died the 21st day of February 1790
> Of RICHARD an Infant Son of their Son JOSEPH who died the 24th day of July 1796
> Of ANN the Wife of their Son JOSEPH who died the 10th day of March 1814
> Of the said JOHN FIDKIN who died the 14th day of January 1815
> Of MARY the Wife of their Son RICHARD who died the 26th day of April 1816
>
> Of ANANIAS their third Son who died […] the 24th day of August 1819
> Of SUSANNA Daughter of their Son RICHARD who died the 17th day of Nov. 1820
> Of GEORGE Son of their Son JOSEPH who died the 8th day of June 1824
> Of their said eldest Son THOMAS BRETTELL who died the 10th day of Dec. 1827
> Of THOMAS Son of their Son JOSEPH who died the 20th day of Dec 1837
> Of JOSEPH Son of their Son JOSEPH who died February 4th 1847 Aged 58 Years.
> Of JOSEPH of Bromsgrove, their third Son, who died March 22nd 1847 Aged 89 Years
> Of JOHN Son of their Son JOSEPH, who died July 6th 1853. Aged 70 Years
> Of SARAH BRETTELL Daughter of their Son RICHARD who died September 3rd 1856
> Aged 69 Years.

Memorial to the Brettell family, first at the old chapel and then moved to St Godwald's church. (M. Dowty, 1968)

The brothers made a little money by selling bits of land to Henry Ellins who had already bought 'lands in this manor called Rigbys ... in occupation of Joseph Ward to pay yearly one penny farthing and sixpence in honey'. They received rent for all their properties – i.e. Benjamin Dugard living at Grimley House and its farm paid an annual rent of £67. Joseph in 1795 bought a third share in a windmill near Halesowen (it was likely he was acting as mortgager for this). Included in that sale were a 'Tenement, Shop, Garden, and other buildings', plus of course the windmill. 'The mill stones, gearing, utensils, wells, and watercourses' were also mentioned, as was the price asked – £250.

Finstall still had some remains of Feckenham Forest woodland, and land needed to be cleared in order to feed more cattle or grow more crops, so sales of timber from their properties brought more income – or should have; on 11 February 1848 at The Dragoon Inn was the first sale of growing timber.

> LOT 1 was forty-four very large ELM, Five ASH, Two POPLAR and one WALNUT TREE ... on the STOKE CROSS FARM, Thomas Buggins, Tenant.
>
> LOT 2 – Eleven OAK, twenty-one ELM, Twenty-one ASH, Thirteen POPLAR, One WITHY, and One ASPEN ... on the TACK FARM, Richard Griffin, Tenant.
>
> LOT 3 – Fifty-four large OAK, Seventeen ELMS, Eighteen ASH, Three POPLAR, and One CRAB ... on the STOKE CROSS FARM, in the occupation of Mr Brettell.

4. The Brettell Family in Finstall House

> LOT 4 – Thirty-three OAK, Twelve ASH, Two ELM, and Three CHESNUTS ... on the GRIMLEY HALL FARM, in the occupation of Mr Brettell.
>
> The Oak and Elm Timber is of first-rate quality, very lengthy and hearty, and suitable for the most valuable purposes.

Unfortunately much didn't sell, and a lot of the wood was offered again for purchase by private contract from 23 March.

Finstall House was possibly rebuilt by Richard Brettell in the 1830s, but there are no descriptions of the house until the Everitts bought it in the 1860s, though in 1866 it was described in the *Birmingham Daily Gazette* as a mansion, a two-storied structure of stone and brick. The building of a half mile sandstone wall that runs down Finstall Road from the railway bridge to the entrance to the house and then along Walnut Lane was a way of indicating the new grandeur of the Brettell family, and the lodge built by the main entrance, also built of stone, added to the estate's importance. However the Brettell family had already achieved their father's purpose – to make them a respectable county family. Their children were being educated – at least one of his grandsons went to Rugby School aged 11 followed by Trinity College, Cambridge, becoming a properly trained solicitor in Chertsey. The Brettells took part in Bromsgrove activities, and Richard was a magistrate and became Deputy-Lieutenant of Worcestershire. In November 1843 Mr and Mrs Brettell of Finstall House joined the procession of carriages driving to make a call on Her Majesty the Queen Dowager who was staying at Witley Court.

Finstall House c.1920. (BC)

It was not all good. In 1799 Richard Brettell died, leaving his son Richard to take his place as head of the Finstall family. In 1824 Thomas Brettell of Summerhill Hall, aged 75, described as 'scrivener, dealer and chapman' – a rather unpleasant way of describing what he himself more grandly would call an attorney – had been made bankrupt. In 1847 the 80 year old Joseph was living in the Clock House at Fockbury with his daughter Mary, who was married to the Rev. Thomas Housman[27], and he died that year leaving a considerable estate to

The stone built lodge to Finstall Park in 1977. (Christopher Pancheri)

---

27 The poet A.E. Housman's grandfather.

his family, including land at Upton Snodsbury acquired from his wife, and his 'freehold messuages tenement farmlands ... situate at Fockbury ... now in possession of the said Thomas Housman'. 1838 brought the threat of the railway to be built over the Brettell land, which was not allowed by them without a fight. In his last complaint in a letter to Mr Burgess of the Birmingham & Gloucester Railway Office, Richard Brettell wrote:

> Luttley near Halesowen
> Nov. 22nd 1839
>
> In reply to your letter received yesterday, I decline accepting the price you offered in your former letter for the Land referred to. And had reason to think that this Land would not enable the Railway Co to make the road so convenient as the Public have a right to require; it is the form of the Tunnel under the Railway much like the letter Z (instead of being carried in a straight line as the Road heretofore was) that is so objectionable.
>
> I am Sir
> Your very obedt Servt,
> Richard Brettell

He didn't, of course, win, and the bridge was known as the skew bridge.[28]

Come the 1850s and the Brettells had all left Finstall, for young Richard died aged 51, leaving his wife Matilda to bury him in the Brettell vault in Finstall Chapel and to rent out the house, which she did for the next 49 years. Of the following tenants there is more in a later chapter.

---

28 For the full story of the skew bridge see *From Bromsgrove to Aston Fields* by this author.

Chapter Five
The Ellins Family and Rigby Hall

When Joseph Blackford, one of the Bromsgrove millers, died in 1814 he left to his son John:

> two copyhold messuages with buildings, gardens, orchards & several closes adjacent or near adjacent of 10 acres called Rigbys in Stoke Prior, in my occupation.

John was a surgeon who lived in Bromsgrove High Street, and his family had long been close friends with the Ellins family, who were also in the High Street; John especially loved the young Ann, daughter of Henry Ellins the Elder, so this inheritance enabled them to get married. And that is how Rigby land came into the hands of the Ellins family.

Henry the Elder had eleven children, four of whom died in infancy. The two of interest to this story are Henry the Younger and George, both of whom were energetic men involved in various activities in the area. In 1778 there were 900 people locally involved in nailing, there were 180 working with flax and linen, and 140 working in linsey. The Ellins family were involved in all three, plus needle making (they invested money in needle mills), and latterly, salt.[29]

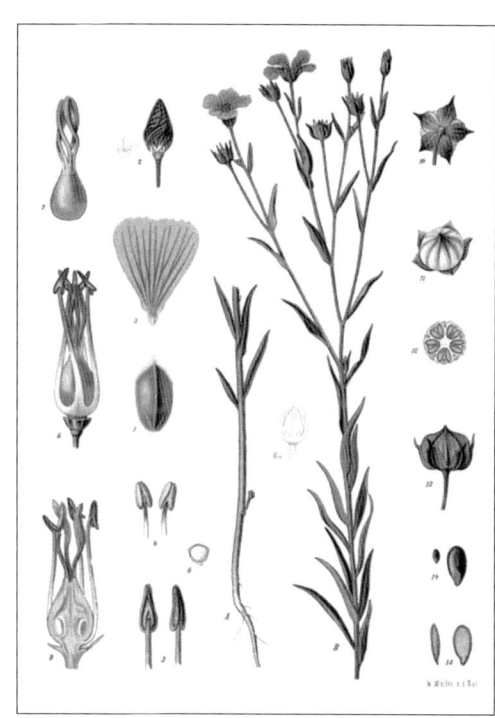

Flax plant (Linum usitatissimum).

In order to encourage the growing of flax and hemp, bounties had been offered in 1781 for their cultivation. Among those claiming for the largest output were William Moore and

---

[29] The article in *The Rousler* number 21, 'Linen Sheets and a Bed of Nails' by John Parker, has been extremely helpful for this chapter, as well as Richard Churchley's articles in volumes 28, 29 and 30. For nailmaking see *Glory Gone* by Bill Kings and Margaret Cooper.

Thomas Overton of Tardebigge, and four men from Stoke Prior, including Henry Ellins the Elder of Stoke Prior who had flax fields in Rushock, Doverdale, Stoke and Hanbury. However when cotton arrived in England the need for linen made from flax declined fairly rapidly – even though flax and cotton could be combined to make velvet, that was only for the well off, and so cotton won, changing the agricultural practices of the country.

But Henry the Elder had been carefully adding to his property and at the time he died in 1817 he owned some fifteen dwellings in Bromsgrove, nailshops, meadow land in Sidemoor used as a bleaching ground for linen, a factory and (nailing) warehouse and around 7½ acres, all left to his wife to 'enable her with the assistance of my eldest son Henry and my younger children George and Sarah to carry on my several businesses and to support educate clothe and maintain them'. His wife was to 'carry on nail business in partnership with Mr Samuel Hedges, then son George'.

Son George also showed himself good at investment in property and bought land in Rigby and Finstall from the Brettells and was on the Register of Electors in 1831 as living at Rigby Hall – indeed there is a map of 1810[30] showing Rigby Hall. His land extended up to and over the Alcester Road at Finstall Heath, including Scotch House, now known as The Vale. What he may not have known until he read *Berrow's Journal* in October 1835 was that through his newly purchased land would run the proposed Birmingham and Gloucester Railroad – through

Rigby Lane before houses were built along it.

'... Cofton, Barnt Green, Blackwell, Rigby (Mr Hillings's)[31] – leaving Bromsgrove a mile to the right; Newton Farm, Sugar Brook ...'

In 1837 George took out 25 shares costing £1,250 in the proposed Worcester and Wolverhampton Railway (never built), but the next year attended the fourth half-yearly general meeting of the proprietors of the Birmingham and Gloucester Railway, of which he also was a shareholder. In 1839 he sold part of Rigby Hall land to the railway company (and also sold Combe Close and Coombe Meadow up at Finstall to Francis Featherstone), and persuaded the company to contract him to build all the bridges needed in Stoke Prior

---

30 A fragile tissue paper map of the Glebe Lands and Corn tithes property of the Dean and Chapter of Worcester. Birmingham Archives.

31 This must be a misunderstanding of the name Ellins.

parish. Soon he was taken to task for the crumbling railway bridges within Stoke Prior that he had been responsible for building.

November 1840 brought the dreadful railway accident at the wagon works when Joseph Rutherford and Thomas Scaife were killed after the boiler of an engine exploded (their gravestones are in St John's graveyard), when the first part of the Coroner's court was convened at Rigby Hall, and George Ellins was the Foreman of the Jury. This was an unusual venue, especially as George had a financial interest in the railway company.[32] It is thought that the railway company was doing its best to avoid criticism for the accident, Ellins also – probably for financial reasons – wanting a quick, quiet result. Being financially involved and with his land so close he continued to take a keen interest in the railway affairs, and in 1842 asked for (but was refused) a special meeting of shareholders because of the 'depressed value of the shares due to the experimental mode of management'. He was the largest shareholder, with 300 shares. He and his nephew Henry Ellins Blackford,[33] who also lived at Rigby Hall, were also shareholders of Joint-Stock Country Banks.

George had had another little tussle, this time with the law in 1829 when he was convicted for paying his workmen other than in money – not an unusual habit of nailmasters and foggers. Despite this, George became an active Liberal magistrate, and was firm with the prisoners, and *Berrow's Journal* reported that in March 1838 he 'gave to 180 poor families one pound of bread and one pound of meat to each person; he also gave to 80 of his poor tenants 2 cwt[34] of coal each'. It could be that an even worse than usual poverty was caused by the illnesses that seemed to constantly sweep through the land. 1838 had seen an epidemic of measles and whooping cough, but there were regular outbreaks of influenza, smallpox and typhus.

In 1837 he was anxious to become a churchwarden of St John's church, and join his brother Henry in that role. This he did not handle well, and resulted in an extraordinary fracas which ended up in court, though George managed to avoid being charged.[35] This was to do with the extremely unpopular church rate, imposed by the church officials to raise funds for church repairs and day to day church expenses. Yet in 1841, it was reported, 'the Pensioners' Club of Bromsgrove have presented George Ellins Esq. with a superb gold seal as a small token of their respect and regard for his kind and generous conduct manifested toward them from time to time'. The man seems to have been a great mixture.

---

32 The most recent and very detailed report on this accident and inquest is in *The Wrangler who went to the Railway*, Neville Billington and Warwick Sheffield, 2010. This also includes the second horrific accident when William Creuze was killed, later buried in Finstall Chapel's graveyard.

33 Sister Ann's son; she died in 1820.

34 1 Cwt = 112 pounds weight.

35 This story was told in full in *The Kidderminster Times*, 18 July 1838, and a shorter version in *Fairly Mounted on a Hill*, pp 203-205, Simon Henderson, 2015.

The income from his nail business probably helped George to build the Rigby Hall we know today, though it is described by architectural historians as being remodelled in the late 19th century. It is probable that, like Finstall House, there had been a much smaller farmhouse before engrandisement. The 1843 estate agent's map shows the house with plenty of coach houses, stables and other buildings, plus a very long 'Conservatory, Vineries, Peach Houses, Walled Garden and nearly five acres of highly ornamental Garden and Pleasure Ground surrounding the house, planted with every variety of the choicest Fruit Trees and Flowering Shrubs'. Other land was bought to enlarge his holding to over 30 acres. He lived well, in company with his nephew Henry Ellins Blackford and four servants. In Bentley's *History, Gazeteer, Directory and Statistics of Worcestershire* written in 1840 it is described as 'a handsome mansion much admired for its tastefully arranged pleasure gardens'.

George Ellins comes across as a man with broad interests; he was a subscriber to Worcester's Natural History Society. He was a keen gardener and was interested enough to want to grow unusual plants. *Dahlia Excelsa* (Tree Dahlia) was a new plant brought into the country from Mexico in 1834 and one was obtained by George Ellins and planted in the border of his conservatory in 1837. By November it had grown from two feet to twelve feet tall and produced 'a handsome corymb of flowers at the summit'; it had no side shoots, but its foliage spread a width of five feet and displayed a single crown of highly attractive pink flowers. His was not the tallest – the one at Liverpool Botanic Garden grew to twenty feet.[36]

Dahlia Excelsa, the tree dahlia brought from Mexico which George Ellins grew.

Henry the Younger was also known in Bromsgrove as a wholesale nail manufacturer and linen manufacturer, but his life also did not always go smoothly. Two nailers in 1838 took iron from Henry, but worked on it for other masters. 'Mr Ellins having forgiven them for the same offence once before, they were committed to the house of correction and to hard labour', one for two months, the other for six weeks. He was a churchwarden at St John's, and got involved in the parish uproar that his brother was involved in which went to the Worcestershire Summer Assizes, reported at great word-for-word length in two complete close-printed pages of *The Kidderminster Times*, when Henry was lucky not to have been included as a defendant. What he did lose was his smart Sunday coat which had been torn from his back.[37]

Come 1843 and the Ellins suddenly had to change their lives – having overstretched themselves financially. Rigby Hall was put up for auction in June:

---

36 Nowadays it is not unusual for these dahlia trees to grow to 30 feet.

37 See *The Kidderminster Times*, 18 July 1838, and *Fairly Mounted on a Hill*, 2015.

5. The Ellins Family and Rigby Hall

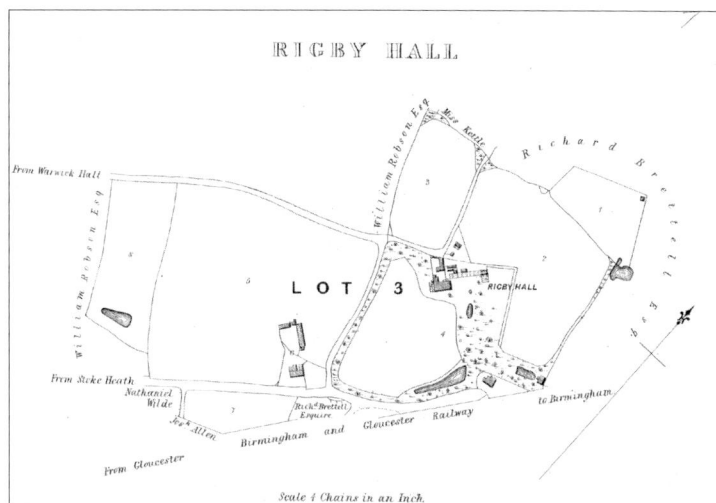

Rigby Hall sale plan, 1843. (BC)

'... a well-arranged DWELLING-HOUSE, with Offices and Garden attached, suitable for the residence of a respectable Family'; and also another 'well-arranged and substantially-built Dwelling House' [Scotch House later known as The Vale] and 'Another Dwelling House, of the same character, immediately joining the last plus four acres of arable land the other side of the railway'.

Lots 5 to 19, mostly in Finstall Heath, were all described as 'valuable Pieces of BUILDING LAND' – the Ellins were always after the main chance!

Lots 20 to 24 were houses and shops and gardens in Catshill and Sidemoor.

Lots 25 to 30 were 44 houses and shops in central Bromsgrove plus a slaughter house, and a warehouse by Holy Lane.

George Ellins had previously ventured into the salt industry in Droitwich, with a Benjamin Smith, but it didn't last long for the partnership was dissolved by mutual consent in May 1844; however George continued his interest because he patented his ideas for improved methods of manufacturing salt. By 1849 there really was a calamity because George, salt manufacturer trading under the name Ellins and Co., was made 'Bankrupt – creditors to receive warrant for second dividend of ³⁄₄d in the pound'. He then lived as a boarder with a cordwainer (shoemaker) in Droitwich. But he wouldn't be beaten, he still continued inventing, and in 1852 patented a 'Method and apparatus for preparing flax straw, for dressing and cleaning'. Some 800 people suffered from the bankruptcy, all left unpaid their due. His brother Henry changed tack completely and got a job as Master at Droitwich Workhouse, bringing with him his daughters Mary as Matron, Dorothy as Schoolmistress, and Elizabeth as Governess. Unfortunately he became ill and the Poor Law Commissioners reported that he died after an illness in 1849.

Chapter Six

The Albrights, Finstall Farm and the Village Hall

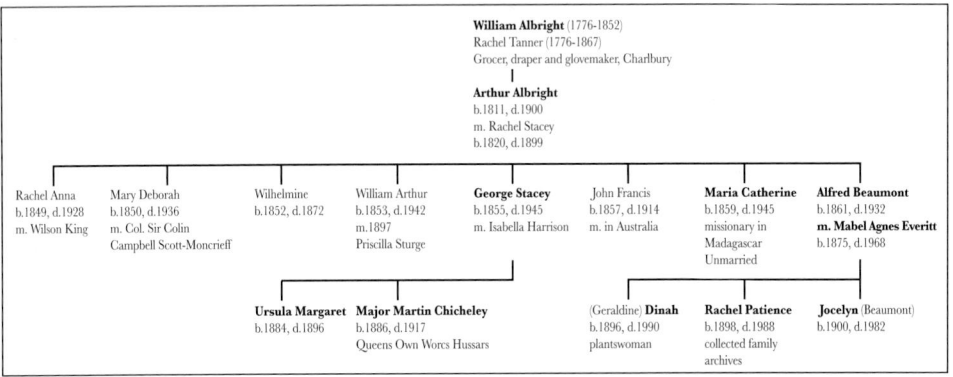

Finstall Farm was finally sold to Arthur Albright in 1874, following the death of R.W. Johnson, and he was the kind of buyer that the estate agents had focussed on. He was another wealthy midlands businessman wanting somewhere to hide from the industrial sites and smoke, and paid £9,550 for the eight bedroomed house, bailiff's house (lived in by Thomas Gardner) and 113 acres of land.

Arthur Albright[38] was a staunch Quaker, as were his family. Arthur moved to Birmingham in 1842 having been apprenticed to a Quaker chemist and druggist in Bristol, and joined his brother-in-law, Edmund Sturge, also of course a Quaker, in a business as a manufacturing chemist. In Selly Oak, Birmingham, Sturge was already making potassium chlorate for the match industry, and Albright added the production of white

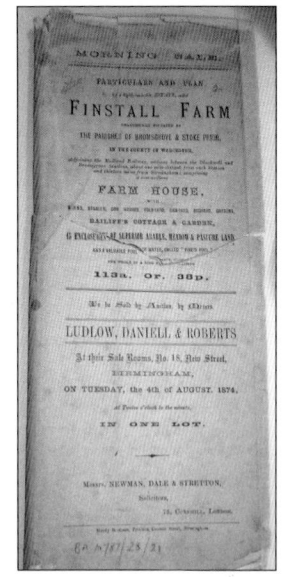

Notice of the sale of Finstall Farm bought by Arthur Albright in 1874. (WRO)

---

38   Arthur was the elder son of William Albright (1776-1852) of Charlbury, Oxfordshire, grocer, draper and glovemaker. He was educated at the Friends' School, Rochester, Kent before becoming apprenticed to the Bristol chemist.

phosphorus in 1844. In 1850 they opened a new works in Oldbury, but they dissolved their partnership in 1854, Sturge not being happy with Albright's management. The production of matches and working with phosphorus at that time caused what was known to the employees as 'Phossy jaw', its proper name osteonecrosis of the jaw, resulting in deformed bones. This horrible disease worried Albright greatly (though didn't stop him working with it), and he began experiments with the safer amorphous phosphorus, with the object of finding some way of making it non-explosive, so that it could be used to make safety matches. Arthur Albright formed a new business with John Edward Wilson[39] in 1856, to be known as Albright and Wilson, which successfully traded as a family business until it became a public company in 1948. Here they worked on phosphorus sesquisulfide, which was dangerous to make but safe for safety matches.

Arthur Albright, painted by Percy Bigland.

Rachel Albright.

Away from work he was a life-long Liberal and sympathised with the Chartists. Amongst other causes he was an early and vocal supporter of the Complete Suffrage Union from 1841, together with Joseph Sturge and Messrs Collins and Goodrick of Birmingham, an active anti-slavery campaigner in the British Humanitarianism and Congo Reform Movement as its second largest donor, and part of the Society for the Promotion of Permanent and Universal Peace. Despite the Quaker background of its founders, Albright & Wilson was involved in the development and production of shells and other armaments, including phosphorus smoke screens and anti-Zeppelin bullets. During WWI W.A. Albright (Arthur Albright's eldest son) on principle refused to take any share dividends during the war. Arthur was subject to depressions, when he 'would think himself the basest of beings, unfit to associate with his fellows', when his family came together to try to lessen his 'black cloud'.[40]

Arthur and Rachel (née Stacey) moved to Mariemont[41] in Westbourne Road, Edgbaston with their family of eight children in 1871. Sadly Wilhelmine, their third daughter, died in 1872 aged 20, a loss that might have encouraged them in 1874 to buy Finstall Farm as a holiday home with no sad memories.

---

39 John Wilson married the sister of Rachel Albright, Arthur's wife.
40 See *Arthur Albright – Notes of his Life*, Wilson King, Birmingham Guild Press, 1901.
41 The house is now demolished and a student hall of residence is in its place, though its delightful lodge is still at the entrance by the road.

Albright & Wilson crate made for bombs; 'Fragile glass, Highly inflammable, do not drop, handle with great care.'

The land Albright bought in 1874 also included Pikes Pool, described in the sale particulars as having springs, and 'a conduit under the railway which irrigates a portion of the estate'.[42] It also had as 'good fishing as any in the county'.

The Turnpike road – Alcester Road – 'gives about ¾ mile of frontage to the estate, and this renders the purchase of the property very desirable for the ultimate object of dividing into Lots for Villa residences'. It was in 1877 that Arthur Albright bought nine acres of Caspidge Farm, 'whereon a messuage formerly stood plus 2 closes near adjoining Finstall Heath called Hill Croft'.

Albright didn't stop at the Caspidge land. He also bought Hollow Tree Farm (23 acres), Old Hill (8 acres) and Vigo Close (3 acres), these in occupation of Thomas Gardner, whose rent was being paid to Thomas Farmer Parkes. In 1881 he bought Tutnall Hall Farm for £10,400 including timber. And in 1894 he bought Caspidge Farm, but sold it on to his friend Francis Corder Clayton the same year.[43] When deciding whether or not to buy Tutnall Hall Farm his solicitor encouragingly said

> there is a growing tendency for Birmingham people to acquire sites for residences in this neighbourhood: this would increase the purchase price.

Advertisement for Albright & Wilson's aspirin, paracetamol and botanical drugs, etc. plus carbon tetrachloride for dry cleaning.

Thomas Gardner, living in Tutnall Hall, was employing several men, including a cowman and waggoner, providing 'liberal wages' and a cottage and garden. An unfortunate incident was that in 1882

> Henry Kings, boatman, a one-armed man, was charged with stealing a turkey value 15s. from Mr Thomas Gardner. Joseph Price of The Cross Inn said he was there that night in the pub. PC Prosser followed footprints to the New Wharf and followed the boat to Oldbury. Kings sold the bird to a boatman for 2s. 6d. He pleaded guilty and was given a month's hard labour.

---

42 See chapter on Pikes Pool.

43 See chapters on these properties.

6. The Albrights, Finstall Farm and the Village Hall

However, in 1883 Thomas Gardner was called before Robert Smallwood Esq and Rev. JRT Eaton and charged with allowing his donkey to stray on the highway at Finstall. He was fined 6d. and 8 shillings costs.

But he and his wife had a sad blow, the suicide of his unmarried daughter Agnes who was drowned in Stoke Works reservoir near to her brother's house at Weston Hall Farm. She was found with her nightdress on, but with her garters and stockings on the bank, so it was no accident. Apparently Agnes had had a severe attack of diphtheria some twelve years previously, followed by a paralysis, and she was 'mentally weak', so had spent a short time in a lunatic asylum. It seems that the Gardners gave up farming around this time, for in 1895 there was an advertisement for both Finstall and Tutnall Hall Farms to let, an offer taken up by George James, who worked the two farms until 1906.

In the end Arthur and Rachel Albright never spent much time in Finstall but enjoyed living at Mariemont, entertaining their large family and friends. They had eight children. Four daughters: Rachel, Mary[44], Wilhelmine and Maria Catherine, who worked as a Quaker missionary in East Africa and Madagascar before retiring to Finstall. The four boys: William Arthur, who lived in Edgbaston, followed his father into Albright & Wilson and married Priscilla Sturge of that Quaker family; George Stacey, who was a fine tennis player and rugby player, was also part of Albright & Wilson[45] and at his death he bequeathed his Bromsberrow, Gloucestershire estate to Alfred Beaumont Albright's three daughters[46], Dinah, Rachel and Jocelyn. The third son, John Francis, was an electrical engineer[47] who became chairman of a number of electrical companies, while Alfred Beaumont was the last, and another investor in Finstall lands.

From the 1890s Alfred Beaumont was living in Finstall Farm, in 1895 marrying

Mariemont, Westbourne Road, Edgbaston, home of the Albright family. Now demolished, though the attractive lodge is still by the road.

---

44   Mary's husband, Colonel Sir Colin Campbell Scott-Moncrieff, KCSI KCMG, who lived with his wife in Cheyne Walk, Chelsea, was known for being Chief Engineer of India's irrigation system, for repairing the Nile Barrage, and reorganizing Egypt's irrigation system.

45   William's only son, a Major in the Queens Own Worcestershire Hussars, was killed in WWI.

46   The eldest of AB Albright's daughters, Dinah, bought out her siblings and lived in the Gloucestershire house until her death.

47   He trained with Bazalgette, famously responsible for London's important and innovative sewerage system.

Finstall Farmhouse in 1900.

Mabel Agnes Everitt (known in the family as May), youngest daughter of Mr Frederick Everitt of Barnt Green House. The marriage settlement was £1,087.10s. which meant that the couple would be very comfortably off, and shortly afterwards they moved into Grimley Hall – a wedding present – which had been bought by Mr Everitt from William Morris in 1894.

Arthur Albright died in 1900, when his will left his property to be divided amongst his family, W.A. Albright being given Finstall Farm. He, living as he did in Edgbaston, then arranged for (Maria) Catherine Albright to take on the tenancy of Finstall farmhouse, for she had retired from her travelling, and in 1942 when he died of broncho pneumonia it was left to her. The farmland was worked by Mr Mebb, whose tenancy was a ten year lease for £225.3.0 per annum.

Miss Albright also inherited five of the cottages in Finstall Terrace, two cottages and gardens and three other cottages on the Alcester Road. She took her position in the village very seriously, and, in 1904, worrying that the people living here had no community facilities and no place for worship, she arranged for the building of the Village Hall on Albright land, designed by local architect Philip Green. This was to be used for 'religious services on Sundays and as a man's social club during the week'. Very soon a small library was collected together, and the men enjoyed billiards, chess, dominoes and ping-pong. An Adult School for Women was allowed to begin in 1914. Miss Albright encouraged religious services which were given

Finstall Village Hall, painted by its architect, Philip Green. This is still hanging in the hall. (Village Hall Trustees)

A 1950s photograph of the Youth Club members, with Topsy Hobbs seated middle front. (Neville Hancock)

monthly by the St Godwald's vicars or their lay readers – including, in the 1980s, Robert Pancheri, the ecclesiastical woodcarver and sculptor. By 1936 she wanted to pass over the ownership of the Village Hall, and a group of trustees was formed – May Albright of Grimley House, Llewellyn Ryland of Walnut Cottage, Major Philip Gunton of Coombe Cottage, and the Revd. Hayman. It was agreed that the hall was:

> ... to be used as a non-sectarian and non-political place of recreation and social intercourse and for any educational, charitable, religious or benevolent purposes for the advantage or benefit of the inhabitants of the Parish of Finstall, under the name of Finstall Parish Institute.

Since then the hall has continued as the centre of the village, soon to be used by the W.I., and other organisations. There have been various upsets – in 1915 there was a fire in the roof, due to overheating of the pipes from the stove, resulting in much rebuilding. In recent times the hall needed a lot of work done on the building and there were proposals to demolish it and build a new one – thankfully this did not happen, for together with the corner shop and The Cross Inn, it makes a most attractive centre for the village.

For the Coronation of Queen Elizabeth II the village pulled out all the stops, holding a service in the hall, organising a sports day, a baby show, a ladies football match and building a float depicting *Finstall* which toured the village. At this time Bill Hobbs was the caretaker, and his wife Ruth, known as Topsy, formed a much appreciated Youth Club. Topsy was worried that there was no children's playground in the village, and wrote a letter to Prince Philip about this. The playground was built by the District Council at the top of Penmanor and it is now leased to the Parish Council. Miss Albright also thought of the children in the village and encouraged them to play in Cart Horse Meadow (known to the children as Cartus) beside Finstall Mount, where she set up swings and parallel bars.

In 1980 a painting by Bertram Priestman (1868-1951), that was hanging in the hall, *Cement Works on the Medway*, was sold to the artist's son-in-law, Lord Pearce, for £1,250 – a useful amount at a time when the hall's committee was very short of funds. The realisation that the painting had a value came when Ferens Art Gallery in Hull asked to borrow it for an exhibition. No-one knew how it had come to the hall, though as the Priestman family were Quakers it would probably have an Albright connection.

The first annual Flower Show, always held in the hall, was in 1905, and among the list of classes in 1906, still nowadays recognisable, were *Plants and Cut Flowers* and *Vegetables* (onions, carrots, runner beans, etc.). Entries for these were confined to 'Villagers, who have no greenhouse nor means of artificial heating'. There was a tiny class *For Women*,

'Miss Finstall' with her five attendants ready to drive round the village. (John Suffield)

with two possibilities: to make a cake with 2 eggs to 1lb of flour, and the second for the best 'Plain Apron. Prizes awarded for the Neatest Sewing and Finish. First prize, Material for a Blouse'. Children under 15 were invited to enter a 'Knitted Sock, small size'. By 1914, just after WWI had begun, an Air-Gun Shooting Competition had been included, women were invited to hand sew a child's pinafore or overall, and children under 15 could enter a 'Child's Chemise, hand sewn and untrimmed'. By 1929 Finstall 'cottagers' could be judged 'For the Best Kept Garden' and 'For the Best Kept Allotment, Size not to exceed ¼ of an Acre'.

Many organisations regularly use the hall for meetings, now including *two* WIs, one in the afternoon and one in the evening. In 1897 Women's Institutes were created in Stoney Creek, Canada and the idea reached Britain in 1915, when countrywomen were encouraged to get involved in growing and preserving food to help increase the supply of food in a war-torn nation. By 1917 the Board of Agriculture was pressing for this. The first WI in Britain was Llanfairpwll, Anglesey in 1915; Finstall waited until 1937, just a couple of years before WWII, when members received instruction on cooking, dressmaking and digging for victory. The five meetings during the first half of that year (with tea at 3d.) included Entertainment by Headless Cross WI, a talk on 'Life in the Monasteries' by Mrs Nettlefold, a demonstration in April of 'A Washing Day Meal' given by Miss Rimmer,

6. The Albrights, Finstall Farm and the Village Hall

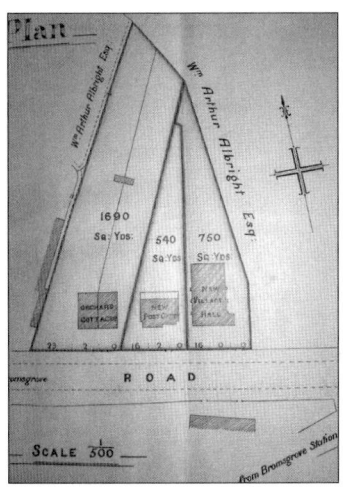

Plan showing the Albright land given to the village for the Village Hall, the Post Office, and Orchard Cottages, 1904. (WRO)

plus a competition for a 'Garden in a Soup Plate'. In May they had a demonstration of 'Thrift' and 'Uses for old Silk Stockings', and a competition for the 'Best Ironed Pillow Case'. However it was during the war that the WI set a high standard in jam making, in 1942 producing 4,550lbs, and members were encouraged to buy stamps from sixpence upwards, saving towards the cost of National Savings Certificates. The WI also did a good service by running the Library boxes which were brought up from Bromsgrove Library so that people could borrow books more easily.

Next door to the village hall Miss Albright built a smart new Post Office, and next to that are the pair of Orchard Cottages. Shortly afterwards Miss Albright decided to use the land opposite The Cross for more houses – three plots of land for three pairs, divided by a Recreation Ground which led to the field of allotments.

In 1938 William A. Albright arranged a Deed of Covenant with the National Trust, offering about 75 of the 98 acres of Finstall farm. This was seemingly to ensure that the land would remain unchanged, for it was agreed that 'no buildings shall be erected other than Cottages for farm labourers and farm buildings, that no mine or quarry shall be opened or worked and that no timber, trees or underwood shall be topped, felled or cut except in accordance with the usual method of forestry'.[48]

Meanwhile in Miss Albright's time Finstall Farm was being run by Mr G. Mebb, who was fortunately on the site when there was a fire in the barn in January 1908; he telephoned for the police (an early date for a telephone to be installed), and put the fire out with water from the farm pond.

Miss Albright's links with Birmingham continued, for she was a member of their branch of the Women's Suffrage Society (its members were largely Quaker and Unitarian), and was one of the many women who refused to have their names on the 1911 census. It's not known whether she was one of their 150 members who went to a demonstration that year in Trafalgar Square by a special train that was decorated with evergreens and purple and white ribbons, with suffrage flags hanging from the carriage windows. The subject of suffrage reached unexpected places – in February 1911 a men's group took part in a debate in Finstall Village Hall on 'Should Women have the Vote'. The discussion proved a very popular one, much enjoyed by the participants. The result of the voting was very close, but the affirmative vote was lost. Another Finstall link to the suffrage movement

---

48   From 1960 sale particulars.

was also in February 1911, when Mr and Mrs Thomas Horton of Coombe Cottage held a 'Drawing Room Meeting' of local people which led to the first large public meeting in Bromsgrove.[49] Women were allowed the vote on the same rules as men after 1928; I hope Miss Albright was able to vote for the first time at her Village Hall as we do today.

Miss Albright was also very much against war – had she been a man she would have been a conscientious objector, and she had great sympathy for those who took that path instead of joining the army. Those who were drafted into the Army and then disobeyed orders faced a court martial, and many of these were sent to prison. Anyone who fled the front could be shot. 'Conchies' as they were known attracted considerable stigma, and there are stories of white feathers being handed to men who were not in uniform. By the end of the war the Society of Friends, the Fellowship of Reconciliation and the Independent Labour Party, but more especially the former, had for some time recognised that many of the men released from prison would be in urgent need of rest and attention before returning to their workplaces. They formed a joint committee known as the Joint Advisory Council to look after this matter, and arranged with volunteers such as Miss Albright to give short holidays in the countryside for some of the conchies who had suffered from unpleasant stays in prison. In a full description of his time refusing to join the army, Harold Blake, a Wesleyan who later became a Worcester pharmacist, was imprisoned twice, and suffered solitary confinement, described his visit to Finstall Farm:

Harold Blake (1889-1980), Conscientious Objector. (Tony Blake)

> On Friday April 25th, 1919, I left Wandsworth [jail] for the last time, being still excessively weak and far from well, although my condition had improved as a result of a more congenial environment latterly. By the first post on Saturday April 26th, I received a letter from Isaac Goss, the secretary of the Joint Advisory Council and it contained three one-pound notes. Thoroughly mystified, I commenced to read the accompanying letter, which explained that arrangements had been made for Mrs. Blake and myself to spend a fortnight's holiday at the home of Miss C. Albright at Finstall Farm near Bromsgrove.
>
> ... The amazing efficiency of the [Joint Advisory Council] and the lightening speed with which things had been expedited quite dazed me. After the harshness and

---

49 For a history of the suffrage movement in Bromsgrove see *Home is the Proper Place for Women – The fight for women's suffrage in Bromsgrove*, Jennie McGregor-Smith, *The Bromsgrove Rousler*, No. 26, which includes the suffrage campaigning by Laurence and Clemence Housman, A.E. Housman's siblings.

6. The Albrights, Finstall Farm and the Village Hall

inconsideration that had been meted out to me for so many months, this kindness so unnerved me that I am not ashamed to confess that tears flowed unrestrained.

When we arrived at Bromsgrove station, we found that Miss Albright, like the other Quakers, was not behindhand in forethought and kindness, for she had sent her pony and trap to bring us up from the station.

... Throughout the fortnight we were blessed with the most glorious weather, enabling us to be out of doors almost the whole time, enjoying health giving rambles throughout the beautiful countryside of Worcestershire. ...

I still slept poorly and was always awake quite early, frequently at dawn. One thing that impressed me about Finstall, above everything, was the extraordinary number of feathered songsters that provided a dawn chorus as the sun climbed above the horizon. It seemed that the multitude of singers trilled out a veritable song of freedom, which found an echo in my own heart.[50]

Miss Albright was plain of dress, and rode a bicycle, though she also had a pony and trap, and later a motorcar. She was described by a villager[51] as 'a gracious old lady who was hard of hearing and carried a lorgnette'. She opened up her Granary barn, next to her house, for Quaker services on Sunday evenings.

After WWI the Albrights were concerned to support those whose gardens were not large enough to provide the vegetables they needed, and in 1918 it was agreed between Stoke Prior Parish Council and W.A. Albright that two acres of the land behind the village hall should be used for this purpose, the Parish Council providing a necessary fence, and paying £4.16.6d p.a. The plan proposed by Mr Albright was for 13 narrow, far too small, allotments on the site. The allotment land, now under the aegis of Finstall Parish Council, is not now used for allotments.

Mr Mebb's stay at Finstall Farm was followed in 1912 by Sherwood Suffield, who had previously been at Stonehouse Farm, and had moved to live in Allotment Cottage across the road from Finstall Farm. He then moved from Allotment Cottage to the newly built Finstall Farm cottage in 1929, paying £122.3s.6d per annum for the farmland, £26.18.0 for Finstall Farm cottage, and £25.0.0 as interest on the cost of a new cow house. His son John Humstone Suffield, Sherwood's son, his wife Mary and children John Sherwood and Marion, lived for a while at No.5 The Terrace.

The family's herd of pedigree jersey cows, started in 1936 by Sherwood, were kept on land behind Ashdene on the Finstall Road, and were milked in a shed in the field. As well as the cows, they kept some sheep and about 200 hens. The family moved up to Finstall Farm, and after the death of John Humstone Suffield in 1951, the younger John Sherwood continued working for Colonel Kerr until 1954. The family finally gave up farming in 1974.

---

50 For the full story go to www.whoseimage.uwclub.net/Chap%2033.htm

51 Mrs Dorothy Knight, *Bromsgrove Messenger* 27 February 1984.

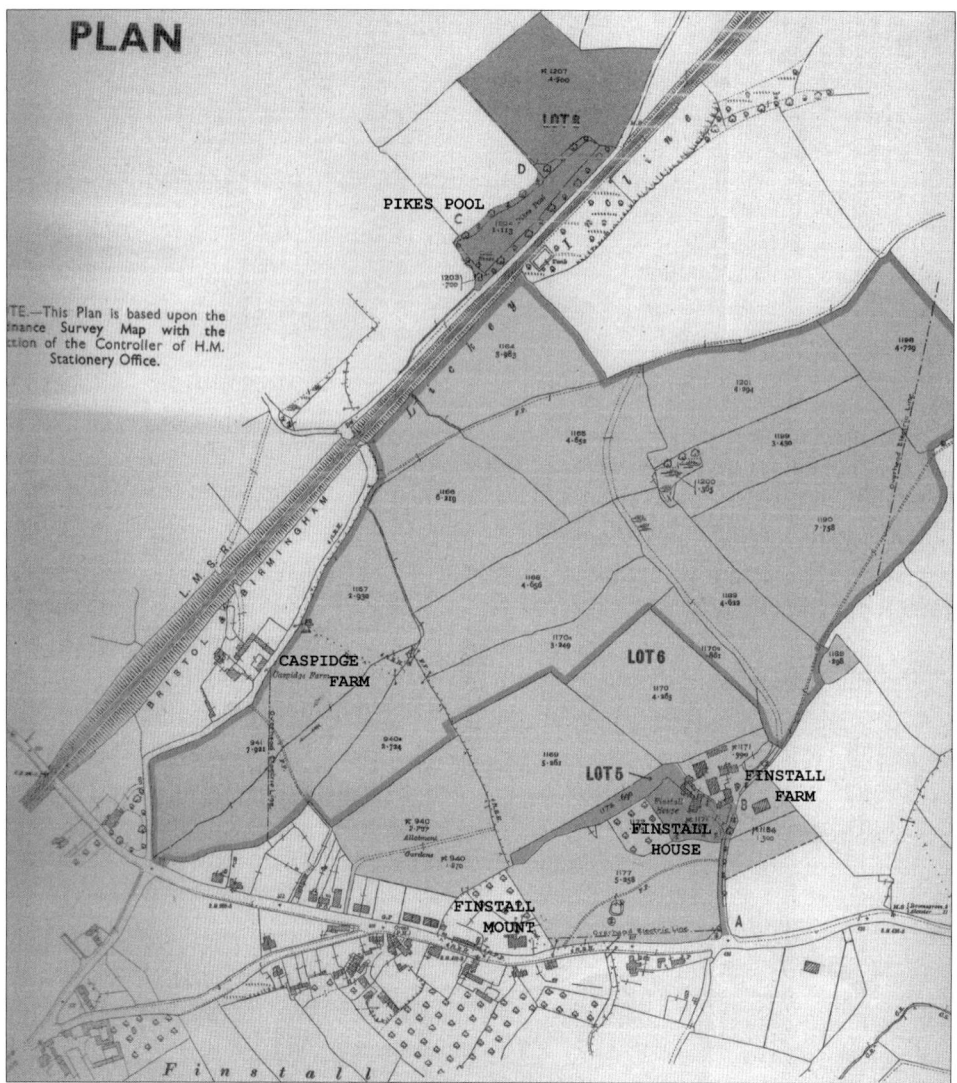

Finstall Farm sale plan, sold by Warwickshire Monthly Meeting (Quakers) in 1949, after the death of Miss Albright. Finstall Farm (Lot 6), Finstall House (Lot 5), Pikes Pool (Lot 8). (BC)

Miss Catherine Albright died in 1945, and her will took an unconscionable time to be sorted out – perhaps one of the problems was that her brother Walter's will (he died 1942) had not been signed off by the lawyers, who must have had a field day when they found she had left Finstall Farm, Finstall Mount and Coombe Cottage, together with Allotment Cottage (next to Coombe Cottage), the Old Smithy and the adjacent allotment land, to Warwickshire Monthly Meeting (Quakers). In order to raise the capital to renovate and

6. THE ALBRIGHTS, FINSTALL FARM AND THE VILLAGE HALL

equip Finstall Farmhouse so it could be used as a guest house for Friends in need of rest, and also as a conference centre, Finstall Mount and Coombe Cottage were sold. But by 1949 it was apparent that the aims were not being fulfilled; Friends were not using the farmhouse as a guest house for quiet recuperation, and though it was being used as a conference centre the majority of guests were not Friends. It was then decided to sell the property, and use the sale to support causes she had been interested in: to enable Friends of Warwickshire Monthly Meeting to obtain respite breaks, help at home for the elderly and for those with small children, and to attend Quaker retreats and summer schools, including help with holidays for Friends with young children. From now on Finstall House was always put up for sale separately from the farm itself.

The rest of her property was to be divided between the three daughters of Alfred Beaumont Albright. This included Allotment Cottage, the old smithy and the allotment land behind the Village Hall which she was renting to Stoke Prior District Council.

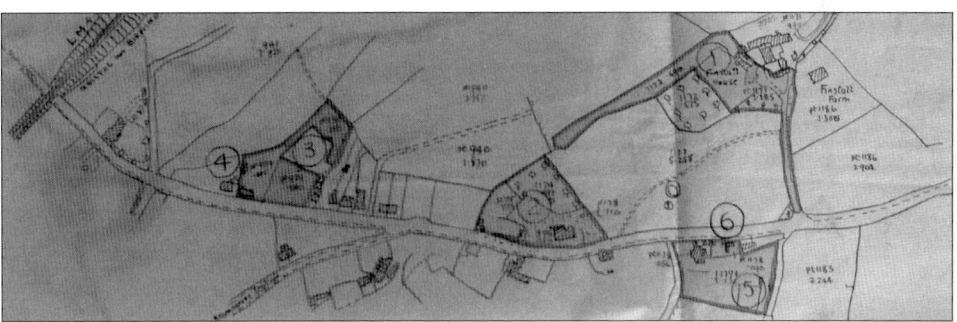

Plan of properties also auctioned in 1949: Lot 1 Finstall House; Lot 2 Finstall Mount; Lot 3 Cottages; Lot 4 Old Smithy; Lot 5 Coombe Cottage; Lot 6 Allotment Cottage. (WRO)

The following were also Albright family property: High Barn Farm at Vigo, Pikes Pool, Clevedon and Vigo cottages, plus Tutnall Hall Farm and Malvern View.

A list of rents paid to Misses Jocelyn, Dinah and Rachel Albright in 1948:

1. Finstall Farm J.A. Suffield   £122.3.6
   Farmhouse J.A. Suffield   £26.18.0
   plus interest on cost of new cow house   £25.0.0
2. Stoke Prior District Council   £4.16.6
3. Cottages Mrs Hathaway   £1.0.0 per week
   W. Mitchell   15 shillings per week
   Mrs N. Hall   15 shillings per week
4. Field adjoining Pikes Pool   £13.10.0

Also from 1931, payment was received for an electricity station on the Alcester Road leased by the Electric Power Company.

So on the death of Miss Albright another Miss Albright briefly took her place at Finstall Farm. Jocelyn Albright was the third daughter of Alfred and May Albright of Grimley Hall, which is where she soon returned for the rest of her life.

Between 1949 and 1960 there was much confusing movement. The Trustees of the Society of Friends sold the house to George Hird, Esq., and Messrs Darby & Co. bought the 84 acre farm. Two years later Hird sold Finstall House to Major I.S.G. Mackenzie, MBE retired, and he sold the farm cottage to Colonel William Harcourt Kerr, T.D., J.P., D.L. of the Worcestershire Territorials and of Tutnall Mount, for £475. Two years after that Darby & Co. – having found they were not allowed to build on the land because of the National Trust covenant – sold the farm to Colonel Kerr for £9,000, and in 1954 Major Mackenzie sold the house to Mr A.L. Evans of Sutton Coldfield. In 1958 Mr Evans sold the Finstall House land to Colonel Kerr, who in 1960 sold the farm's 98 acres, but not Finstall House, to George Bridges. It was a well equipped farm by then, with modern cow sheds for 30 animals, a dairy block, a bull pen and yard, three pigsties, loose boxes and calf pens, two barns plus stock shed and a tractor house. Judith and Michael Maguire and their children came to Finstall House after the Evans.

The ownership of the property became even more confusing in the late 1960s when the County Council bought the house and part of the land in order to build the new Bromsgrove/Redditch highway. Finstall House was left untenanted and fell into disrepair, though Mr Bridges continued farming throughout the road building period and after, and Finstall Farm is still in the ownership of that family.

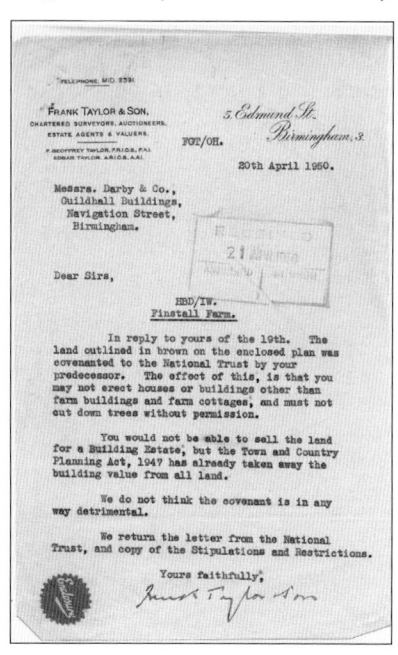

Letter to Messrs Darby & Co. in 1950 regarding the covenant to the National Trust by Miss Albright, which still stands today. (WRO)

The poor house deteriorated greatly. In 2001 Bromsgrove Council found it necessary to register the house – which is Listed Grade II – as a 'building at risk', after which the house was well restored, was sold in 2005, and is now in good condition again, and is what the estate agent described as a 'fine family home'.

Chapter Seven
Finstall Heath and The Cross

Having looked at some of the grander people of Finstall, the other half of the village in early days was the group of cottagers living around Finstall Heath and what is now The Cross, which has been open as an alehouse since at least the 1780s.

Possibly the earliest building was the first Finstall blacksmith's shop, which in the mid 1700s was tenanted by James Macmillan but owned by Mr Brettell of Finstall Park. He was followed by William Allbutt, sadler and whipmaker, then his son John, blacksmith. In 1796 the tenancy transferred to John Albutt, Yeoman. This was a small pleck of land with

> ... ¾ of an acre lately part of and inclosed from the Common called Finstall Heath by virtue of the Act of Parliament lately passed for dividing and inclosing the commons and waste lands with the said manor and bounded by turnpike road leading from Bromsgrove to Alcester, land of John Ashmore and a cottage and garden of William Orford and land of ... James Macmillan deceased.

This was the only building on the northern side of the turnpike road for many years. It changed hands many times, and grew to be two cottages, but because of the regular traffic of horses and carts passing up the hill from Bromsgrove or down the hill from the canal wharf it was well known to the travellers and also to local farmers, so it was a successful working forge for at least 100 years. In 1853 a plan of Finstall Farm showed that the blacksmith's plot had belonged to Mr Ellins of Rigby Hall. In 1885 a poster announced the sale of a:

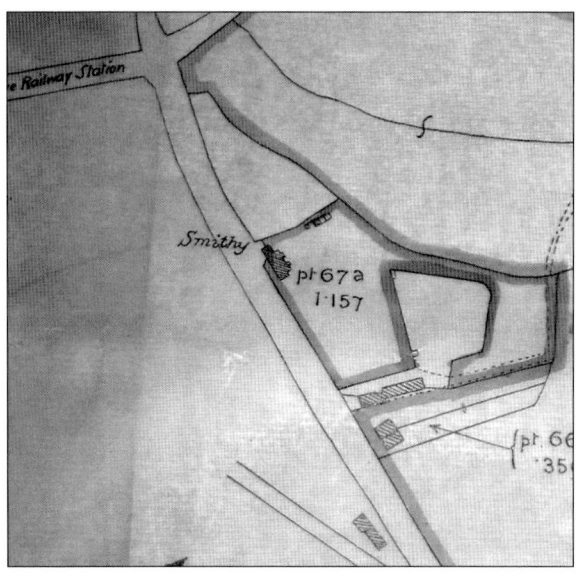

Sale plan showing the first smithy, together with the other early cottages – one of them becoming the first Post Office – on Alcester Road. (WRO)

'Dwelling House with blacksmith's shop and large pleck of garden ground on the Alcester Road Finstall. Mr Cotton has received instructions from the mortgagee to offer for sale on 1st September 1885 at the Dog and Pheasant. ... The Dwelling House has a sitting room, kitchen, pantry, 3 bedrooms, brewhouse, blacksmith's shop and Pent House [a shed or lean-to attached to the house], pigstye, necessary out offices and large productive garden well stocked with choice fruit trees. 1 acre 0 reams 16 perches. ... supplied with water.'

This was bought by Mr Albright of Finstall Farm and soon the buildings were known as Old Smithy cottages. The last recorded blacksmith in Finstall was 1901, but he was employed to work at the wagon works at Aston Fields, as were many of the people living in Finstall at that time.

The aptly named Stone Cottage, though half built with brick.

In the two groups of cottages high above the road to Aston Fields, known as Finstall Terrace, originally there was one pair, and another row of five. In the 1720s the two freehold (formerly copyhold) cottages were owned by Stephen Abbott, who passed them on to his son, S. Abbott junior. By 1822 Thomas Rogers, son of farmer Thomas Rogers of Caspidge, owned them and lived in one. These were later inherited by Mary Ann Rogers, and Mary left them to her son-in-law Henry Dowley, who in turn sold them to Miss Harriet Harris who bought the pair of cottages in 1876 for £198.

There was a 'messuage and tenement at Finstall Heath with copyhold barns, stable buildings, land and pastures in the possession of Thomas Strafford' owned by Thomas Farmer, a Bromsgrove ironmonger[52]. Farmer left this property in his will dated 1723 to members of his family, and also said that if his wife (who must have been pregnant when he wrote the will – but he didn't die until 1737) had a daughter, he'd leave the girl £600 when she was 21; if she had

Part of the Terrace showing the stone wall alongside Finstall Road. Painting by Frances Rogers

---

52 This is at Birmingham Archives, MS 3101/A/3/6/1. I have not identified the property.

a son he'd leave him £800. Farmer already had three daughters – Hannah, Elizabeth and Mary – to whom he left £600 each, instructing them to dress 'in a sober plain manner ... as used ... by people commonly called Quakers'.

The five cottages next to Finstall Terrace were owned in 1754 by John Betts, then by Francis Featherstone[53], thus beginning another family history in the village. A little later one of the cottages was taken by W. Hedges, machinist (a name familiar to many of us today), who paid off his copyhold, as had Featherstone.

William Hedges, machinist.

The next important name in the village was that of Cund, for Jeremiah Cund, a 30 year old wheelwright was there in 1841, living next door to his wheelwright father aged 60, down Alcester Road at the old blacksmith's. Jeremiah's business obviously did well, for in 1866 he was advertising for 'several wheelwrights – good wages and constant situation', and also worked hard on his little bit of land, having his hay ricks and winter beans auctioned at The Cross in 1868. The family line continued, with young Richard following in their footsteps. Others in this practical family became shoemakers, Christopher was a coach builder (probably at the wagon works), David was a blacksmith and a later Jeremiah called himself a carpenter but also became a provision dealer and sub-postmaster, work that his wife took over on his death. He did his bit for the community, being appointed a Constable or Overseer in Bromsgrove, accompanied by his friend Thomas Gardner of Finstall Farm. There was one blip in the Cund reputation in 1878 when one of the Jeremiahs was charged with being drunk in Worcester Street; Mr Housman of Perry Hall appeared for the defendant, but the Bench (Major Bourne of Grafton Manor and Mr R. Smallwood of Rigby Hall) considered it proved and fined the defendant 10 shillings plus 10 shillings costs. This seems a tremendous amount of money for that period. However, as there was another Jeremiah Cund living in Bromsgrove at this time we shall hope it was he, not the Finstall Jeremiah, who had misbehaved.

Jeremiah senior died early in 1899, and his son Jeremiah junior died a few months later aged 48. An executor of Jeremiah senior's will was the friend and once neighbour of the family, William Hedges, machinist, who had moved to The Crescent, Bromsgrove. He had total responsibility for carrying out the terms of the will because the other trustees had died. A big sale was held in October that year. The two cottages in Lot 1, next to each other, were the family homes – Jeremiah senior in one and the other, nearest Alcester

---

53 Fetherstone is spelled many different ways in those papers – Featherstone, Featherston, Fetherstone, Fetherston. All are the same family. I am using whichever was used in the original paper describing each event.

Road, was the village shop and sub-postal office run now by Martha Cund, Jeremiah junior's widow. This Lot was bought by T. Horton for £450, who was later to live in Coombe Cottage.

Lot 2 was the five cottages of Finstall Terrace, which was withdrawn but bought later by Mr Albright. Each cottage contained 'kitchen, pantry, 2 bedrooms and joint use of two brewhouses'. Lot 3 and 4 were a brick and tiled cottage and Mr Prescott's garden, with 'kitchen, back kitchen, 2 bedrooms with out offices and good front gardens'. These were bought by Mr John Boultbee Brooks of Finstall House for £180. Lot 5, two cottages next to Lot 4, was sold to Joseph Tilt, builder, of Bromsgrove. This was a complicated Lot, sold subject to the right of the joint use of the well by the occupant of Lot 4; ... the purchaser shall at own cost disconnect the present slop-drain of the houses which emptied into the corner of Lot 6 and shall construct a fresh dumb-well on his own land and connect the house drains therewith. ... The present gateway leading out of Lot 5 into Lot 6 is to be closed. The purchaser of Lot 5 will be entitled if he thinks fit to make a new gateway close against the side of the end house to give him an entrance to his back garden.

Mr Tilt didn't seem to mind these restrictions, and paid £275 for the cottages. Lot 6, described as 'Valuable building land adjoining Lot 5, having extensive frontage of road to the station, together with erection of wheelwright's shop and timber shed now ... in occupation of Richard Cund'. This was bought by Thomas Ince, a Bromsgrove stationer.

The Finstall Post Office first opened under the rule of Miss M. Rose in 1855, to be followed in 1865 by a tailor, John Hooper. After a couple of years he relinquished it to the Bevan family, William taking over from his mother Susannah as sub-postmaster and shopkeeper in 1881. In the 1860s the post arrived from Bromsgrove Post Office by 7.00 am and 3.35 pm, ready for distribution in the village. The shop itself was open on weekdays from 8.00 am until 8.00 pm, with the last post at 8.10 pm; by 1896 deliveries began at 6.30 am and 3.35 pm, the Letter Box being cleared at 6.30 pm. The shop was open every day from 7.00 am until 8.00 pm including Bank Holidays, while Christmas Day and Good Friday it was open in the morning only. By 1921 the wall letter box at Finch End was cleared at 6.50 pm on weekdays. In 1949 deliveries were from 6.50 am, every day including Christmas Day and Bank Holidays, though not Sundays, and there was a 'Telephone Kiosk outside from which telegrams may be despatched at any time. Dial "O" and ask for "Telegrams"'.

The Cund family had taken over in 1882, led by Jeremiah Cund junior and Martha his wife – who personally delivered letters as far as High Barn, Burcot. The family stayed in Finstall, either running the Post Office and shop, or working as Richard was, as a wheelwright, until the 1960s, though the Post Office moved around. First from the blacksmiths, up the hill to the cottages on the corner opposite the Village Hall, then in 1904 it moved to Miss Albright's smart new villa next to the village hall, where it was run by Mrs Ivy Routh, a Cund niece.

7. Finstall Heath and The Cross

In September 1908 the new old age pension came into being for those aged over 70; 5 shillings a week, 7s 6d for married couples, though only those with a good character could receive it. The Post Offices administered the scheme in order to remove any perceived stigma that there could be if it were dealt with by the parish or under the Poor Law. The first day that people could apply there were long queues in Bromsgrove, and no doubt in Finstall too, when, because the majority of applicants were unable to read or write, the Post Office staff had to fill in the necessary forms on their behalf.

Next to the new Post Office were built Orchard Cottages, also Miss Albright's, and a few years later, on the field known as Finstall Piece – the land between the Village Hall and The Mount – she built three more pairs of houses, leaving space between two of them which she proposed should be a Recreation Ground (now another pair of houses). The Allotments were behind this.

The allotment movement had begun by the 1840s and as early as 1848 Nash, writing of Tardebigge and Stoke Prior, said

> The allotment system, I rejoice to find, has been adopted in this parish, and uniformly attended with the happier effects; and although the last three seasons, owing to the lamented failure of the potato crop, have been most unfavourable for a criterion, none of the occupiers of allotments, I hear, are behind hand in the payment of their rents.

In 1893 the Stoke Prior and Stoke Works Allotment Association held their first show, so Finstall was rather late in having their allotments behind the Village Hall. There was a boost to development of allotments during the wars and as early as 1903 Finstall Field, behind Coombe Cottage and where Allotment Cottage would be built, was also being used for allotments. There are now only allotments at the top of Penmanor.

A wedding celebration opposite The Cross. See motor with ribbons on the left of the picture, and decorations hanging from Highbank Cottages, with a band playing under the eye of a policeman.

The two pairs of Highbank Cottages were aptly named, being high above the road, their east side against the land belonging to Finstall Mount.

* * * *

Francis Featherstone was the son of John, who had died in 1812 leaving Finstall Inn and its 9 acres 3 roods 11 perches to Francis, these acres being Quarry Close, Barn Close, Great Fearnhall (later Pear Tree Piece), Little Fearnhall, Far Piece and the Earl. He was henceforth described as a victualler. The Cross Inn, as it became to be known, had been built extremely close to another dwelling lived in by James Green, resulting in a complicated legal agreement between the two men in 1824.

> 'Agreement between Francis Fetherstone of Finstall and James Green, shoemaker, ... a messuage or dwelling house near to the said messuage in occupation of Francis Fetherstone and separated therefrom only by a passage between the houses of the said respective parties. Whereas Francis Fetherstone and James Green are also entitled to the use of a well and water at the top of the passage ... And whereas the said James Green for the enlargement of his said dwelling house and for the better and more convenient occupation of the same is desirous of building a room across said passage, such building to commence at the distance of six feet and a half or thereabouts from the ground and extending upwards.'

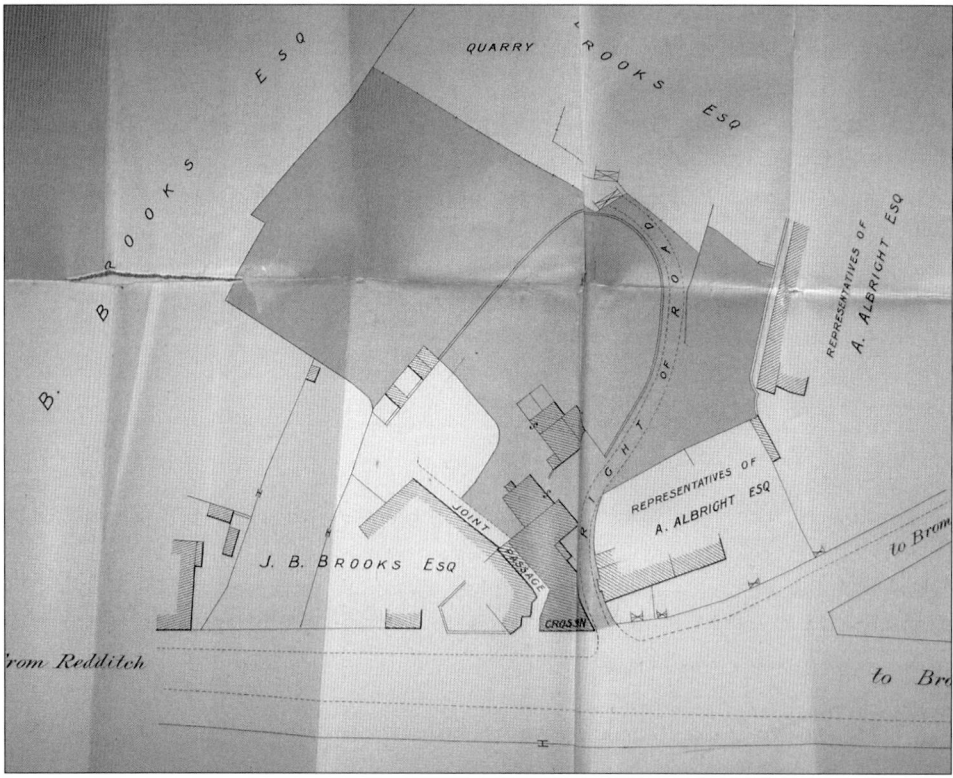

Plan for the sale of The Cross Inn showing a rather exaggerated narrow passage between it and the cottage next door.

7. Finstall Heath and The Cross

The Cross Inn in 2017, with Finstall Croft shown further up Alcester Road.

The sign of The Cross Inn in 2017.

Anyone who knows The Cross and its neighbour will understand the need for the above agreement. And the matter of wells is really important, because all water had to be got from them. It wasn't until 1884 that piped water came to Finstall, and that would only be bought by people who could afford it.[54] It was quite normal for wells and pumps to be shared, for they were expensive to create, and it was also quite usual for house deeds to state which group of houses would share a well.

Most housewives made their own ale or beer for the family to drink. Water often being unclean, even from wells, meant that ale was preferred. Ale was made from malted grain and water but had a short shelf life, took four days to mature, and was a complicated business to make. However by the 18th century hops were generally available and were used for beer that had a longer life, and most country homes had a small pleck of hops near the house where they could grow what they needed for their own consumption. Some estates had much larger areas, growing hops commercially, like the Hopgardens Farm, but there were other smaller hop fields in the area as well. Commercial hop crops were taxed by the government between 1720 and 1862, and it was a risky business, very dependent on the weather.

In Finstall at this time there were at least three places for gathering to enjoy ale or beer; one of course was The Cross, which had its own brewhouse, and Mrs Mary Wilde who kept an ale house by Finch End farmhouse but also there was The Boot Inn (later Coombe Cottage) further up the hill, where in 1871 shoemaker and beerhouse keeper George Harford and his family lived.[55] Living on Alcester Road where both horses and men got thirsty struggling with the steep hill was an ideal situation, and if the local Aletaster approved of the brew then it was worth making a business of it.

---

54 The story of water is told in detail in *From Bromsgrove to Aston Fields* by the present author.

55 It was pleasing to find that there are still hops growing in a hedge at The Boot (now Coombe Cottage).

The Cross was run and owned by Francis Featherstone, victualler, until 1830 when his daughter Martha took it over. Francis Featherstone had died in 1830, leaving after his wife's death:

- to dear daughter Martha Featherstone dwelling house known by name of The Cross, together with brewhouse, rickyard, pigstye, garden with fencing. Also to use jointly with son Francis the stable and fold yard, also 2 freehold dwelling houses adjoining, together with gardens.

- to son Francis dwelling house with garden ground and stone quarry now in occupation Thomas Higgins and barn, cow house, pigstye. Right of way through The Cross ... Quarry Piece, Garden Piece, Orchard, Barn Piece, Pear Tree Piece (previously Big Fernall), Little Fearnall, Far Piece, and the Earl (which dwelling house and garden are copyhold and in his occupation).

- to my daughter Sarah, wife of James Warr, brickmaker of Kingswinford: two dwelling houses at Finstall Heath.

He also left £15 towards placing James, son of John, as apprentice to some trade or business. The dwelling houses left to Sarah, wife of James Warr, who most usefully was a brickmaker, were higher up the Alcester Road – Finstall Hill – from The Cross.

There were several publicans over the next few years. One who had ideas for improving his takings was Alfred Townsend who was happy to apply to the magistrates for late opening hours when there were events in the area – in 1875 he applied for permission to keep open an extra hour on a Thursday and Friday when there was an army camp in Hewell Park. Townsend had numerous interests, including pigeon shooting and pig keeping. He had one prizewinning boar who he named 'Sir Roger Tichborne' following the scandal that continued in the 1860s and 1870s when an Australian butcher claimed to be the missing heir to the Tichborne baronetcy. There were restrictions for the customers; in 1872 a publican was fined for allowing card playing, and for this he had a heavy punishment. Sadly, however, Townsend's ideas didn't bring him enough money and he was made bankrupt. Joseph Price, who became keeper of The Boot up the road in 1872, decided to close and come down to The Cross, but he soon gave up and in 1902 passed the inn to Josiah Deague who was there until 1928, when the property was bought by Flowers of Stratford-upon-Avon.[56]

Before he died Featherstone added to the nine acres that were with The Cross and bought two fields called Combe Close and Combe Meadow which had been part of Stonehouse Farm. Joined by his son John, the Featherstones were known as 'farmers of Finstall Farm' – not the present day Finstall Farm but the land described in Francis's will. In 1861 after Francis's death John sold another 15 acres near the railway station – they were bought by John Jones of Stoke Court for £1,280, showing an increase in the value of

---

56   New owners had just restored the building as this went to the publisher.

7. Finstall Heath and The Cross

A token for 3 pence issued by Josiah Deague of The Cross.

the land locally, probably because the coming of the railway brought much more financial benefit to the area.

John Featherstone was involved in local activities; he was a churchwarden of St Godwald's church, a member of Stoke Prior School Board for six years, and, chosen by a considerable majority, elected Guardian for Stoke Prior Board. A generous gift he made to the parish was to provide the stone from his quarry to build the new Finstall church in 1883. As he grew older his land was rented out, and it is thought he lived in the house on Finstall Hill nowadays known as Finstall Croft. When he died in 1898 he left 'Far Piece, Fern Hill, the Earl and Quarry Bank, Pear Tree Piece, Barn Piece with part of the Quarry; four garden fields, two cottages and gardens and one house and garden (presumably Finstall Croft), Combe Close and part of Coombe Meadow, and Stonehouse Farm'.

In 1898, after Featherstone's death, J. Boultbee Brooks bought a lot of the land. Within the conveyance ran the following:

> ... at all times hereafter by day or by night and for all proper purposes with or without horses carts carriages or wagons laden or unladen to go pass and repass and to drive cattle sheep and other animals along over and upon the road delineated on the said plan ... the said J. Boultbee Brooks his heirs and assigns from time to time paying his or their due proportion with such owners or occupiers as aforesaid of the expense of maintaining the said Road in proper repair ... to be holden to the Lord of the Manor.

This means, I think, that he must pay a proportion of the costs of running the road to the Lord of the Manor (who were the Ecclesiastical Commissioners). I hope he or his lawyer understood it better than we do.

When in 1843 George Ellins of Rigby Hall had to sell his properties, the big field of approximately four acres known as Finstall Heath (now bounded by Finstall Road and Heydon Road) seemed to him to be ripe for building, and he hopefully divided it into no less than fifteen lots. The land was sold to Mr Everitt, but no building was done on the site until the nineteen thirties. The only buildings already on Finstall Heath in 1843 (not owned by Ellins) were the two cottages (which became the Post Office and shop opposite the Village Hall), and the three 18th century sandstone ashlar terraced cottages which were owned by Ellins and still are on the corner of Finstall Road and Heydon Road. They would have been built with stone from one of the Finstall quarries.

An early photograph of the three stone cottages, showing a long wall up Finstall Road towards the Cross and fine stone steps up to the Stud Farm Cottage.

In 1924, when in the Everitt sale, the descriptions show the stone cottages were still much as they had been for 100 years; the two cottages nearest Heydon Road had two rooms up and two down, with 'Pantry, Back Kitchen with sink and furnace, and outside EC (earth closet); the End Cottage ... three rooms up and three down, with Back Kitchen, Pantry, Cellar and outside EC'. However, water was laid on, and there were large gardens. For the smaller cottages the tenants were paying £12 per annum, the Landlord paying half rates, while the larger one was 3/6d per week, the landlord paying the rates. Mrs Dorothy Knight, who grew up in one of the cottages, said in 1984 that when she lived there as a child 'there was no gas and the toilet was up the end of the garden'. The two smaller cottages were being rented by Mr Everitt to Mr J. Boultbee Brooks of Finstall Park, who was then letting them to workers on his property. Later, when Mr Hugh Chance was living at Caspidge House, his chauffeur, Mr Davies, was living in one of the cottages, and Mr McHale, a pigman at Caspidge was on the Finstall Road side. They were then owned by the Albright family. The central cottage has a plaque reading 'God defend the Right'.

Chapter Eight
Finstall Park Estate from the 1850s

When the Brettells moved out of Finstall House in 1851 (or Finstall Hall as Mrs Matilda Brettell then called it) she took with her three young children and moved to The Heath near Bewdley, advertising the house To Let. Mr Thomas Payne came for a very brief two years, after which he had a sale of his household goods including a 'capital Phaeton with useful Grey Pony and Harness .... and an Alderney Cow'.

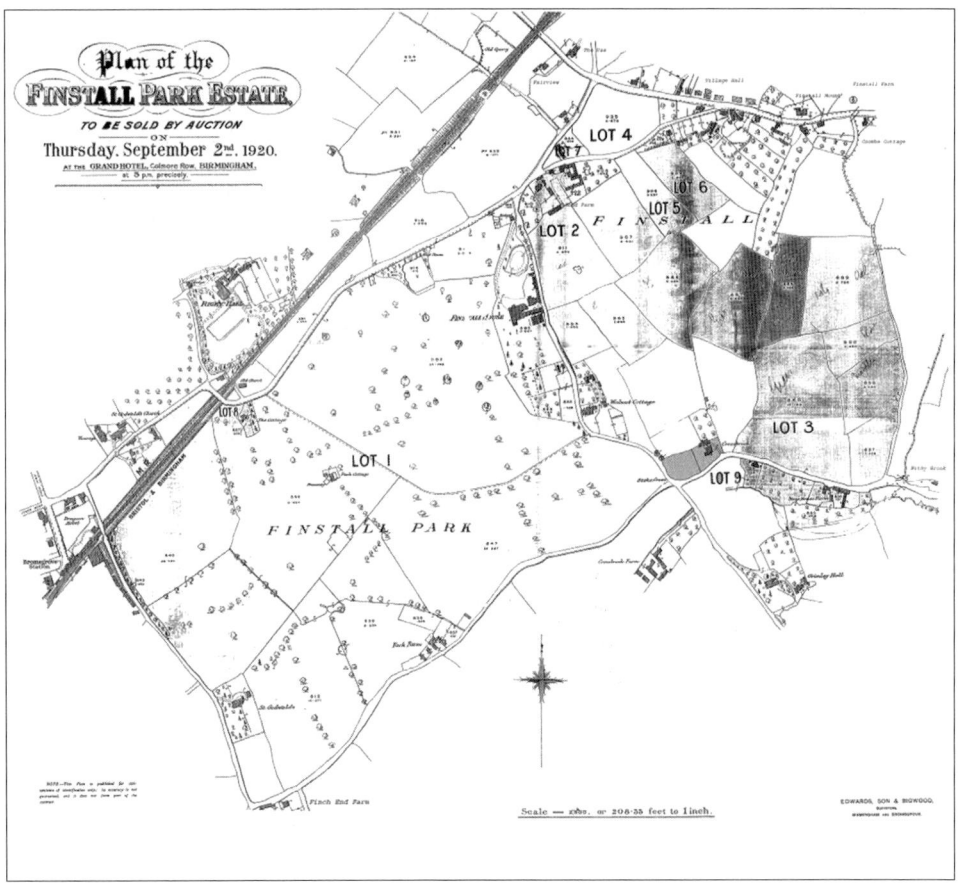

The map shows all the land owned by the Everitt family, put up for sale in 1920. (BC)

Next was James Shaw, merchant of Birmingham, and acting magistrate in Bromsgrove, who was a tenant for seven years, and during his time his daughter Edith married Robert Smallwood, who then went to live at Rigby Hall. Shaw seems not to have been a well man, and in 1862 was 'laid up in London from an attack of paralysis'. However, during his time he gave permission for the Second Worcestershire Volunteer Rifles to hold a Battalion Drill in Finstall Park. This was no little event, for it was regarded as a holiday by the public and many of Bromsgrove's shops were closed. The commanding officer Lieut. Col. Scobell and his mounted officers were Major Vernon MP (of Hanbury Hall) and Major Wilton. There were 60 rank and file in the Bromsgrove company, plus 52 from Pershore, 68 from Malvern, 35 from Evesham, 52 from Worcester, and 58 each from Droitwich and Redditch. There were also Cadet Corps from Worcester and Bromsgrove schools. After they had gone through a series of manœuvres, 'the volley firing really admirable', the officers and friends of Mr Shaw were entertained with 'an elegant collation, laid out in the house' while the non-commissioned officers and men were taken to a very large tent where they were 'most hospitably entertained'.

Finstall House front. (BC)

James Shaw died in 1865, the family moved out and another sale was held, including much furniture, about 2,000 gallons of prime cider and perry, 100 dozens of prime old Port, Sherry, Madeira and Claret plus forty-eight ewes, 73 tegs[57], a thoroughbred Cotswold Ram, seven in-calf Cows and Heifers, six Horses, and a lot of farming equipment.

Next came Mr Palmer, Birmingham solicitor, in 1866, and it was during his time that there was a terrible fire. Seeing the smoke the Stationmaster telegraphed for Mr Palmer to come from his Birmingham office, while the local vet galloped to Bromsgrove to call the volunteer fire brigade's horse-drawn fire wagon. A body of about a hundred men from the Wagon Works rushed to help and made a human chain with buckets, scooping water from the pool near the Finstall Road. They were joined by numerous Bromsgrove people, including some boys from the Grammar School (Bromsgrove School), who had seen the flames from the town and ran along the New Road to help. The roof was entirely destroyed, together with the floors of the rooms down to the basement, though much costly furniture and many valuables were saved, for the men fighting the fire were throwing carpets, furniture, paintings and other chattels out of the windows. A day or so afterwards Mr Palmer, who had been completely uninsured, went down to the Wagon Works and gave a day's wages to each man who had helped with the fire – for which generosity the men

---

57 Tegs are sheep in their second year, or before being shorn.

in turn, through *The Messenger*, thanked Mr Palmer. This must have been a tremendous shock for William Palmer, as well as very costly, and two years later on Good Friday afternoon he 'expired suddenly while sitting in a chair at his residence, Finstall House. ... The deceased gentleman was in his 56th year and in his usual health up to a few minutes before his death'.

Though most Birmingham industrialists or business men coming out to the quiet countryside with their families did not suffer such a dramatic end to the dream life, it is notable that hardly any of them stayed more than four or five years. Maybe their wives found that getting their milk from an Alderney cow was rather more time consuming and messy than having it delivered to their home from a churn; that needing to catch a train to take them shopping in Birmingham made the outing very long; that the number of neighbours of like mind and like interests were few and not living nearby as they were in Birmingham suburbs.

However, the next tenant of Mrs Brettell was William Everitt, metal merchant and tube and wire manufacturer, whose stay in Finstall was 23 years. He was a member of a progressive family, whose business named Allen Everitt and Sons began in Birmingham but moved to Kingston Metal Works in Smethwick, a state-of-the-art factory. The works covered a wide area of ground on both sides of the canal, and employed several hundred hands. Apart from the smelting of ore Messrs. Everitt carried on every operation connected with manufacture within their works, from refining the pig copper and casting the ingots to the final scouring and annealing of the articles. They manufactured sheet and foil copper and brass, non-ferrous tubes, copper-nickel condenser tubes and in 1878 Everitt took out a patent for a ploughing engine.

William's first wife, Fanny, had two children but she died shortly after; William married Emma in 1875 and she had two boys and a daughter in quick succession, with the support of five servants – cook, parlourmaid, housemaid, footman and kitchen maid, plus a live-in nurse when the babies were young and a coachman living in the lodge. Despite several attempts to sell Finstall House, the elderly Mrs Brettell was not successful, but maybe because of the fire and the reduction of its value, William Everitt did manage to buy the house. And he bought other property too; Mrs Housman's estate sold Tack Farm (now Finstall Park Farm) to Everitt in 1883, seventeen acres for £1,450.

Finstall House however wasn't up to the standard expected of a gentleman's residence, still needing some restoration and improvement following the fire. The Bromsgrove architect John Cotton was asked to plan the work needed, which was restoration of the public rooms in the centre of the house, and to build a new kitchen wing (on which is still the date – 1884).

William involved himself in Worcestershire life, becoming a magistrate, being High Sheriff of the County, and as an active member of the Conservative party, when in 1885 he offered his parkland for 'A Conservative Demonstration in Finstall Park, when the following Noblemen and Gentlemen have promised to attend ... viz., the Rt. Hon.Earl Beauchamp; the Rt.Hon Lord Windsor; Mr Staveley Hill, QC, MP; Mr Bosanquet QC. and others'. Apart from free entry they offered reduced rail fares for those brought by train 'from Kings Norton, Redditch and other intermediate stations'.

It wasn't all politics; in 1870 several notable women in the area including Mrs John Corbett of Stoke Grange, Mrs Dickens wife of the vicar of Tardebigge, Mrs Bourne of Grafton Manor and Mrs Everitt offered collection points for contributions in money or useful articles for the Association for Giving Relief to the Sick and Wounded in the Boer War. William was on the Bromsgrove Cottage Hospital committee. And for pleasure, in 1886 the couple were elected as members of the Worcestershire Archery Society, together with Lord & Lady Windsor. They were always pleased to show off their parkland, and in July 1889, with Lady Mary Lygon from Madresfield and Miss Lea Smith from Halesowen Grange in the company, and Mrs Everitt acting as Lady Paramount,[58] they welcomed a special train of archers from Shrub Hill, Worcester, leaving the city at 11.10 am and returning from Bromsgrove at 12.00 at night. Queen Victoria's Jubilee in 1887 was also celebrated at Finstall:

> This place, which is near Bromsgrove, though not in that parish, and not being invited to join in the Jubilee celebration at the other end of the parish, at Stoke Prior, seemed likely not to have any festivities ... However, on Tuesday, some residents in the upper end of the parish had a sheep roasted, and a party of about 80 persons sat down to dinner ... under the shade of trees. The women and children had tea afterwards. ... On Wednesday, the thanksgiving service was held in the church in the evening, when the National Anthem and the hymn *'Awake! O happy nation'* were sung. On Thursday two beasts, given by the High Sheriff, Mr W.E. Everitt of Finstall House, were roasted and distributed to the poor and to working people; and 360 children had tea in the Board School Rooms, medals were given them, and the day closed with sports.

William also had a hobby, which was the breeding of racehorses, though this did not continue after the Everitts tried to sell the lease of the property in 1891, and after William who was 60 and, presumably intending to retire, moved to Bournemouth. The Stud Farm was included in a big sale with all the farm stock and agricultural implements (you could book lunch beforehand).[59] Another sale notice offered Finstall Park to be Let, on Lease unfurnished, or Sold, with up to 200 acres of land. Once again it did not sell, so it was rented out once more. However when the Everitts moved out the contents of the wine cellar were auctioned, including about 150 *dozens* of bottles (that is 1800 bottles), including some rare vintages of port, champagnes, sherries and other wines. The best prices were 160 shillings per dozen for Moët and Chandon champagne, vintage 1880; 180 shillings

---

58   A woman in supreme authority (chiefly in Archery), a woman appointed to present the prizes and (in some cases) to act as supreme arbiter in any disputes that may arise.

59   See Chapter 11 for the Stud Farm.

for one dozen of Pommery and Grano, vintage 1874; 180 shillings per dozen for ten lots of Perrier Jouët; 152 shillings per dozen for three lots of Madeira port, bottled upwards of fifty years. Some wine cellar!

By 1893 the house was rented to Dr. E. Jebb Scott MA, FRCS. and his wife Kate. On 25 March 1896 an inquest was held in Finstall House concerning the death of Kate Scott. Dr. Scott said that four months before, his wife had a baby, but since the child died Mrs Scott had been depressed and out of spirits. Dr. Scott, he said, had six months previously ordered for his own use a liniment containing what to us seems an extraordinary collection of agents – chloroform, aconite and belladonna – which was later used to rub Mrs Scott's arm for rheumatism. It was wondered whether Mrs Scott drank the liquid thinking it was her own sleeping draught – no-one thought she had shown any tendency to take her own life. The jury found that Mrs Scott had died from the effects of an irritant poison, but how taken, or with what intent, there was no evidence to show. Sad.

But to cheer us up, in 1894 the Scott's gardener, Mr A. Tennant, had grown a stick of celery from seed, weighing 5.5lbs, 13 inches in circumference, 4 ft 6¾ inches in height! This was displayed at the third Bromsgrove Horse and Flower Show on fields off New Road. A great feature of the show was a group of greenhouse plants shown by Mr Tennant for which he won first prize, joined by honorary exhibits from the local gentry, including Lord Windsor and Mr Smallwood of Rigby Hall.

Dr. Jebb Scott sold up, and Mr John Boultbee Brooks and family moved in. He had clearly been attracted by William Everitt's stud farm, for he immediately bought the Finstall Heath estate from the Featherstone trustees. This land is behind the stables and bailiff's house in Finstall Road.

John Boultbee Brooks.

John Boultbee Brooks was only 51 when he came and left his mark on Finstall, but he was another inventive imaginative businessman and had done extremely well. He had left his birthplace, Hinckley in Leicestershire, when he was in his thirties, and with just £20 in his pocket he went to Birmingham, where he opened a leather works in Great Charles Street, specialising in horse harnesses. In 1878 his horse suddenly died, and Brooks borrowed a bicycle to get him to work. The wooden seat was so uncomfortable that he determined to design one that would solve the problem, and four years later he patented his new leather saddle which was an instant success. J.B. Brooks saddles, together with saddlebags and

The workers who made the newly invented Antler suitcases, 1914. (Antler Ltd)

panniers, motor car trunks and other leather goods were made in the workshop, and by 1914 there were 700 craftsmen employed.[60]

Young Edmund Page of The Vale wrote this in his unpublished memoirs:

It was in these days that the first Motor Car appeared on the roads. Automobiles they were called by the best people. J.B. Brooks, ... who lived at Finstall Park nearby, was the first neighbour to possess himself of one of these early devils. Preceded by a man on foot waving a red flag, this engine careered up and down our roads, generally enveloped in a cloud of smoke, which was dispersed periodically by fearful detonations called 'backfires', the more destructive of which brought the machine to a halt during which it evacuated a shovelful of red hot castings. If the wait were a prolonged one an enormous blow lamp was produced from the boot and the vehicle's business end hotted up again for the re-start.

Dr. Beilby soon followed with a more reliable make of car. He kept a succession of Red Flag men, whom he trained and sent to an early grave as a result of the speed at which he drove. The noise these early cars made was prodigious and their passing caused a universal terror on the narrow roads. Horses would seldom face them and farmyard animals, dogs and fowls were very slow to understand and accommodate themselves to their rapid movement. Horn-blowing, gongs and bells were much used and were more necessary as a signal of approach than they are nowadays.[61]

As others before, the Brooks involved themselves in local life, being helped in their 25 roomed house by 8 servants (housekeeper, butler, cook, housemaid, parlourmaid, housemaid, kitchenmaid, boots [none of them local people except Dinah Poole of Linthurst, housemaid] who helped with the seven Brooks children. Edward VII's coronation in 1902 was celebrated by the local people with sports in Finstall Park after a

---

60 J.B. Brooks & Son later produced Antler suitcases (christened thus and using a stag's head as trademark because Boultbee Brooks' son Boultbee was keenly interested in wildlife), but it wasn't until 1930 that Antler launched the first ever lightweight, soft-top suitcase – the story is that a leading London store bought up the whole of the first consignment, which all sold in a day. The firm expanded and introduced new styles of luggage and improvements to bicycle and motorcycle equipment, until during the 1950s they were bought up and the name Brooks disappeared.

61 Dr. Julius Henry Beilby was a respected Bromsgrove doctor who lived at Perry Hall, was in the Worcestershire Yeomanry in 1916 east of Suez Canal. He was killed at Oghratina at the Battle of Katia, described by A.V. Holyoake as 'an unmitigated disaster'. *The Road to Yozgad: My War 1914-1919* Ed. Douglas Bridgewater, Menin House.

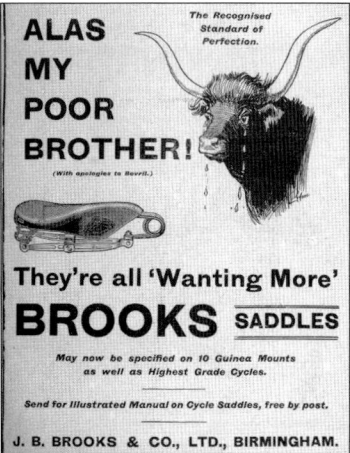

Left: A Brooks saddle. Right: An advertisement for Brooks saddles, 1904.

service in St Godwald's, coronation mugs for the children, a dinner for the old folk and performances by the local Red Star Minstrels. The considerable expense of all this was helped by Boultbee Brooks' donation of £50.

In 1910 the East Worcs Liberal Association held its summer outing in Finstall Park. 1,000 people attended, and speeches focused on the political lull since the death of King Edward VII, and how the party had been in the wilderness for 20 years. Their eldest son, christened Boultbee, moved to Blackwell Court in 1906 as a tenant, and bought it in 1909.

An Agreement was signed in 1904 between John Boultbee Brooks, William Weaver, the builder, and G.H. Gadd, the architect, for eight cottages and outbuildings to be built in Aston Fields, as yet unidentified. A much later legal document relates to numbers 11 and 15 Carlyle Road, Aston Fields. Other land he bought was in 1898 from John Featherstone, being the fields surrounding The Cross, no doubt needed for grazing for his horses at the Stud Farm.

In 1910 they had three weddings – Elizabeth, their youngest daughter, married Oliver Smith, the second son of Mr & Mrs Martyn Smith of the suitably named Brooklands in Bromsgrove; at Hanover Square in London Wilfred Brooks married Miss Pauline Duboc, daughter of Edmond Duboc, gentleman, and Mme. Duboc, née Lallemert, court dressmaker – presumably she designed the lovely dresses for the bride and bridesmaids. This marriage ended far too quickly, for within ten years, when living with Pauline at Finstall Croft, Wilfred aged 35 died from influenza. Marianne, the second daughter, married Charles Michael Tallack, a banker of Lahore, Punjab, at Finstall church, later moving to Australia. The final Brooks wedding was that of Leslie to Miss Blanche Birley of Yorkshire, in November 1914. The date probably tells us why they married then, for Leslie, aged 23, had already joined the 4th West Yorkshire Regiment (Prince of Wales's Own) and was granted a commission in September 1914. He was 'killed while gallantly leading his men' in the charge in the Battle of Loos in France on 25th September.

Meanwhile, following the death of William Everitt, his son Ernest[62] decided the time had come to sell the Finstall properties. 1917 saw the auction of the Everitt farms: Finch End with 114 acres (sold for £3,100) and The Gambolds with 79 acres (sold for £2,400, both tenanted by Mr Quinney), 'The Valuable Small Farm known as The Dust House' (71 acres), which with the six acre Withy Brook pastureland was let to Miss Taylor.[63]

In the centre of Finstall Park was a small two-up two-down stone house known

The wedding photograph of Wilfred Brooks to Pauline Marguerite Duboc on 19 October 1910. Bridesmaids were Kitty and Maisy Coleman (children), Marie Brooks, Lucille Duboc, Patricia Horton. (© Victoria and Albert Museum, London)

as Keeper's Cottage or Park Cottage, where in 1905 there was a Pheasantry. Many of the inhabitants of the cottage were farm bailiffs or grooms or agricultural labourers such as William Griffin and Benjamin Wheildon, connected to Finstall Park as a farm. The little Park Cottage continued to be occupied until the 1940s, latterly by a very elderly lady regarded by the local children as a witch. When she left the cottage it was allowed to moulder away.

In 1920 the Everitts unsuccessfully put Finstall Park with Tack Farm on the market, withdrawn at a bid of £16,000. Finstall (School) Cottage, lived in by architect John Cotton's stepmother, the three stone cottages, and Cross Brook cottages were all withdrawn, but the Stud Farm and Clovelly House plus 55 acres of pasture was sold at £4,600. Stonehouse Farm was sold to Mr Ted Goodman, some land behind the three stone cottages was sold part to Mr Charles Lane and part to Mr Deague of The Cross, and Cross Brook Cottages were sold for £330 to Mr Kemp.[64] John Boultbee Brooks, who still had the tenancy of the estate and the Stud Farm, was not well at the time and died two days after the lease of the Stud Farm ran out. Aged 74 he left a fortune of £320,614, of which £219,732 is net personalty. That is not a bad return on the £20 he started off with. His will left £1000 to Birmingham Children's Hospital and £500 each to the Birmingham General Hospital, the Queen's Cottage Hospital Hinckley, and Bromsgrove Cottage Hospital.

---

62   Ernest Montague Everitt, JP, was living at Sillins, Tardebigge. Having been in Worcestershire Hussars Yeomanry between 1881 and 1895 he was now an Income & Land Tax Commissioner.

63   For more about these farms see Chapter 14.

64   For more about these properties see Chapter 14.

Come 1924 and the Everitts and the agents went through it all again. In 1921 the sale prospectus had proclaimed it as 'A Freehold Residential Estate'; in this second sale they called it 'a Charmingly Situated Freehold Mansion', and in large black type announced 'The Lounge Hall and Ground Floor generally is heated by a central system. Electric light is generated on the estate; there is a gas service and the Post Office telephone is installed.' This time Tack Farm sold separately for £3,800, and Finstall Cottage for £500, but the main house still did not reach the reserve. After the sale, and probably with a lot of negotiation, the house, this time with 46 acres, was bought for £3,536 by J&A Brazier of Bromsgrove, the successful building firm who were well known for the excellence of their work,[65] and the house was rented by Brazier to Mr Gerald Lee Waller and his wife Mabel (known as Gerry and Bunny) who opened a preparatory school the same year. Gerry, according to John Pugh (later a Bromsgrove solicitor), was 'slightly tubby with a moustache and he wore glasses and he always seemed to wear a brown sports jacket and when out, a cloth cap. Bunny had a pretty face with a gentle smile – but she could shout'.

Finstall Park Preparatory School[66] for boys lasted from 1925 to the late 1940s. These were difficult times, though Waller did his best, the numbers attending being between twenty and a never-reached hoped-for fifty. During WWII there were staffing problems, Waller regularly advertising 'urgently' for assistant masters to teach general subjects, games and Latin. Waller and his wife Mabel took part in local activities and took the boarders to St Godwald's church on Sundays, where for a few years he was Vicar's Warden, and the youngsters in the private school had to put up with jeering from local children about their green and brown school caps, known as 'cabbage and gravy'. For many years Mabel was President of Finstall WI, and a Scout and Cub group was founded by staff member Keith Murray (who spent most of his time in khaki shorts), which later moved up to Finstall Village Hall and still runs today, with the addition of Beavers. The School grounds had a big vegetable garden, and the Head Gardener, Mr Avery, his son Frank and assistant Ernie Woodward took vegetables, fruit and flowers by horse and trap to several shops in Bromsgrove. Mr Avery was also a big chrysanthemum man, winning many prizes for them.

During the war the boys aged 7-14 were taught to knit for the war effort, sending their work to the Daily Sketch War Relief Fund, and getting their photograph in the *Bromsgrove Messenger*. John Pugh was at the school during an air raid, the boys hiding in the cellar as they did most nights, when a German plane dropped high explosives and incendiary bombs in the school grounds; it was thought the target was a searchlight and AA battery in the field which later became the Rugby Club. Also during the war there was talk of the park being used for a prisoner of war camp for Italians, but when this news came out, with great alacrity the land was ploughed for wheat by John Suffield of Finstall Farm.

---

65 See *Braziers, Builders of Bromsgrove*, 1850-1990, Alan Richards, 1996.

66 See Finstall Park School, Revd. Alan White, *The Bromsgrove Rousler* December 2009; *The Bromsgrove I Knew*, John Pugh, 2005.

Finstall House as it was in 2012, having suffered a second fire in the 1970s. The roofless area is on the left.

In 1951 Waller gave up, and sold the school to Ardenvale Schools Ltd. They were not successful either, and in 1955 applied to the Council to put up an estate of 200 houses, which thankfully was refused. The house with greatly reduced 7.23 acreage was bought by Mr Lou Thomas and his wife Jessie (landlords of The Dragoon at Aston Fields, now The Ladybird), and in 2014 they sold it to the present inhabitants who are looking forward to restoring the house. Its condition was bad when they bought it – there had been yet another fire in the 1970s, and a comparison between the 1920s photographs and those of 2014 is dismal indeed. As can be seen in the later picture the stone part of the house is completely roofless. The brick part of the garden front was probably designed by John Cotton, and is certainly Victorian.

Lou Thomas, who had bought the parkland, sold it to Miss Jocelyn Albright who offered part of the land for the Rugby Club. Miss Albright entered into a covenant with the National Trust that the parkland should never be built upon, excluding the Rugby Club from this condition. The Club persuaded her to sell them enough land for the second pitch, and after her death they bought the Club land from her executors.

Over the last sixty or so years the land between Finstall Farm and the Rugby Club has been used as pasture land, and there are notable trees both in the gardens and surrounding the small pond which is half way down the still fine ashlar sandstone wall (despite its considerable damage from road salt) which reached from Finstall House gardens to the railway. The stone lodge by the gate to Finstall House drive has been extended several times, and there are now three houses built at the back of Finstall House where there were once stables, apple store, engine house, dog kennels and manure pit.

Chapter Nine
The Oakalls and Hopgardens Farm

The name Oakalls (or Oakhalls, or Okholt in 1250) indicates the growing of crops of hemp, and the name Hop Gardens Farm does not need explaining. But apart from these the Oakalls was well known for its agricultural production, with herds of cows, and the cultivation of potatoes at a time when they were still regarded as luxury goods. Throughout much of their history the Oakalls and the Hopgardens Farm were owned by the same person, often with the owner or a gentleman tenant in the Oakalls and the farming folk living at Hopgardens or in cottages nearby.

During the 17th and 18th centuries Bromsgrove was known for its growth of flax and hemp. So important was it that in 1781 bounties were offered for their cultivation. Among the names of those from Stoke Prior and Tardebigge claiming their bounties were Henry

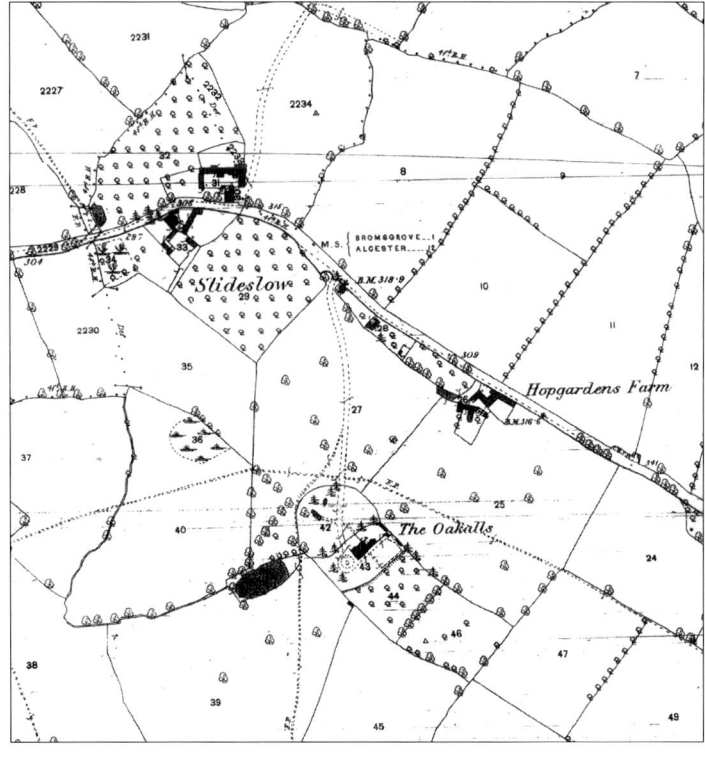

Early 20th century map showing The Oakalls, Slideslow Farm and Hopgardens Farm. Hopgardens were the first buildings to go when the Redditch Highway and the Oakalls were built.(BC)

Ellins and William Moore of Tutnall.[67] Most farms and cottages had their own hemp plecks,[68] the words sometimes reduced down to hen-plecks, where they grew their own flax, to spin for their own use or to sell to those in the thriving Bromsgrove linen industry.

Oakum is the coarse part of flax (*Linum usitatissimum*) and hemp (*Cannabis sativa*), separated in hackling or heckling, which is the last of three steps in preparing the fibres to be spun. Its coarse fibres, loosely twisted together, and mixed with tar, were used both in the making of rope, and for caulking or packing the joints of timber in wooden sea vessels. 'Picking oakum' was a common, horrible punishment for criminals (and even the poor people in the workhouse), who had to pick out the oakum strands from old rope with their fingers so that it could be used again. One famous man who suffered this punishment was Oscar Wilde, when in Reading Gaol, who found it was only the company of the other prisoners which saved his sanity. Oakum pickers developed thick black scars on their hands from this work and also suffered tendonitis, bursitis, nerve damage, and all those other conditions that result from repetitive stress motions.

Hops were also grown in small plecks near the house, but in the 18th century they became a worthwhile crop to grow commercially and by the mid 19th century beer made with hops was in demand. This did not last, for the demand for beer fell, possibly because clean water was more easily available. In 1908 there was a huge demonstration in Trafalgar Square when some 500 Worcestershire hop growers and their labourers joined the 50,000 represented from the rest of the country, in protesting against the dumping of foreign hops in England. Nevertheless, hop growing in Bromsgrove faded out, apart from small personal hopgardens. It was only the hop cultivation in Kent and Sussex that continued, together with Herefordshire, which continues in a small way today.

Left: From flax to linen: flax seeds, green flax straw with seed pods, broken flax, Scutched flax, combed flax, linen fabric. Right: Hops on the plant.

---

67 See Richard Churchley's two articles in *The Bromsgrove Rousler*, Nos. 28 and 29, 2013 and 2014.

68 A pleck is a small enclosure, usually nearby the house.

9. The Oakalls and Hopgardens Farm

Henry Dugard, clergyman and Master of Bromsgrove Grammar School between 1606-1611, lived at the Oakalls, where his son William was born in 1606. After William's education at one of Worcester's schools (Kings School was founded in 1542 and the Royal Grammar School in 1561) and Sidney Sussex College, Cambridge he received a BA, followed by an MA in 1633. He married twice, had nine children, and in 1644 became headmaster of Merchant Taylor's School, London. Although becoming official printer for Oliver Cromwell he was later imprisoned for printing material in favour of the royalist cause, but on his release he continued printing both political and educational books. He died in 1662.

The Oakalls farmland was well known for its agricultural production, but now we must investigate Dr. Collett's behaviour in 1827. Dr. Collett had been an eminent surgeon in Bromsgrove, but 'for a long time past resided in rural retirement at the Oakalls'. He had gone to court to justify stopping up a public highway which ran close to his home, the Oakalls, thus depriving the public of a right of way between the Alcester Road turnpike and the Bromsgrove to Rigby Hall roadway, long used by local people to go to church services. In 1814 Dr. Collett had diverted this road to a greater distance from his house, and covered the old road with a paddock by the house. Dr. Collett, as the newspaper said, thought he would be 'more comfortably situated if he could drive people away altogether'. He went to two magistrates who were his friends – the Right Hon. Lord Aston and the Rev. William Vernon – who signed an order in June 1827 to stop up this 'useless and unnecessary' road – though they left out of their order the part of the road which went through the lands of Mr Ellins of Rigby Hall. However the appeal to the Court of King's Bench was accepted, Ellins himself leading the fight, since the stopping up of the road was appearing to benefit Dr. Collett only, and the result of the case was used as precedent for similar road-stoppage court cases elsewhere in the country.

After his death in 1832 the house was advertised to be let, with seven bedrooms, kitchen, dairy, brewhouse, coach-house, stable, etc. with garden, paddock, and shrubberies in four acres. An important piece of information was that a London coach passed daily. Another advertisement three years later told us that the Rev. G.F. Jessey was living there, and also mentioned an orchard well stocked with fruit trees and surrounded by a row of excellent filbert trees (hazel nuts), and a well stocked fish pool. The Worcestershire County Council geology department says that the two pools (one of which has now gone) are thought to be part of an old manorial complex.

During 1838 William Robson was living at the Oakalls, renting it while he was working on the tithe apportionment of many places in the area. The Stoke Prior tithe map was published in 1846, by which time he and his new wife – Sarah Sanders, daughter of Charles Sanders Esq. of Bromsgrove – were living in Bournemouth. He must have continued to have some sentimental attachment to the area, or maybe his wife had persuaded him, for he donated the site for the new St Godwald's church in 1883.

It was not only hops and flax that were grown at the Oakalls; potatoes were also a good commercial crop. Nash in his *History of Worcestershire* reported:

> Potatoes are cultivated here [Bromsgrove] with great success; 42,000 bushels of them are supposed to have been raised in 1774. The produce of an acre is generally about 300 bushels. Many barge loads of them are sent annually to Bristol and other places; so that they are become an article of commerce.[69]

During the 1840s John Adams of Perry Hall became interested in the state of potatoes when farmed in Bromsgrove, the Oakalls regularly growing a crop each year. For some time there had been worries nationally because so many different types of potato were suffering from blight, and in 1845 the Irish potato famine and the 1846 Highlands potato famine were very serious and unexplained. The Horticultural Society in 1847 experimented with some forty-five ideas for remedies, including adding sulphate of soda, coal-tar sprinkled over the sets, Moberly's sulphate of magnesia, powdered oil cake, or planting them alternately with beans. Their report said:

> In consequence of the strong opinion entertained by many persons that the potato disease is caused by exhausted vitality and that therefore it would disappear if the vitality were re invigorated by raising seedlings, some experiments directed to that point have also been instituted. Potato seeds were received from Baden through Mr John Adams of Bromsgrove, from Mussooree through the East India Company, from Poland sent to Lord Palmerston by Colonel Du Plat, her Majesty's Consul at Warsaw, and from Messrs Hardy Maldon in Essex.[70]

John Cotton said in 1908:

> About one hundred years ago, potatoes were more rare than oranges are now ... and have proved of much more use than tobacco. In the History of Virginia ... 1722, we are informed that potatoes are ... "either red or white, about as long as a boy's leg; and sometimes as long and big as the leg and thigh of a young child, and very much resembling it in shape." ... It is but of very late years that they have been common roots in this county. ... The Spaniards had them before the English brought them from the southern parts of America: a merchandise which has proved less destructive ... than that of the gold and silver to those countries.[71]

Potato growing continued to have an element of risk from potato disease, and in August 1872 it was reported that the potatoes in Bromsgrove were 'diseased to an alarming extent' – so much so that 'they will not pay for getting out of the ground'. It was the lightest crop known for many years. Experiments with potatoes continued for many years with

---

69 *Notes & Queries No.1*, page 41, from the *Bromsgrove Messenger*, 1908.
70 *Journal of the Horticultural Society of London*, Volume III, 1848.
71 *Notes & Queries No.1*, page 41, note (b), from the *Bromsgrove Messenger*, 1908.

9. The Oakalls and Hopgardens Farm

A view of Hopgardens Farm.

not a lot of success. Even today work is still being done to try to eliminate potato blight.

In 1843 William Brooke, gentleman, was living at The Oakalls; in 1846 there was a newspaper report that the Oak Halls had been 'robbed of all the wall fruit and onions, together with a number of fowls, rabbits, etc.'; by 1851 the farmer of the 60 acres was John Jones, working the Hop Gardens and Oakalls with just one labourer. The next year his 'only and beloved son' Edwin died aged 10 months.

Mr Edward Perkins, a nail manufacturer who owned business property in Bromsgrove High Street, followed John Holyoak, the retired Bromsgrove draper, who died in 1855. Perkins was doing what so many nailmasters were doing – moving to a larger house with land, outside the perimeter of the town. Perkins not only made nails but was superintendent of the children's Independent Sunday Schools, some 220 of whom he entertained each summer with plum cake and milk while the teachers took tea together on the lawn. He was heavily involved with the Mechanics Institute, being Chairman for several years, was a supporter of Windsor Street Congregational Chapel, and gave £100 to the bicentenary of Nonconformist Memorial Fund. But all was not good, because the nail industry was in a bad way.[72] For some years the nailmasters had regularly reduced wages, nailers were striking and the truck system[73] was having a disastrous effect. In 1869 Perkins claimed that the trade was in good shape, despite the need for a soup kitchen while men were on strike. By 1887, because pay had been reduced so much, on one day in October 1,100 children and 150 adults were served bread and soup.

It was not only the nail trade problems which affected Edward Perkins; in 1870 his tenant's five cows were hit by foot and mouth. This particular outbreak began in December 1869 in Chaddesley Corbett. The following week there was a case east of Bromsgrove, and it spread through much of east Worcestershire in spring 1870. There were 1,200 farms affected in the county, and by 1872 there was no district free of it. In the Finstall area there were outbreaks at Broom House, Ford House, Mr Jeptha's farm (Crossbrook Farm) and John Harvey's five cows at the Oakalls.[74] Cattle had previously

---

72 See *Glory Gone – The story of nailing in Bromsgrove*, Bill Kings and Margaret Cooper, Halfshire Books 1989.

73 Forcing workers to accept payment of wages in kind or enforcement of nailers to shop, having been paid with tokens, in businesses owned by the nailmaster or middleman (fogger).

74 John Harvey moved to Crossbrook Farm the next year, taking the place of Jeptha.

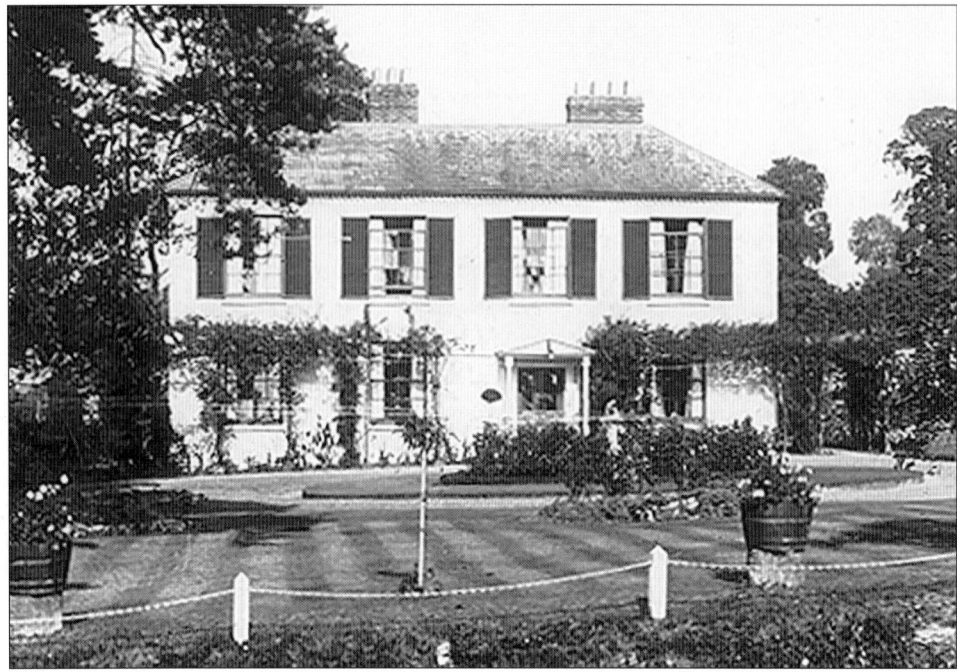

The Oakalls in 1900.

been hit in 1865 by Rinderpest (Russian plague), an infectious viral disease which seems to have spread quickly all over the county, with half of the county's cattle suffering the illness. Foot and mouth returned in 1881, and was rampant throughout the county for a year. The epidemic of 1883 was not so severe, and then things quietened down until early 1914 – not the best of years to be dealing with such a problem. That outbreak was at Bradley Green, and there was soon prohibition of cattle moving, and Bromsgrove, Hagley and Barnt Green markets were among those closed.

After the death of Mr Perkins in 1872 Mrs Perkins continued to live in the house until 1880, relying on Thomas Hewson who was the farm bailiff. From the late 1870s Edmund Albutt had been farming the Hopgardens, staying there until the turn of the century.

In 1880 there was a sale by tender of timber: 21 elm, 14 ash, 13 poplar, 12 larch, 8 oak, 5 spruce, 5 willow, 3 alder, 3 chestnut, 1 scotch and 1 beech, standing on the Oakalls. 'Some of the Timber is of large dimensions, to be seen by contacting Mr E. Albutt'. A similar sale was offered at Crossbrook Farm, both farms then owned by Mrs Barrow of Grimley Hall.

In June 1883 at an 'Important Sale of Properties' there was a large assembly for the sale of the properties of Mrs Barrow, who had recently died. Lot 5 was the Oakalls, with outbuildings, pleasure kitchen garden, orcharding and piece of turf land, together with the

9. The Oakalls and Hopgardens Farm

Hop Gardens Farm – farmhouse, farm buildings, three cottages, the total area being 64 acres. It was Mr Newton Jones, son of Mrs Margaret Jones, tenant of the Oakalls, who bought this lot for £5,350. On the death of Mrs Jones, Droitwich solicitor John Holyoak bought the house; he died in 1897 and Frank Impey came to live there.

During the 1880s the house named Rockville was built on Alcester Road, lived in first by A.H. Godsall, then Frank Swann, then from 1901 by J. James Hall, a carpenter with six sons, including George who was a stonemason (there was the quarry close by), and Roland who at 16 was a railway porter. William became a coal merchant, and Douglas later became a market gardener at Finstall Gardens up the road, joined there about 1913 by his father. There is a well in the garden, which had a pump, and there was also a pump inside the house. Next door to Rockville were built semi-detached cottages, one named Rock Cottage. Even in 1974 the living quarters were just a living room with quarry tiled floor, a scullery with a cold water tap, and a cupboard and staircase leading to two bedrooms. The names of the houses give the clue to the fact that this part of Alcester Road cuts through solid rock.

Rockville in 2017.

Frank Impey, an accountant and a Quaker, was a keen hunter. In July 1899 he entertained the members of the North Worcestershire Beagles for a presentation to Mr E.H. Humphreys who had been Master for 16 years. The hounds had been sold, and nine couples with their huntsman had gone to Carlisle. The extremely generous gifts were a silver salver, a cob (a small strong horse with short legs), harness and a Ralli cart (a light two-wheeled horse-drawn cart for four people). And not only that – the ladies of the hunt presented Mrs Humphreys with a silver teaset, a diamond pendant and an illuminated address. However Mr Impey did continue to hunt, and the same year he advertised saying he needed a groom – 'at once – who must understand a hunter, and be of good character and be willing and obliging'.

He was followed in 1902 by A. Charles Cutler, Birmingham stockbroker, his wife Clara Ellen, and their only son Herbert. After his Bromsgrove School education Herbert trained as a mechanical engineer and worked at Messrs Taylor and Challen, the well-known Birmingham engineering firm, until WWI, when he enlisted and went into the Royal Flying Corps, to be killed in France on 10 May 1917 aged 26. He was buried at Templeux-Le-Guerard British Cemetery, France. By this time the Cutlers had moved to The Cedars, Bromsgrove, where they stayed until 1946. During their time William Pearman was farming at, he said, 'the Oakhalls and The Heath'. Presumably he meant Hopgardens land, and the Oakalls. Pearman had been a tenant at various other local farms, and was here just for four years.

In 1915 a short-term tenant, Bombardier Raoul de Paravicini Simon, of the Honourable Artillery Company, and his wife Florence (née Sheldon) caused no end of a twitter in Finstall when Simon petitioned for dissolution of their marriage because of Florence's adultery with Llewelyn Slingsby Bethell (whose daughter was born that year). The shocking behaviour alleged by both sides of the petition was reported in lurid detail for four days by *The Times*, involving Simon's heavy drinking, coarseness and cruelty, their 'motor-car driver' having seen Florence sitting on Bethell's knee, and the co-respondents' nights at the Plough and Harrow Hotel in Edgbaston. Having achieved his divorce Simon cut short his stay in Bromsgrove, and died, having married a lady named Blanche, in 1963.

After this came Edward B. Martino, who lived at Oakalls until around 1932, to be followed by Major Douglas J. Vaughan who put the estate up for sale in 1941. This sale was advertised in the newspapers, the sale notice loudly proclaiming that the house had MAINS ELECTRICITY AND WATER. The house had been much improved and enlarged since its sale nearly a hundred years earlier. There was central heating 'by means of electric tubular radiators in Hall, Cloakroom, China Pantry, Landing, Bathroom No.1 and Maid's bedrooms'. Strangely there is no mention of heating in reception rooms (though the dining room had an electric fire). It is remembered that the staircase was made from beautiful oak, and there were Stubbs paintings on the walls (received as part of a debt). There was a big decorated lead water tank on legs at the back of the house, dated 1711, but that unfortunately was stolen. There was now a billiard room, a heated garage with car wash, a hard tennis court, a heated greenhouse, and dog kennels for five dogs. The entrance lodge, partly stone built, was down by the Alcester Road, near to the Hopgardens Farm which was included in the sale. Including the Hopgardens he was selling 76 acres.

Another tenant in the house was Mrs Joan Winn, a former actress and mother of the writer Godfrey Winn. Godfrey, who was born in 1906, did come to stay with his mother and wrote part of his autobiography – *The Infirm Glory* – in the Oakalls in about 1966/7. He had been educated at King Edwards School, Birmingham. His career started as a boy actor, and as an adult he became an author, writing numerous novels and autobiographies, with a secondary life as a journalist, writing for the *Daily Mirror* and the *Sunday Express*. In 1939 he was the first British war correspondent to cross the Maginot Line, and later during WWII he served as an able seaman in the Royal Navy on HMS Ganges. Having been discharged because of an injury he began to be heard on radio, often compèring

Housewives Choice. He continued writing for newspapers and magazines as well as appearing in films such as *Billy Liar* and *The Great St Trinian's Train Robbery*. His social life was as part of the gay community in London, including Cecil Beaton, Beverley Nichols and Kenneth Tynan. Homosexuality was finally decriminalised in 1967. Godfrey Winn died in 1971, having given a lot of pleasure by his writing, particularly to women readers.

Ordinary Seaman Godfrey Winn.

Edgar C. Marsland and his wife were the last inhabitants of the Oakalls; an industrialist with iron foundries around the country, who acquired the Hayseech Foundry and the Great Bridge Disposal Co. in Brierley Hill in 1967, which he wound up in 1985. He also had a financial interest in Dudley Zoo. The Monte Carlo Rally attracted him in 1954, when he made his debut in the arduous event driving a Jowett Javelin (Terence Hall, the Bromsgrove pharmacist, had taken part in the two previous Rallies in his Morgan car). Marsland died on 13 July 1988.

In 1987 sadly the Oakalls house and the Hopgardens farm buildings had received their death warrant, for the planners gave the go-ahead to developers to build on 100 acres, demolishing the buildings, despite it being green belt land. The developers were first given permission to build a 'modern rural village', to include a general store and 400 houses. The next year, with the new roads being built, construction started on the Parklands. The developers were given five years to develop suitable amenities but they reported no businesses were coming forward and so they were given permission to continue building more houses on the proposed village green where the shop was to have been built.

Chapter Ten

Grimley Hall

When the Albrights came to Grimley Hall it was already at least 100 years old, and was owned by Thomas Brettell of Finstall House. In 1275 it was known as 'de Grimley'. In 1801 it was important enough to be one of only two Bromsgrove houses mentioned in *Kearsley's Guide to Great Britain*,[75] however, we start in 1796 when Benjamin Dugard lived at Grimley Farm.

One interpretation of the meaning of Grimley is that it is derived from a pagan name, referring to the god 'Grim', while 'ley' would be 'leah' – i.e a woodland clearing,[76] because the old Feckenham Forest stretched over the Grimley lands. Another theory is that Grimley is 'Wood and hill haunted by a ghost or spectre'.[77] So the Grimley estate was, like Finstall Heath, made up of a mix of pasture and orchard, as well as having a hopyard.

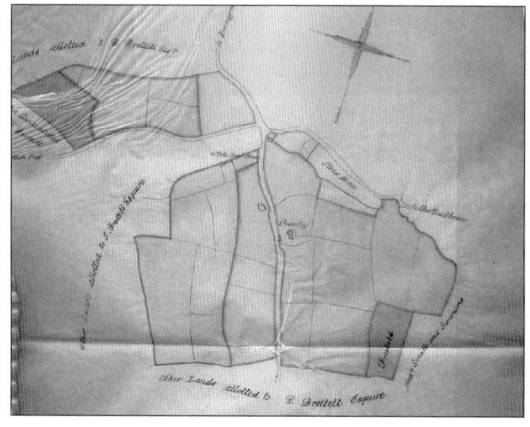
Sale plan c.1856 of Grimley House land.

Benjamin Dugard, probably related to the Droitwich Dugards, Henry Dugard, clergyman schoolmaster of Bromsgrove Grammar School (Bromsgrove School) and the Dugard of the Oakalls, paid rent of £67 to Thomas Brettell who had bought the farm and land in 1771. For £4,000, a huge amount of money at that date, Brettell had bought 'a parcel of land 2 closes known by the name Point of Size 7 acres, lane leading from Stoke Cross towards Webbs' Farm and part of Sheltwood Farm and land belonging to Whitfield Esq. in the holding of Widow Page, and another coppice or woodground belonging to Smith of Worcester.'

---

75 *Kearsley's Traveller's Entertaining Guide Through Great Britain*, George Kearsley, 1801. 'Between this place [Bromsgrove] and Tardebig is Grimley-hall; also Finstall-house, Brittel [Brettell], esq.'

76 *Dodderhill through the Ages*, Derek Hurst et al, 'Early medieval landscape of the Droitwich to Bromsgrove Region', Della Hooke, p35, 2011.

77 *Concise Oxford Dictionary of English Place-names*, Eilert Ekwall, OUP, 1936.

10. Grimley Hall

In 1796, Thomas Brettell's will left Grimley House with all outhouses, barns, stables, buildings, gardens, orchards and lands to his wife. To Ananias, his cleric son, he left all buildings and land (except 'Poole Meadow SW side of the lane from Stoke Cross to Grimley, ill divided with rails from land in holding of Thomas Bourne') and a close at Cross Brook (then a hopyard), and 10 acres of Grimley Hill, bounded in the north by part of Grimley Farm, on the east by Lower Coppice, on the south by Heifers Croft and on the west by Grimley Hill Lane.

To his son Joseph he left Grimley's appurtenances in 'Aston End close, Turby Croft 6 acres, Fearned Field 6 acres, Wheat Field, Upper Heifers Croft, Tardebigge Croft, all part of Grimley estate and Grimley Homestall; Lower Meadow, Peas Close, Hither Tardebig Croft, Further Tardebig Croft, Cow Pasture, Grimley Orchard, the west part of Grimley Hill, Poole Meadow, the lower part of Hawkcroft Hill, upper part of Hawkcroft Hill, little Wheatfield, Brown's little Meadow, Wheatfield meadow' – in all, 67 acres, in occupation of Thomas Horton, William Griffiths, Thomas Buggins jnr, and Richard Holden.

I wonder how many of these fields still are known by the same names.

In 1856 the Brettells conveyed Grimley House and Crossbrook Farm with 111 acres for £1300 to James Barrow, who was a Wolverhampton corn and butter merchant, cheese factor and tallow chandler, with a large warehouse on the Union Canal Wharf at Tettenhall, Wolverhampton. He was another who invested his savings in property, buying both the Oakalls and the Hop Gardens farm. However just eight years later James Barrow died, aged 58, leaving his wife Dorothy – they had had no children. However she died in 1882 and the next year her 'highly important' estate was sold at auction. The then tenant of Grimley Hall, William Morris, bid £1575 for his home with 67 acres, and the bidding for the other farms was quite intense, for the two big local landowners wanted to add to their properties. Crossbrook Farm was bought by W.A. Albright for £3000, while W.E. Everitt of Finstall House paid £1880 for two cottages and two fields. The 31 acres of Stoke Cross Farm, previously owned by the late Mrs Housman, was bought on the same day by Mr Everitt for £2000, as was The Tack farm, 17 acres for £1,450.

Following Mr Morris's death only a year later in 1894, Grimley Hall and just 8 acres were bought by the Everitts and given to Alfred Beaumont Albright and his new wife Mabel Everitt as a wedding present; their marriage settlement being £1,087.10.00. Albrights were in residence now until Miss Jocelyn Albright's death in 1982. Alfred Beaumont Albright, the youngest son of Arthur Albright, died when he was 69 in 1932, leaving £21,720, despite, it is said, being a bit of a gambler. After he left school he travelled to many different countries, and then settled down in Finstall to become a farmer. He farmed at Finstall, Tutnall and Crossbrook farms from 1884, and hunted with the Worcestershire Hounds. He was involved in local government, and was nine years on Worcester County Council for the Stoke Prior division. When the Finstall war memorial was planned he took a prominent role in raising the funds.

Mabel (known to her family as May) Albright died in 1968, the day before her 94th birthday. She had taken a quiet interest in the village, and for a short time was on the Parish Council, always taking part in the Finstall Flower Show, and enjoyed gardening, fly-fishing and walking. She worked with Lady Plymouth of Hewell Grange to form the Hewell and District Nursing Association – much needed in the days before the NHS – and was also a member of many other organisations such as the women's section of the local British Legion, the W.I., the Worcester Cathedral Embroiderers and the Bromsgrove Women's Luncheon Club. In the 1960s she presented St Godwald's church hall with a much needed new kitchen.

Alfred Beaumont Albright. (Reproduced with permission of Library of Birmingham MS 1509/7/24 & 30)

Three daughters were born to Alfred and May. (Geraldine) Dinah in 1896, Rachel Patience in 1898 and Jocelyn in 1900. When their uncle George Stacey Albright died in 1942 he left his Gloucestershire estate, Bromesberrow Place, near Ledbury, to the three women, because he thought of them as his poor relations. Dinah bought out her sisters, and lived at Bromesberrow until her death aged 94. During the First World War she had been an ambulance driver, but had no possibility of following that independence after the war; but as well as being a successful 'lady of the manor' she became a keen plantswoman – she loved orchids, and employed a specialist gardener, Alan Greatwood, who developed several new species named after her, such as *Promenaea Dinah Albright gx 'Pendock'*. She was very happy to invite evacuee children to the house during WWII; the worst part of that war for her must have been when a German bomb fell near her greenhouses. On her death she left much of her estate to the National Trust and to the Diocese of Gloucester for the restoration of

Dinah, Rachel Patience and Jocelyn Albright. (Reproduced with permission of Library of Birmingham MS 1509/7/24 & 30)

10. Grimley Hall

the Arts & Crafts gardens of Glenfall House, Cheltenham – now a hotel.[78]

The second sister, Rachel Patience Albright, was also a country girl, being brought up at Grimley Hall, and at the beginning of WWII she was Farm Bailiff to the Quaker Lady Godlee at Coombe End Farm, Whitchurch. Later in her life she became interested in her family history and it is due to her that Birmingham Archives has a massive collection of papers about the Albrights which, they say, 'displayed very few traces of any original archival order', but include letters from Miss Maria Catherine Albright when she was in Madagascar as a Quaker missionary and from their grandfather Arthur Albright who travelled in Turkey and Italy in the 1850s while working on the manufacture of phosphorous.

Another country girl was Jocelyn, who lived at Grimley nearly all her life. Miss Albright jnr was a keen fisherwoman and enthusiastically rode to hounds side saddle; she was a hands-on gardener like her sisters. She inherited much of Finstall, including Finch End Farm plus two cottages, five Finstall Terrace cottages and two of the stone cottages on Finstall Road, the Post Office by the Village Hall and the two cottages adjoining, plus the land behind the Village Hall which was rented to the Stoke Prior District Council for allotments. For a time there were more allotments in Finstall Field behind what came to be known as Allotment

Bromesberrow House.

Dinah Albright with puppies. (David Myers)

A lime yellow orchid named Promenaea Dinah Albright.

---

78 A typical comment from someone writing about her 'My school, Wanstead High School, ... was evacuated to Newent, summer 1940. Eight of us and a teacher were billeted at Bromesberrow Place for a couple of months and no-one could have been kinder than Miss Albright. We four girls slept in the late son's bedroom [Dinah's cousin Major Martin (Toby) Albright, Queens Own Worcs. Hussars, killed 1917] which was decorated with rowing trophies, caps and scarves, and deer heads ('please don't hang your hats on the antlers' she said).

Cottage (later the home of Topsy and Bill Hobbs). She built more cottages and houses along Alcester Road. All of these brought in rent, including a small amount for the electricity station on Alcester Road, leased by Electric Power Co. And all of them were painted in Albright colours – dark green doors and cream windows.

Miss Albright II was very much the lady of the manor. Times were different then – a description of Finstall School said it 'was a very happy school ... it was very strict, we had to know our manners, ... (if we met) the governors on our way to school, [or] going past the Albrights from Grimley Hall. ... the boys had to raise their caps and the girls had to curtsy; we got punished if we didn't.'[79] When Miss Albright entertained, one of her employees, Len Tansell, normally an outdoor worker, had to come in to be butler, wearing white gloves.

Mrs May Albright dressed to go fishing. (Bromsgrove Messenger)

One of the farm buildings was known as the Egg Shed, where daily Miss Albright and her staff – Len Tansell, Doreen and Bill Baylis – helped to pack the eggs ready for sale, after cleaning them with sandpaper.

A story told by solicitor Matthew Horton of Thomas Horton's law firm and a relation of the Goodman family, tells of his memorable first contact with Miss Albright when he was newly qualified in the late 1970s. Tim Brotherton[80] of Luce and Silvers, the local auctioneers, who acted as land agent for the Albright Finstall estate, arranged for young Matthew to meet him outside Grimley Hall and instructed him to be on his best behaviour during a meeting with Miss Albright.

> I duly turned up at the hall with shoes blacked and an important looking briefcase at the pre-determined time and date. After being ushered into the anteroom to Miss Albright's study, we seemed to wait for a long time before it was announced that 'Miss Albright will see you now'. I followed Tim reverentially into a large room where the diminutive Miss Albright sat behind a large desk engaged in correspondence. After a brief introduction by Tim, Miss Albright said 'Mr Horton, Mr Brotherton informs me you will be a trustee of the Albright Village Hall'. Taken aback, I looked at Tim with surprise, whilst Miss Albright continued with her correspondence, only to see him nodding furiously in my direction and with a finger to his lips.

---

79   Georgina Stokes (née Harris) on the centenary of Finstall School.

80   R.B. (Tim) Brotherton was a collector of photographs and sale particulars of buildings around Bromsgrove. Now being looked after by Bob Richardson, this amazing collection has been freely available to all local historians, including this writer.

Grimley Hall 1982.

>I mumbled an incoherent 'yes, thank you' at which Miss Albright dismissed us by saying 'Good, that's settled. That will be all'. At which point we were summarily shown out.
>
>Driving back to the office, Tim said 'Well I thought that went rather well!'. Notwithstanding being disappointed in not achieving multiple legal instructions, I greatly valued and enjoyed my 25 years serving the interests of the Finstall Village Hall upon the orders of Miss Albright. She who would be obeyed!

There was a popular BBC radio programme called *Down Your Way* which for many years visited towns and villages around the country, talking to the inhabitants. The programme came to Finstall in the 1970s when Rev. David Tonge, who came from Antigua, was a popular vicar at St Godwald's. Miss Albright was interviewed, and asked to comment on Rev. Tonge: 'Well, I thought it rather funny at first having a black fella ....'

She became less active as she grew older, and when she was 70 she advertised in *The Times* for a full time helper – 'Country woman wanted to assist with Garden and Poultry. Furnished flat in country house supplied. Albright, Grimley Hall.'

She died peacefully at home on 12 March 1982, leaving an estate worth £1,021,976. She left £112,000, some property and effects and other bequests to personal legatees, half the residue to charities for helping and housing old people, and the other half to the National Trust.

Chapter Eleven
The Stud Farm and Penmanor

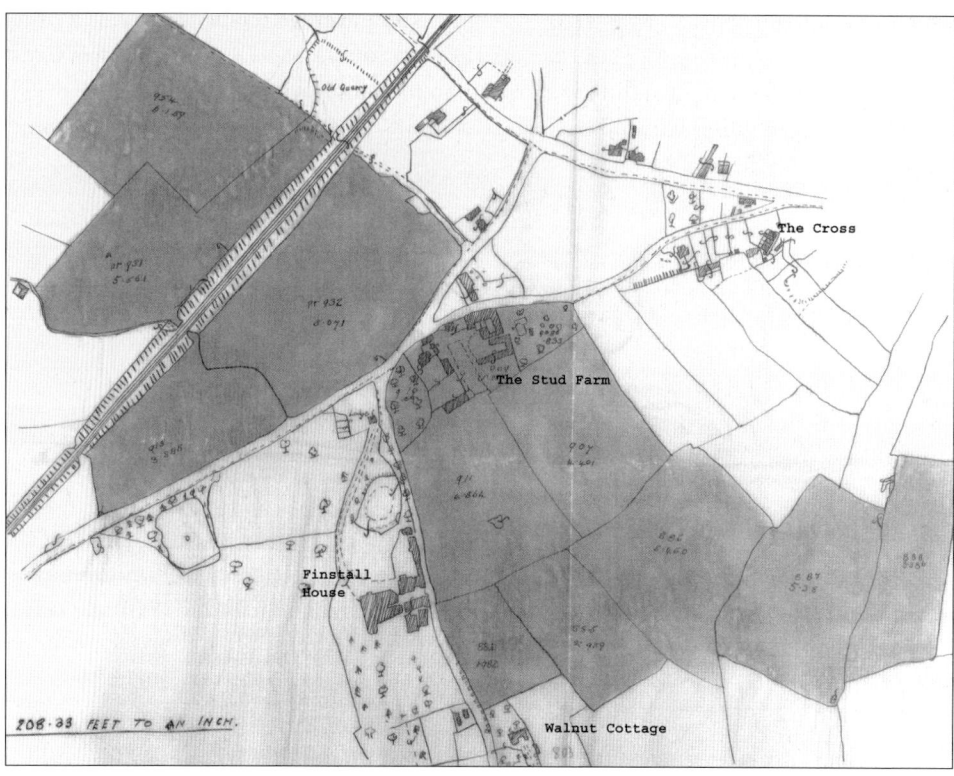

Sale plan of the Stud Farm 1923. (BC)

William Everitt, who was living at Finstall Park from 1868 until he moved down to Berry Court, Bournemouth in 1892, was passionate not only about his wine cellar, but also about racehorses. To indulge his enthusiasm he built a specially planned farm (where Penmanor is now), with a newly built five bedroomed house for his stud manager, and a complex of looseboxes and everything else needed for his horse breeding. By 1920, after John Boultbee Brooks had taken the site over, there were no less than 21 looseboxes and even more corrugated-iron ones, plus saddle room, men's mess room, a foaling box, timber built foal shed, cart shed, harness room with granary over, a barn, stack yard, a stallion yard and even a chicken house. Plus 55 acres of pasture land, half of which was behind the stables (bought from the Featherston trustees), and half across the Finstall Road (bought from Brettell trustees).

The Everitt racehorses by the 1870s were well known throughout the country, and his collection was mentioned in newspaper blood stock reports with regularity. In 1871 at Birmingham Horse Show in Bingley Hall he was selling 'thoroughbred stallions for getting hunters', including Paul Jones, the winner of the Chester Cup and the St Leger, which was 'a horse made for speed and far more than average quality'. It seems he was showing off Paul Jones at the show, for in 1874 it was published that 'Cardinal York and Paul Jones will stand at Finstall Park Farm upon the same terms as last year'.

The horse breeding vocabulary is very specialised. In 1875 Mr H. Bird, the Stud Groom, was offering

> STALLION – ORNE, at Finstall Park Farm,
>
> Thorough-bred Mares, £3; Half-bred Mares, £2.
>
> ORNE is a Bay Horse, without white, 15 hands 2½ inches high, sound, good tempered, with excellent bone and fine action. He is by Feruck Khan, by the Baron (sire of Stockwell and Rataplan) – Princesse de la Paix by Gladiator. His blood comprises Sir Hercules, Sultan, and Partisan strains (the stoutest known), exactly the same as Blair Athol, the most fashionable sire in England. Fees to be paid at the time, and Mares to be taken away same day.

A review of the Worcestershire Agricultural Society show in New Road, Bromsgrove, said:

> There's seldom been seen a better lot of horses in the Society's yard. The stallions were a very good class – Paul Jones, the property of Mr Everitt (13 years old) by Buccaneer out of Queen of the Gypsies was rightly placed first. He is a beautifully coloured horse, a bit slack in the back perhaps, but a very fine mover and good jumper, who won a first prize. And two further prizes.

In 1910 Mr Everitt died, aged 80 at his home in Leamington. An obituary said:

> The deceased ... was held in high esteem in the counties of Worcestershire and Warwickshire, and some years ago filled the office of High Sheriff to the former.
>
> In Mr Everitt's colour Day Dream won the Great Eastern Counties Handicap in 1873, while the next year with Genevieve he succeeded in winning the Portland Plate at Doncaster. The best horse he owned was Martley, bred by him at Finstall. Paul Jones, the Chester Cup winner, and second in Formosa's famous St Leger of 1868, the Cesarewitch winner of 1870, Cardinal York, and Pellegrino were also bred by Mr Everitt. Another well-known mare owned by Mr Everitt was Zelle, the dam of Zealot, who won many races for the late Lord Bradford.

A more spikey comment in the Victoria County History was 'His best sires were Paul Jones, Cardinal York for whom he gave a long price, Martley, and Knight of Malta. This stud never turned out anything first rate, but Mr Everitt ran several that ran races. Paul Jones unluckily died prematurely, and Cardinal York failed to beget any stock as good as himself.'

During Everitt's ownership he employed a stud groom who lived in the newly built Finstall Cottage on the corner of Walnut Lane and Finstall Road, and he was responsible for the various sales. There was a second line of horses being bred – in 1890 they were selling '5 VALUABLE YOUNG CART HORSES, the property of W.E. Everitt Esq, of Finstall Park, Bromsgrove. These horses had been worked on the farm up to date, and are sold for no fault, only to make room for Colts coming on. ... They are big, upstanding, sound Horses, suitable for town work, and all warranted quiet and good workers.'

On 7th March 1892 there was a big auction held at the Stud Farm of the farm stock, agricultural implements and building materials. This included 47 head of cattle, a pedigree red and white bull calf, four very valuable young cart horses, well-bred in-pig sow, and 100 head of poultry. So when Mr Boultbee Brooks began his breeding he would have had to set up with everything new, though he probably bought many of the lots in the auction.

During Everitt's time the stud grooms regularly changed: Henry Herman, Jas Elliott and Thomas Peacock Marshall (sometimes known as Thomas Marshall Peacock) were responsible for the horses in quick succession, and when Mr Boultbee Brooks, with W. Maddocks as Farm Steward, took over the operation there seem to have been similarly speedy changes.

Portrait of Finstall Ryman, 1919, who had 'proved himself a sure sire, his first crop of foals realising up to £170.'

Boultbee Brooks was interested in prize winning cattle and shire horses, and in his time won many medals. In 1909 at the Herefordshire Horse Show in a strong cart horse section he won a silver medal for Finstall Surprise; the same year he won 3rd prize at the Birmingham Fat Stock Show with his Aberdeen Angus Finstall Princess, and by 1913 it was a prize for Finstall Meadow Queen at the Shire Horse Society Show, Islington and a medal at Madresfield Show for the best mare, filly or foal. Brooks was successfully moving in a world which included the Earl of Coventry, Lord Hindlip, and Earl Beauchamp of Madresfield Court, who were all keen breeders.

The Stud Farm land, however, still belonged to the Everitt family and it was put on sale as Lot 2 of the big Finstall Park sale in 1920, with 55 acres and the stud groom's home now known as Clovelly House. John Boultbee

Brooks was unable to buy the farm, which was a good thing since he died the following year, two days after his lease ran out. Thomas Rawes bought the farm for £4,600, and Arnold William Cadbury Butler[81] took over the stud breeding. 1923 brought the sale of the farm, still 55 acres, to Barrow Cadbury and William Adlington Cadbury[82] for £3,550.

AWC Butler and his wife Rhona had a daughter in 1927, and in 1928 he took second prize for the open stallion class, foaled in 1927, at the Shropshire and West Midlands Society Show. In the early 1930s H.T. Jordan was breeding the Penmanor herds of pedigree large and middle white pigs.

Barrow Cadbury.   *W.A. Cadbury.*   *Rev. Percy E. Warrington in 1928.*

1930 also brought a big sale of several stallions in Peterborough and yet another sale of the property, this time with 31 acres (and a description offering 'excellent road frontage of about 575 yards affording a number of choice building sites ... some of the Buildings suitable for use as Cowhouses have been passed for Grade A Milk Production'), while Lot 2 was 20 acres going back from the opposite side of Finstall Road, and Lot 3 was a narrow field bordered by Finstall Road and the railway line. We can see that the estate agents and the two Cadburys had an eye for the new housing market. Lots 2 and 3 were sold before the sale and Lot 1 was withdrawn at £2,400, but 16 of the 31 acres were bought a few months later by the Rev. Percy Ewart Warrington.

---

81   AWC Butler (b.1902) was son of Edith (née Cadbury), grandson of Richard Cadbury who was second son of John Cadbury, founder of Cadbury's chocolate company.

82   William Adlington Cadbury and Barrow Cadbury (in 1931 was Chairman of Cadbury's) were sons of Richard Barrow Cadbury and grandsons of John Cadbury.

Stud Farm stables as they are today.

The garden front of what was Clovelly House, home of the Stud Groom, taken in the 1960s. Now No.86, Finstall Road. (Rob Oldaker)

And that was the end of the Stud Farm, and the beginning of Finstall's house and bungalow building that we know today.

The Rev. Warrington was an interesting character. He was described as 'a financier in a surplice' who had previously had no connection to Finstall, and by this date had completed his sixth deal around the country in the acquisition of large buildings with land to create public schools. At this time he was aged about 40, and had the living of Monckton Combe in Somerset. He was born in Derbyshire to a father who was a lamplighter for Burton Corporation. He saw his enterprises as the vanguard against 'the insidious wiles of Rome and the even more treacherous machinations of the Anglo-Catholics'.[83] He was responsible for creating five schools, mainly with the support of the Martyrs Memorial Trust, which were Wrekin College (which he bought for £110,000 in 1921); Stowe House in 1922, then the home of the Duke of Buckingham, which is now Stowe College; Wimborne College, Dorset, also in 1922, bought from Lord Wimborne; Harrogate College for Girls (which he bought for £120,000 with support from the Church of England Trust in 1924); and Weston Birt, Gloucestershire also for girls (which he bought after its auction had failed to find a purchaser in 1927). However any ideas he might have had to create a major school in Finstall came to naught, but he did buy the 16 acres and three houses as an investment for his sister, Miss Lilian E.M. Warrington – though neither of them lived here.

Wartime slowed up the building of houses on Penmanor.[84] On 26 October 1940 all deeds and papers relating to the property were destroyed through fire caused by enemy action in Newhall Street, Birmingham. Nevertheless there were a few houses built – Innisfree and Four Winds among them. Come 1944 the owner put the Penmanor site to auction in three Lots, with about a dozen houses already built, and with it the regulation

---

83 *From Controversy to Co-Existence: Evangelicals in the Church of England 1914-1980*, Randle Manwaring, CUP, 2002.

84 The name Penmanor is unusual, and there seems no reason for it. BCG Nokes, in his *Finstall Parish Handbook*, 1958, calls the estate Penn Manor.

11. The Stud Farm and Penmanor

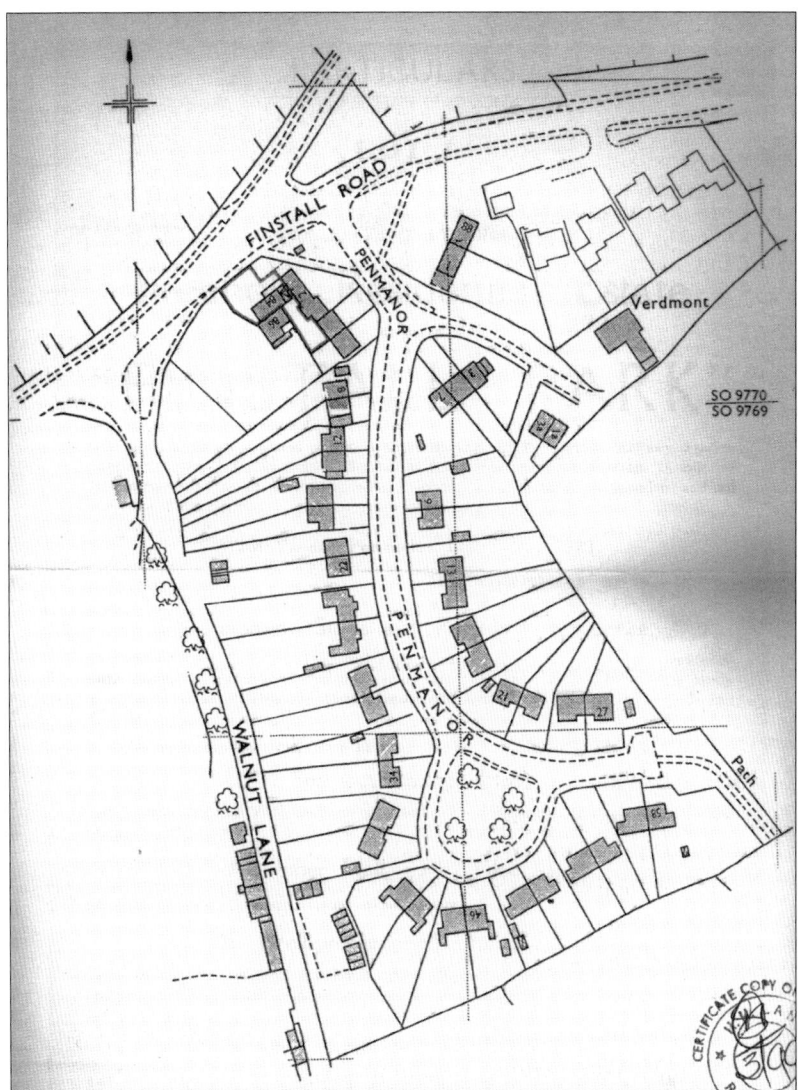

Proposed layout of Penmanor, c.1944. (Chris Milton)

that 'No building may be smaller in size or value than the largest of the dwellinghouses already in existence, nor shall buildings be used or occupied for any purpose that would be detrimental to the use and enjoyment of such adjoining properties.' By 1955 there were 24 houses built, most of the most recent ones being council houses (or as they are known today, social housing). At the top of the site there is a field gate leading to the children's playground, the idea of Topsy Hobbs who wrote to the Duke of Edinburgh successfully asking for his support. In 1945 to celebrate the end of the war a 'Penmanor Peace Picnic' was held for Finstall children, who were taken on an outing to Weston-Super-Mare.

Chapter Twelve

Pikes Pool: Fishing Pond or Waterworks?

In the 1500s Bordesley Abbey had fishing rights to all waters in the Tardebigge area, which would include Pikes Pool. A deed of June 1729 describes 'a great fishpool lying near Burcot' and two other pools called the 'Pink Pools'.[85] The latters' site is now the opposite side of the railway line. Pikes Pool is fed by five springs and when full should be over twelve feet deep, and some 60 yards long, which must be why it was such a good fishing place, for there were always a quantity of pike, perch, roach and tench, and there were always gentlemen who wanted to fish it.

Most of Pikes Pool was part of John Ashmore junior's estate in the 1840s, though that land was later owned by Thomas Wilson Esq of Worcester. The land abutting the northern end of the pool was owned by Baylies' Charity School of Dudley.

There were several happenings connected with Pikes Pool, including what was a nasty accident in 1847 'which might have been attended with very lamentable consequences'.

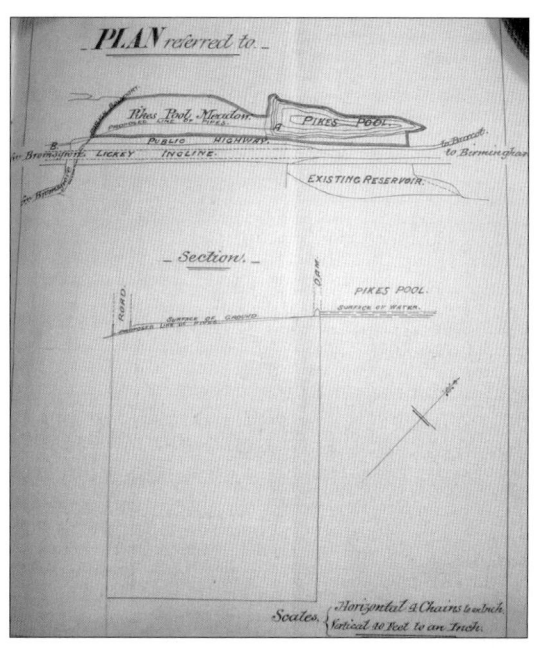

1882 plan of Pikes Pool showing the 'proposed line of pipes' sloping down to the road, taking water to the Wagon Works at Aston Fields. (WRO)

Mrs Gaunt, wife of Mr Gaunt, surgeon of Alvechurch, was being driven in her phaeton along Pikes Pool Lane (previously called Turnpike Lane) from Burcot. They were driving close by the railway line, with the Pool – also very close by, and considerably below the road – on the other side of the lane, when a train came up. The horse took fright, dashed

---

85 This is a quote from Leadbetter's *Story of Bromsgrove*, 1946, who does not give any further information about the deed.

12. Pikes Pool: Fishing Pond or Waterworks?

off towards the bridge, and collided with it. The vehicle was broken to pieces and the horse – apparently a very valuable one – was killed instantly. Mrs Gaunt had only a few bruises, but the Gaunts' servant who was driving was much more seriously hurt.

There was an area of wetland by Pikes Pool where watercress was grown very easily, and was a valuable crop, thus encouraging thieves: 'John Stanton, nailer, was charged (in 1867) with stealing watercresses, value two pence, the property of Mr Thomas Gardner (Finstall Farm farming tenant) ... PC Workman saw prisoner gathering watercresses from Pikes Pool, on Sunday morning, and charged him with stealing it. Prisoner said Mr Gardner had given him leave which was contradicted by Mr Gardner. The case was dismissed on defendant paying the costs, 7s 6d.' John Stanton seems to have been regarded as not too serious an offender.

However, another case that took Thomas Gardner to the petty sessions as a prosecutor was when three Birmingham men appeared before Dr. Collis and John Corbett Esq charged with stealing 164lbs [74 kilos] of watercress from Pikes Pool. Watched in the night until four o'clock in the morning by two police constables, the men were seen picking the

Pikes Pool in autumn.

watercress. One of the prisoners had already been convicted for stealing Mr Gardner's mushrooms and also with stealing watercress from another pool, and Superintendent Bevan said he had several times been convicted for similar events. Mr Gardner asked the Bench to deal leniently with the other two prisoners as it was their first offence, and they were fined 21 shillings each. The leader of the three was sentenced to six months' hard labour. This was not a light sentence; prisoners were often used as the main work force in quarrying and building roads, but if they misbehaved the chain gang was used to punish the convicts – men were shackled together with heavy chains whilst they carried out their labouring jobs.

Pikes Pool as we know it became seriously under threat in 1866 when there was a move to supply both Bromsgrove and Droitwich with water from Pikes Pool stream and Spadesbourne Brook, which runs towards Bromsgrove from Lickey End. Mr E. Wilson, engineer, of Worcester (was he related to the owner of the land round Pikes Pool?) had worked out that Pikes Pool could yield 66,000 gallons of water per day if the Spadesbourne were diverted into Pikes Pool, to be stored in a reservoir built near Mount Pleasant[86], and be sufficient for both Bromsgrove and Droitwich. At a public meeting Mr Dipple 'at great length' urged that the water should be provided by the Local Board not by a private company. However Dr. Fletcher, who knew the damage unclean water was causing, was in favour and asked the Local Board to support the proposal – 'fever feeds on filth', he said. A few months later it was reported that Pikes Pool would supply Droitwich only, and Bromsgrove's water would come from the Spadesbourne Brook from Burcot. The directors of the company included Messrs F. Watt and W. Llewellin of Bromsgrove, R.W. Johnson whose wife happened to own Pikes Pool, and T.G. Smith and J.H. Bradley of Droitwich, Mr Wilson being the engineer. Numerous shares were sold, with the newspaper wisely telling its readers that 'Water works always pay well', and would make a profit of 30%.

Fortunately for Finstall, the Pikes Pool idea never happened. Piped water from the Burcot waterworks came to Bromsgrove in 1882, to Finstall in 1884 and Aston Fields in 1886.[87]

However, despite the piped water reaching Finstall in 1884, it didn't reach every household, for Caspidge House even in 1951 was reliant on water for the household from a well 130 ft deep, and the farm buildings and fields used water brought from Pikes Pool by means of a petrol-driven pump and pipe works which took the water to storage tanks.

By 1874 the pool was part of the lands bought by Arthur Albright from Sarah Booth Johnson. The sale particulars said that Pikes Pool had springs and a conduit under the railway, irrigating a portion of the Finstall Farm estate, and had 'as good fishing as any

---

86 Mount Pleasant is the hill coming out of Bromsgrove, on what is now called Stratford Road.
87 For more detailed information about water, see *Victorian Greenhill*, Jennie McGregor-Smith, 2000 (out of print), Coombe Cottage Books, and *From Bromsgrove to Aston Fields – A Story of Victorian Expansion*, Jennie McGregor-Smith, 2008, Brewin Books.

in the county'. Arthur Albright was no countryman, and he did not go fishing like his daughter-in-law, so he was pleased in 1894 to sell Pikes Pool and the fields surrounding it to his Birmingham Quaker friend, Alderman Francis Corder Clayton, who two years earlier had bought some land from Mr Edward G. Capon who owned Caspage Farm. It was Clayton who built the new Caspidge House up the hill.

Part of any agreement about the pool included the right of the pool owner or renter to empty the pool over the land below it as long as seven days' notice was given. Before this, in 1882, the Midland Railway Company and Arthur Albright were discussing their earlier arrangement that the Company could use water from the pool. James McConnell, Chief Engineer of the Railway, had had a problem with mud in the well at the station, and his answer to that problem was to lay a pipe from Pikes Pool to the wagon works – a mile and a half away! Albright's solicitor wrote to Albright telling him that the Midland Railway Company would not approve a clause in their agreement limiting the amount of water they could draw. The solicitor comfortingly says 'of course we have an additional indemnity in respect of any riparian proprietors who may be damaged', and, amusingly, 'the Company say they will only draw the minimum amount of water which they need lest they should get themselves into trouble'.

An ancient pollarded oak tree in the hedgerow of Pikes Pool Lane.

The discussion continued in 1893 when Robert Smallwood wrote from Rigby Hall to Mr Albright:

> I have written to the Midland Railway Co. as to taking all the water from Pike Pool ... I am advised I must first apply to you as the injury done to the property of several of us is so severe that we shall be compelled to take some proceedings to regain the supply of water wrongfully taken away.

For if too much water was taken by the Railway for their purposes, it meant that the brook which passed through Smallwood's land lost its water. The solicitor having sorted this out, Arthur Albright decided in 1896 to buy back from the Railway the right to use the boathouse and boat on Pikes Pool, for which he paid £4. Then Mr Clayton who was renting the pool must have found he had no time to go fishing because in 1897 he rented out the pool, its boat house and the grounds round it, to Charles R. Sayer (who was then at Finstall Mount) for seven years. The solicitors must have had a fine time sorting all this out.

At a time of great misery and unrest among the nailers and nailmasters in Bromsgrove because of the expansion of the much cheaper machine-made industry in the Black

The flood that hit The Vale in May 1971. (Bromsgrove Advertiser Messenger)

Country (hand-wrought nails were now only 10% of the nails made in the region) it does not seem surprising that one nail manufacturer, John James of New Buildings, Bromsgrove,[88] who was depressed, in ill health and short of money, should have been found drowned in Pikes Pool in March 1908. James apparently knew the area well, for he had helped his brother on Caspidge and Tutnall farms for many years. The Coroner agreed that James could not possibly have fallen down the bank into the water (though members of the jury thought that there should be a better fence between the road and the pool – the Coroner's response being that there was no law to compel an owner to fence his land except to keep his cattle in). James had not left a note, so the verdict was 'found drowned'.

John James was not the only person who had lost their life in Pikes Pool, and the stokers on the engines grinding up the incline would keep an eye on the pool as they passed it, just to check that there was no floating body. There were rumours, not confirmed, that even one of the Albright family died in that way. The latter may have been why Leadbetter in his 1946 description of Pikes Pool should end with the words 'In recent years the pool has obtained a sinister reputation'.

---

88 New Buildings were a row of thirty nailers' cottages built c.1808, opposite the Crab Mill pub, between Victoria and All Saints Roads. They were demolished as slum-clearance by the Bromsgrove Urban District Council in 1962. See *The Bromsgrove Rousler*, number XXII, December 2007, 'New Buildings Deeds and Documents' by David C.B. Nokes; later memories by Shirley Brittan in the same edition, and in *A Bromsgrove Carpenter's Tale*, ed. Margaret Cooper.

12. Pikes Pool: Fishing Pond or Waterworks?

1949 brought an auction of the pool with the pasture adjoining it – just over six acres, including the boathouse and flat bottomed boat; the pool was unsold. The sale particulars noted: 'The Owner of this Lot has the right to occasionally empty the Pool by causing the water therefrom to flood over land to the south-west of the Pool provided that not less than seven days' notice is given to the occupier of the land.' However, sometime before she died Miss Jocelyn Albright gave the pool and more fields towards Burcot to the Boy Scouting organisation to be used for camping and activity holidays, an idea so popular that there is now an organisation called Blackwell Adventure. This is based at Blackwell Court, which had been built in 1874 on some 42 acres for Mr George Unite, one of the family of silversmiths and jewellers in Birmingham Jewellery Quarter, and where Boultbee Brook, son of John Boultbee Brook of Finstall Park, lived. In 1971 the Birmingham Boy Scout Association bought Blackwell Court with 52 acres as a conference and activity centre. Initially it was known as the Douglas and Mary Turner Scouting Centre because they generously provided the money.

The Scout organisation has built various useful wooden buildings near Pikes Pool, but there are regularly small or large groups of tents with camp fires set up, which are used by a variety of organisations. Often one sees small groups of teenagers walking slowly round Finstall and Tutnall anxiously studying maps for their Duke of Edinburgh Awards.

In May 1971, when the new owners were draining the pool to clean it for scout use, the water flooded over the field (3,000,000 gallons, it is said), into the lane and down to Finstall Vale where it swept into the cellars and a shed, leaving flooding on the lawns. Not a happy thing to happen when you have just moved into the house, as Jill and Brian Findon had just done.

Chapter Thirteen

Rigby Hall after the Ellins

What of Rigby Hall? Rigby Hall itself was bought from the Ellins by Bromsgrove solicitor James Holyoake who asked Birmingham architect Charles Edge[89] in 1844 to design a new Lodge and some improvements and alterations to the house. Holyoake asked for the 'cornice to be continued round the south, west and eastern fronts of the house, and the blank windows on the west front to be taken out and the openings bricked up and cemented as other parts'. It was then let to Mr Charles Taylor in 1846, a regular and grumpy passenger on the train to Birmingham. One day he was taken to court by the Midland Railway Company. The newspaper report says:

> It would seem that between the plaintiff ... and the officers of the company, some differences had arisen, which had the effect of inducing them to annoy each other as much as possible; the company's officers always weighing every bit of Taylor's luggage on his various passages to and from Bromsgrove, and the plaintiff standing on his strict right. ... Taylor arrived at Bromsgrove and showed his ticket to a porter, who moved to him, as much as to say it was all right. Taylor then went into the booking office, and he was asked by a railway constable for his ticket. Taylor said he had shown it, but would not give it up, as it was his [Taylor's] receipt. He was therefore taken into custody. Taylor was taken before a magistrate some five miles from Bromsgrove, ... but was instantly discharged.
>
> Mr Whitehurst [for the Company] stated the plaintiff formerly kept a beer shop, but somehow or other had latterly got hold of an old farmhouse bearing the proud name of Rigby Hall. He usually travelled by the third class, and was in the habit of annoying the company's officers as much as he could.
>
> Verdict for the plaintiff: £5 damages.

It seems that Mr Taylor was not really happy with his new home either, so that same year he put up for sale his 'superior and modern' household furniture, including an elegant circular rosewood loo table, a 'Piano-forte in mahogany case' and a handsome mahogany chest of drawers. His farming stock was more rural, including eight handsome young fat

---

89   Charles Edge (1800-1867) was a Birmingham architect, working from about 1827 and designing classical Greek Revival buildings, mainly in Birmingham. Unfortunately many of these have been demolished.

13. Rigby Hall after the Ellins

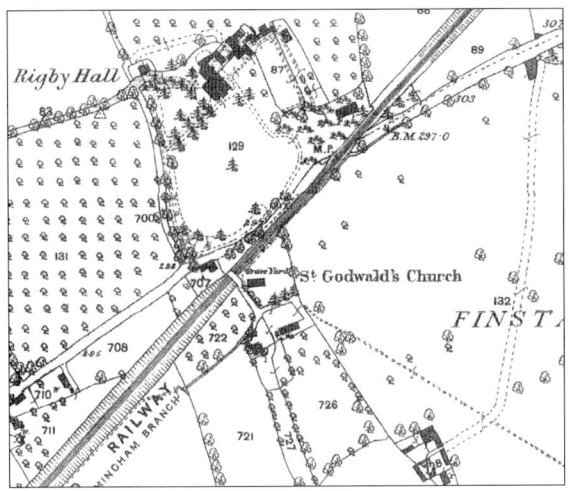

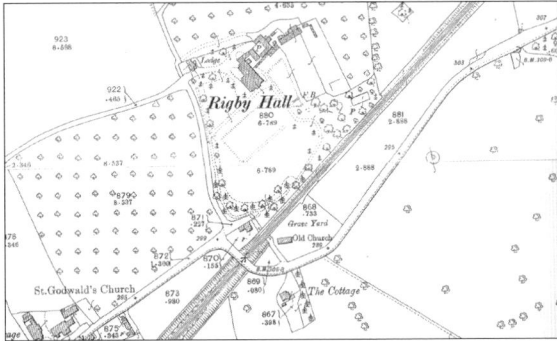

The 1883 and 1901 mapping of Rigby Hall and the Finstall skew bridges, the first running under the railway and the second showing the new bridge over the lines and the newly built St Godwald's church.

bullocks, three excellent milking cows, two gilts[90], two porkers, fifteen Southdown ewes, four wethers and a hay rick.

There were two more short lived tenants before the Corbetts came. An announcement in March 1851 in the Births column of *The Standard* read 'Birth at Rigby Hall, to the wife of Thos. William Kinder Esq., a daughter' – the name of the mother was clearly not important![91] Kinder was owner of the railway coach building company at the Wagon Works. Then came Mr Thomas William Vernon, who sounds a much more pleasant man:

> Charles Bates and Richard Hall, the two youths charged with stealing pears from the garden of Mr Vernon of Rigby Hall, the hearing of whose case had been adjourned for a fortnight, were again brought up, and Mr Vernon declining to press the charge against them, they were discharged ... and admonished not to similarly offend again.

> MARRIAGES On April 2nd 1856, at the British Embassy, Paris, John Corbett, Esq., of Rigby Hall, near Bromsgrove, to Anna Eliza, daughter of John O'Meara, Esq., of Paris and the county of Tipperary, Ireland.

John Corbett, 'the Salt King', owner of the British Alkali Company at Stoke Works, had met Anna O'Meara in Paris when he was travelling to market his company. During the six years they lived in Rigby Hall they had three daughters, and the youngest was baptised at Little Malvern Roman Catholic church in April 1859, with Camille Du Bois and

---

90 Gilts are young pigs; wethers are castrated rams.

91 At this time, and for many years more, children were the sole property of the father; the mother was not legally a parent.

Birmingham Architect Charles Edge's 1844 design for a new Lodge for Rigby Hall. (Reproduced with permission of Library of Birmingham)

John Corbett, 'the Salt King' of Stoke Works, who lived at Rigby Hall from 1856-1862.

Gioachino Rossini (the composer) of Paris being her Godparents. The baby was christened Anna Camille Olympe, named after her Godmother and Rossini's wife Olympe.[92]

The Corbetts were to leave in 1862 to go to the recently built Stoke Grange [now Bromsgrove Pre-Preparatory School at Avoncroft], while waiting on the completion of the Château Impney, the exotic mansion into which they moved in about 1870. While living in Rigby Hall the Corbetts gave the children at the Stoke Works school regular treats, both in the summer and at Christmas. Eighty children came on the Annual School treat in 1860; 'The little folks arrived by train, and after many a frolic and much fun partook of a substantial repast of tea, plum cake, ham, bread and butter, jam, etc. ... Games of all kinds resorted to in the beautiful grounds of Rigby Hall, at which all the children obtained prizes of toys, books, handkerchiefs and a merry and happy evening was spent. ... About six o'clock the merry party took their departure.' The Christmas visit of about 100 children in 1861 were given hot roast beef and plum pudding, and enjoyed an 'elegant and well laden Christmas tree before being given a toy, or some useful article of clothing'.

The Grange, now Bromsgrove Pre-Preparatory School at Avoncroft, painted by Miss A. Aldham, 1878. (WRO)

---

92 This information provided by Julian Hunt from records at Worcester.

13. Rigby Hall after the Ellins

In April 1859 Mr Holyoake had put the estate up for auction again with no result, but after the Corbetts left Robert Smallwood and his family moved in during 1864 and stayed for 34 years. This Birmingham wine merchant and JP had come across the estate when visiting the daughter of James Shaw then living in Finstall Park, visits that ended in marriage and first renting, then purchasing, Rigby Hall. And what a wedding it was! Despite being in February several triumphal arches were erected between Stoke Prior church and Finstall Park.

> At half-past eleven o'clock the bridal party arrived at the Church in nine carriages and pairs. The bride [was] attired in an elegant white glacé silk dress, with a beautiful veil of Honiton lace, and attended by six bridesmaids. ... the party returned to Finstall Park and partook of an elegant and sumptous dejeuner. ... A ball in the evening terminated a very happy day. The children of the three Schools in the parish were not forgotten, being, by the generosity of Mr Shaw, regaled with buns and wine.
>
> (There was one little blip...) A merry peal was attempted by the ringers, but the Stoke bells sadly required the Churchwardens' inspection, one being cracked, and the others inharmonious.

Robert Smallwood's business premises were in Lower Priory, Birmingham.

Robert Smallwood, JP, who lived at Rigby Hall for 34 years, until 1900.

> ... at the bottom of the said Lower Priory, [is] a sedate and solid brick building. He will see a brass knocker on the door and a brass plate bearing the name of Smallwood and sons – only this, and nothing more. This is the business house of the oldest firm of wine merchants in Birmingham, and I believe that these premises ... have been in the possession of the Smallwood family since the days of the Commonwealth; and, further, that the present active members of the firm are the fifth and sixth generation of Smallwood and Sons, wine merchants. There is no big shop window full of bottles of cheap heterogeneous wines and spirits. It might be the house of some good old doctor, or the office and home of some ripe old lawyer.
>
> If you step inside the office you see few signs of Bacchus or his bowl, but you do see some antiquated rooms, some quaint furniture, and a nice dry, well-seasoned appearance that denotes age. There are full and capacious cellars on the premises of course – cellars containing a sort of well in which the books of the firm were buried at the time of the Birmingham riots; ... With regard to Messrs. Smallwood's cellars, their

Rigby Hall, 1900. (BC)

> subterranean premises are honeycombed with catacombs containing the remains of some grand old spirits and big bins of choice vintage and various other wines.[93]

The Smallwoods settled in well, having five children and being looked after by a cook, housemaid, kitchenmaid, no less than three nurses (in 1871), a footman and a groom. Robert Smallwood regularly took the train to Birmingham where the firm had branched out into unfermented cider and perry (in casks of 30 gallons), the drinks possibly made from the fruit grown in Rigby Hall orchards and taken by canal to Worcester Wharf in Birmingham. He also was a JP – often sitting with John Corbett – and chaired the magistrates for twenty years. He was on the Bromsgrove Cottage Hospital Committee, and took part in politics. When he became ill aged 69 he retired to Birmingham, and died in 1898.

The estate came up for auction in 1900, now with an area of 87 acres – Smallwood had bought it with just 24. The house was much as one would expect for a wealthy gentleman:

> three reception rooms and a billiard room, a downstairs lavatory with w.c., a strong room with a Whitfield's door. In a separate wing were the Servants' Hall, a Cooking Kitchen with Kenilworth range, a Rufford sink (made in Stourbridge), hot and cold water supply and soft water pump. 'A Scullery, Dairy, Vegetable Larder, Meat Larder,

---

93 *A Tale of One City, The New Birmingham*, Thomas Anderton, c.1900, from a collection of articles from *Midland Counties Herald*, republished online by 1st World Publishing 2005.

13. Rigby Hall after the Ellins

Cook's Pantry, Housekeeper's Room and Butler's Pantry, Serving Hall and Back Passage. In the Servants' Yard are Knife House, Coal House, Ashplace and w.c.'

Upstairs continued with much the same quality facilities, though just one fitted Bathroom and w.c. on the first floor, and the second floor, with six Bed Chambers, had only a Dressing Room.

Outside was equally well provided, with three-stall Stable and Loose Box, Saddle Room, with Groom's Room over; Meal House with Corn Room over; roomy Carriage House, Boot House, two Piggeries, and three-tie Cow House, Hay Shed and Loose Box, in two enclosed paved yards. Also Cart Sheds, Carpenter's Shed and Timber Shed; Feeding Shed, Wagon Shed, and Pigsty in fold yard.

Edward Ansell of Ansell's Brewery, who lived at Rigby Hall 1900 until 1908. (www.midlandspubs.co.uk)

Could you really want any more than that? Well, yes – there were Glass Houses comprising Hothouse, early and late Vineries, Peach House, Peach Case, Conservatory, Melon House and Potting House with Store over.

The purchaser was Mr Edward Ansell, brewer, who bought it all in 12 Lots for £18,350. These included land alongside Finstall Road and Rigby Lane and cottages on Finstall Road and in Middlefield Road. During his time Mr Ansell gave an acre of land surrounding St Godwald's church, where the 'Institute' hall was built, and also the land for the War Memorial.

Ansells Brewery in Birmingham was thriving at this period and Edward was to become Chairman in 1904. Living at Aston Fields when working in Aston, Birmingham must have been quite difficult and he tried to sell the property, presumably without land, in 1905, when it was withdrawn at £7,000. He was more successful in selling his Aston Fields housing plots, which in 1907 were the land opposite St Godwald's church, and six plots in New Road, opposite Wellington Road, and in 1911 were five plots up Rigby Lane and eleven plots from the corner of New Road and Rigby Lane up to Finstall Road, which were later used for very attractive council houses built by Braziers. Dragoon Fields followed in 1930, Braziers building ten council houses for £3,342. 6s. 6d.

In 1908 Albert Eadie of the Enfield Cycle Company in Hewell Road, Redditch bought Rigby Hall and stayed there for four years. Highlights of the Eadies' stay was a burglary (when 'not much was stolen'), and a garden party in 1910 when they entertained the Unionists of the Finstall Polling District only a couple of days after a similar Liberal meeting had been held at Finstall Park. The elder daughter Olivette married Herbert Judge, and later lived at Finstall Croft. His younger daughter Dorothy was married to an

Irishman in January 1912 when there was a fire in the 'temporary reception and ballroom' [marquee] which destroyed it. Not the best thing to happen during a wedding celebration.

By 1911 Eadie also had works in Smethwick, Birmingham, manufacturing not only top quality bicycles but also rifles and small arms – probably doing well, having just had

Eadie MFG. Co.'s 1900 autocar. (Grace's Guide to British Industrial History)

the Boer War and with the Great War still to come. Again, not an easy daily journey, so he sold the house for £4,000 – probably just the house, given the money he got for it. The lucky purchaser was Ernest R. Jones, who was Chairman of Jones & Attwood Ltd in Stourbridge (whose Titan Works were very near to Brettell Lane) and also Chairman of Activated Sludge Ltd.[94] The firm was known for its care of the workforce, and in 1898 had been a forerunner in fair payment, at a time when there was much restlessness about low pay; an 8 hour day was introduced, payment for a 48 hour 6 day week being the same wages as their previous 54 hour week. It was in 1919 that the firm began to use Messrs. Impey, Cudworth, Lakin-Smith and Goode as their auditors.[95]

Rigby Lane with houses, the road still looking very rural.

Between 1923 and 1940 Ernest Jones' wife involved herself in parish activities, and maybe was interested in the suffrage movement because in one register of occupants in 1939 she described herself as living in Rigby Hall with 'unpaid domestic duties' – though that was a regular description at that time. She helped set up St Godwald's Sewing Party in 1926 which attracted about 50 members. During the Second World War their daughter Catherine was a VAD (Voluntary Aid Detachment) and their son Walter Stringer-Jones ended the war with a DFC (Distinguished Flying Cross).

The Jones's became the last people to live in Rigby Hall as a family home. During WWII a Government Ministry used the buildings, and in 1940 Worcestershire County

---

94 Jones & Attwood were market leaders in the technology of activated sludge, making heating apparatus, enamelling stoves, pipes, boilers, castings, their patent pipe cutters, sewage distributors. In 1935-1938 Ernest Jones negotiated in Chicago to sell and manufacture in Europe the Comminutor – a screening and disintegrating machine installed in a flow of raw sewage. Solids too large to pass through ¼" slots in the machine's drum screen were cut up by the machine until small enough to do so.

95 See Chapter 9 on The Oakalls.

13. Rigby Hall after the Ellins

Rigby Hall in the 1980s. (BC)

Council bought it for £6,250, since when it has had several lives. A special school was built on part of the grounds, and the main house was a maternity home in the 1940s, then a Shenstone Teachers Training College hall of residence, and since the 1980s it has been used by commercial firms. The Lodge has gone and other dwellings have been built in the grounds, but it still has some of the mature and beautiful trees planted by the Ellins and Smallwoods.

Rigby Hall side elevation in the 1990s.

Chapter Fourteen
Dusthouse Lane: Finch End to the Dusthouse

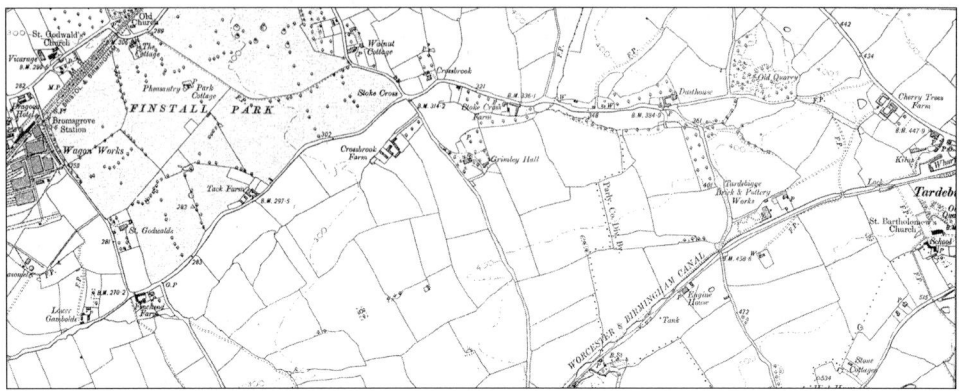

From 1903 OS map showing all the buildings in this chapter.

The ownership of the farms that range eastwards from Finch End to the Dusthouse – Finch End Farm, Tack Farm (now Finstall Park Farm), Crossbrook Farm, Grimley Farm, Stonehouse Farm and finally Dusthouse Farm – are so interlinked it seems impossible to write coherently about them. So this chapter is a collection of notes about the farms and other early properties along Dusthouse Lane, including mention of some of the big sales of lands that were in the ownership of the Brettells, Barrows, Mrs Housman, and the Everitts. Nowadays there are more buildings than those covered in this book, and we do hope there won't be any more built. The naming of the lanes often changed over the years; that between Finch End and Stoke Cross was known as Tack Lane during the 19th century, and in the 1540s the lane from Tutnall was known as Quarry Lane, but the full length is now Dusthouse Lane.

    Dusthouse Lane is still really 'country', a change from the more built up part of Finstall, with a tree lined narrow road that gently winds eastwards from Finch End to Dusthouse Farm. Here it turns right down London Lane towards the canal, turns left towards the group of houses of Curtis Close and Tutnall, and straight ahead as an early, and probably well trodden footpath in years gone by, that goes past the old quarry and the badger sett, and across the old orchard to Cherry Trees Farm on Alcester Road, Tardebigge.

14. Dusthouse Lane: Finch End to the Dusthouse

Finch End Farmhouse painted by Miss A. Aldham, 1870. (WRO)

The second Finch End Farmhouse, as it was in 1987. (Jean Harper).

* * * *

Finch End Farm, or Wheat-fields as it was earlier often called, in the area south of Aston Fields known as Finch End, was one of the first properties that Thomas Brettell bought, from the Lilly (or Lilley) family after the death of John Lilly. After Thomas Brettell's death his estate was left to his sons, who divided up the Brettell farms amongst themselves and it was Joseph, the Bromsgrove solicitor, who took over Finch End Farm. The tenants over the years included John Gardner (whose later family moved around from farm to farm), William Griffin and his son Richard (who did the same), the Parish Clerk John Wilde (whose wife Mary kept an ale house by the farmhouse), and J.W. Wheeler until 1872 when he gave up farming and his property was auctioned:

> The truly valuable FARM STOCK included 'three capital In-calf Dairy Cows. 2 Barrens, and 5 Yearling Heifers; Team of 4 valuable CART HORSES, SOW and PIGS, well descended IN-PIG SOW, poultry and AGRICULTURAL IMPLEMENTS including carts and wagons, ploughs, Turnip Slicers (by *Samuelson*), a 2-knife Chaf Engine,[96] plus numerous other Effects and a RICK OF BEANS'.

Although most of the farming families were tenants this did not mean that some were not people of substance; many of them were interested in the community, were involved in the church, and the Quinney family's finances seemed secure.

William Quinney, who came to Finch End's 127 acres as a young man, had no children and worked the farm until 1901, when his place was taken by his cousin Edward. The Quinneys (whose antecedents originally came from Ireland, and at this time were Quakers) were, apart from one, a family of farmers, William's and Edward's generation being born on a farm in Fenny Compton near Banbury. Members of the family around this time worked Rowney Green Farm and Seecham Farm near Alvechurch amongst others, and

---

96 A small handworked machine to cut up hay and straw for feeding animals.

before coming to Finch End Edward was tenant of Waseley Hill Farm near Rubery. One part of the family began the very successful Quinney's Dairies in Redditch and south Birmingham during the 1960s.

The Quinneys also took over the farming of Lower Gambolds, which is just one field west of Finch End Farm, finding it worthwhile to pay £80 per annum to Mr Everitt. In November 1887 a Mrs Susannah Heath of Upper Gambolds (just south of Finch End), was summoned for allowing six pigs to stray in Finch End Lane – she was fined one shilling for each pig, and eight shillings costs. Six years later fourteen year-old George Green of Little Gambols (Lower Gambolds) was knocked down by a horse he was leading and received injuries from which he died a few hours later. The runaway afterwards collided with another horse, which was so severely injured that it had to be put down. Farming life could be dangerous.

William retired first to Fairview in Finstall, then moved over the road to the newly built Elmwood. He also owned Penshurst in New Road, which was later lived in by his niece Florence. Of Edward's four children three worked the farm with him, while Horace, the second son, being a bright boy, became a science master in a Birmingham school; his son, also Horace, was sadly killed in WWII. Allan R. Quinney took over from his father in the 1920s, when the 114 acres cost them £145.50 on an annual Lady Day tenancy.[97]

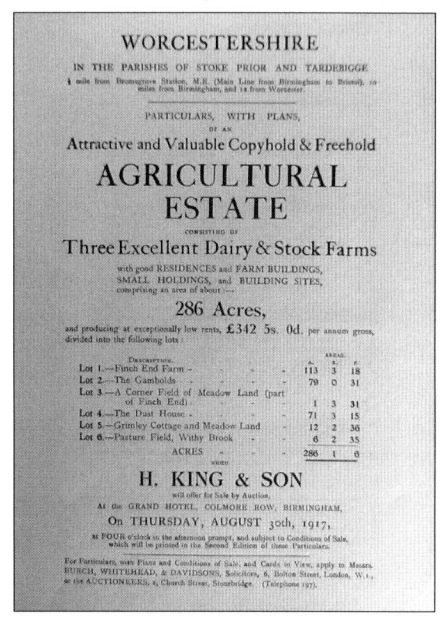

Cover page for the Everitts' 1917 sale selling Finch End Farm, The Gambolds, Dust House Farm, Grimley Cottage and Withy Brook field. (BC)

It was in 1917 that there was the first of the big sales that included Finch End Farm, The Gambolds, Grimley Cottage, several meadows and the Dust House, sold by the Everitt family. Despite the fact that there had been three years of WWI there was considerable interest in the properties. Finch End's 113 acres of mainly good pasture land sold for £3,100 plus £190 worth of timber, Gambolds' 79 acres brought £2,400, and the Dust House's 71 acres was sold for £2,400.

By that time there were good farm buildings at Finch End – 18-tie cow houses, open feeding houses and a calf pen, a four-stall stable and various sheds and barns, piggeries,

---

97 Lady Day, 25th March, the first quarter day, was the traditional day on which year-long contracts between landowners and tenant farmers would begin and end in England.

etc. There were also two generous sized cottages for farm workers, each with 3 bedrooms. The old timber framed farmhouse shown in Miss Aldham's painting had been replaced by a smart early 19th century five bedroomed brick house, possibly built by Joseph Brettell.

A realisation that there was something special and extremely frustrating in one of the Finch End arable fields came to Philip Harper, who took over the farm in 1972. A giant boulder appeared in the field, half hidden underground, which prevented him from ploughing. Because it was too big to remove it he dug round it and let it sink down out of the way of the plough, but over the years the boulder rose again causing the same problems. Helped by a neighbour, Philip Harper dug round the stone with a huge 13 ton 360 digger, easing it out of the ground and then, spinning it bit by bit, they moved it off the field. It is thought it must weigh over 15 tons, measuring 4ft high by 10ft in diameter. There were numerous other boulders around Bromsgrove[98], thought by geologists to have travelled down from the Arenig Hills, part of the Snowdonian range, during the Ice Age. Most of them, like the three in Station Street, Bromsgrove, have disappeared, but there are another two, originally found beside the weighing machine previously at the junction of the Strand and Rotten Row, which are now one each side of the gates to Bromsgrove cemetery[99]. John Humphreys wrote in 1902, describing the numerous 'erratics', or far travelled ice-borne stones:

Molly and Philip Harper with their Ice Age boulder. (Jean Harper)

> A ... (boulder) was removed from the cross roads at Finstall. Another, of intensely black colour, stood in the brook by the roadside near Cross Brook Farm, Finstall, measuring 5ft 6in by 4ft high and 2ft 6in wide. It has since been moved with many others to the grounds of Mr Wilson's house, Lydiate Ash. On Finstall Farm several stones lie on the side of the pool near the railway [Pikes Pool]. At Burcot several large specimens may be seen, one lying against the cottage in the middle of the village, another fine one near the entrance to Burcot Grange.

* * * *

---

98   In 1924 a 'monster' boulder, weighing probably more than a ton, was found in the footpath on the east side of Bromsgrove High Street. 'An attempt was made to break it up, but it was so hard that the electric drill was not able to cut through it. A piece as large as a loaf was detached, but the main boulder remained in the trench, and this relic of the Glacial Age will lie side by side with that modern production, an electric cable.' *The Bromsgrove Messenger*, 19 July 1924. One wonders whether it is still there.

99   Northfield's 'Great Stone' was outside the Great Stone Inn in Church Lane, until in 1954 it was moved to the 17th century Animal Pound within the grounds of the inn.

Just down the road on the north side, past the fields of Finstall Park, was Tack Farm (now known as Finstall Park Farm). The Tack is a name for pasture, grass or clover, hired out by the week, month or quarter for cattle or horses, often in winter. If cattle were on the lands of another for payment they were 'out at tack'. This may well be where Tack Farm got its name. It was the home of Richard Griffin in 1850 who acted as farm bailiff for the Brettells, and presumably was in charge of farming all the land within the curtilage of Finstall House. Inherited by Mrs Housman from the Brettell brothers it was sold to Mr Everitt in 1883 for £1,450 for its 17 acres 1 rood 33 perches.

Tack Farm was then absorbed back into Finstall Park, and was in the 1920 Finstall Park Sale as part of Lot 1 with the main house and 136 acres, described as a cattle farm, let to J.B. Brooks, and not sold. The second Everitt sale in 1924 put the farm as a separate lot with 86 acres, and stated how the land along St Godwald's Road would be ideal for building houses.

Those who lived at Tack Farm included Samuel Robinson, a young carpenter in the 1860s, and in 1870s William Griffin who was farm bailiff, and Joseph Partridge, farmer. In 1900 Charles Powell was farm bailiff and in the twenties A.R. and R.Y. Quinney were renting the farm, and gave notification they wished to quit on Lady Day 1925.

In 2014 there was great shock in the community to find that Robert Whitehouse of one of the recently built bungalows had been arrested as part of a huge international drugs smuggling ring. Three years later he was ordered to pay back £442,945.67 and was sentenced to 22½ years in prison. A total of £13.5 millions worth of drugs had been seized. Not what you expect in Finstall!

* * * *

Crossbrook Farm – sometimes known as Grimley Farm, for they tended to be worked together – was approached from what was then Grimley Hall Road (the access being behind the present Crossbrook Cottages). In the sale of 1856 both Grimley Hall and Crossbrook Farm were bought by James and Dorothy Barrow of Stourbridge, and he described himself as a farmer, though he really was a dealer in corn, butter and cheese. There were always real farmers and labourers living at Crossbrook. In 1871 William Jeptha, butcher, farmer and cattle dealer, moved up to Finstall Heath, no doubt still remembering October 1867 when a set of silver plated harness was stolen from his stables. But also remembering that in 1870 Foot and Mouth disease came to his farm (as well as the Oakalls, Broom House and Ford House Farms).

James and Jane Harvey came to Crossbrook Farm about 1872. In 1874 the *Berrow's Journal* reported under the heading Petty Theft, before Captain Bourne and Robert Smallwood Esq.:

> John Stanton and Edward Packwood of Stoke Prior charged with stealing two hens eggs ... the property of their employer James Harvey of Cross Brook Farm. Both received good characters, but were committed for seven days hard labour.

14. Dusthouse Lane: Finch End to the Dusthouse

In 1875 after her husband's death Mrs Harvey, left with five children – sons 14, 12 and 7, daughters 13 and 6 – continued at the farm but took on Henry Drury as her farm bailiff. Just before her husband died there was an advertisement in *Berrow's Journal*: 'WANTED a married man as Cowman. A good cottage and garden provided. Apply Mr J. Harvey, Crossbrook.' Presumably this was in addition to Henry Drury. When Mrs Harvey gave up farming Crossbrook in 1886 she held a sale of stock, describing them vividly: '24 genuine dairy cows, ripe fat cow, young bull, 60 well bred sheep and lambs ...'. A few years later there was an auction by order of A.B. Albright of Grimley Hall, who had bought the farm, and now had 'given up dairying and let the farm', including '20 head of dairy cattle, ranging from 3 to 5 years old, the whole being in full production and in calf or with calf'. The fruit in the orchard and hedgerows were included.

1897 brought Frederick and Eliza Tilt, with their four children – the eleven month old requiring a nurse – and a farm servant who was 18. They stayed until 1910, after which there were various short-term tenants, including Frederick Carter, William Pearman who also worked land in Alcester Road, and Henry Hughes who described himself as a dairy farmer and heavyworker.

Tom Pugh-Jones of Cross-brook Farm with his First Prize heifer at the Bromsgrove Farmers Show. (Jill Banner)

In the early years of WWII Tom Pugh-Jones, known to everyone as Pugh, moved from Llanpumpsaint in Wales to Crossbrook Farm with his wife and daughters Deirdre, Bronwen and Dilys. The rent he paid to Miss Albright was £225 p.a. and he undertook to personally reside in the farmhouse, and that the fields would not be used for camping without Miss Albright's consent. She also made it a condition that she would have the right to use five of the fields for her poultry, subject to £1 per annum per 100 birds, and she also rented his grazing for her horse at £10 per annum, and he had to pay £12 towards the cost of a new Dutch barn. Later he swapped several fields with her, though she kept the right to shoot over this land. She was an unusual landlady, to whom you didn't say no! David Banner of Banner's the butcher at Aston Fields remembered Pugh as 'a man of the highest principles' having been brought up with a chapel background in South Wales. Having 'loved a game of darts or snooker' he had many friends, and helped and guided many people during his years in Finstall.[100] He was one of the farmers who provided milk for local people from his cows, which was sold in Park Stores, opposite the beginning of Walnut Lane.

---

100 David J. Banner, *Piano Row – Childhood Memories 1940's – 1950's in Aston Fields and Finstall*, 1996.

* * * *

On the north-east corner of Stoke Cross is Crossbrook House, which until 1900 was known as Crossbrook Cottage, lived in by a shepherd. When it became the home of Dr. Henry Swinson, being looked after by his long time housekeeper Anne Williams plus a general servant, the house was extended to be suitable for the gentry, and in 1875 it was sold with 10½ acres for £2,070. Swinson was a churchwarden at St Godwald's, was very generous financially, and was 'the last of the trio of centenarians who at one time lived within a stone's throw of one another'.[101] Swinson trained as a surgeon but when aged about 22 he had been diagnosed with haemorrhage of the lungs, and told it would prevent him working, so, being comfortably off, he wasted his medical training and spent

The Crossbrook crossroads.

the next 80 years to his death in 1900 enjoying life as a gentleman of leisure. *The Bromsgrove Messenger* noted his death with deep regret, saying 'We were all proud of the grand old man who bore his great number of years so bravely. ... very few of the centenarians retain the vigour of mind and body that Dr. Swinson possessed up to the last.' Relating this to the other two centenarians, the newspaper said 'Surely so many instances of contemporary longevity have never been heard of within so small an area, and there really must be something conducive to long life in the air of the Bromsgrove neighbourhood.' [Though it should have read 'air of the Finstall neighbourhood'!]

As soon as the faithful housekeeper Miss Anne Williams had left Crossbrook the house was bought by Thomas Hanbury Ward, who used its eleven acres for six cows, pigs, and fowls plus the still needed two-stall

Crossbrook House in 1999. (BC)

stable, coach-house and harness room with groom's rooms over. Calling himself a school riding master, he maybe gave riding lessons at Bromsgrove School or perhaps the Stud Farm. When he tried to sell the house in 1911 the description of the grounds showed that a keen gardener had lived there – the lawn surrounding the house, 'Flower Borders,

---

101 See Joseph Guise, Caspidge Farm chapter and Mrs Perkins, Dusthouse Lane, this chapter.

14. Dusthouse Lane: Finch End to the Dusthouse

fine Ornamental Shrubs; a large Kitchen Garden well stocked with Fruit Trees, Vinery and Conservatory with healthy Vines in full bearing, also Orchard planted with choice Fruit Trees'. 'The Property offers many inducements to gentlemen in search of a country residence.'

Edwin Goodman, a wire and safety pin manufacturer, who in 1918 did describe himself as a gentleman, came to Crossbrook in 1913 with his wife Muriel. He became a Captain in the Worcestershire Yeomanry in 1915, serving until 1921. One of their sons, Robert married Peggie Booker from Elmbridge in 1935, and they soon moved over the lane to Stonehouse Farm. When WWII came their son Oliver joined the RAF and as a Leading Airman he was on HMS Daedalus of the Royal Navy, to be killed on 17th January 1941 when he was 23. He is commemorated on the Lee-on-Solent memorial and the Birmingham University memorial. Edwin died in 1969, aged 89.

* * * *

The Crossbrook Cottages on the crossroads that we know today were built about 1904, but there were two other cottages on Dusthouse Lane lived in by agricultural labourers, or 'ag labs' as they were usually described in the censuses. 1871 brought William Mason, his wife, two daughters and a son, and William Hunt who was a groom – presumably for Mr Auster of Grimley Hall. George Allcock was in the second cottage, another ag lab with his wife, two daughters and three sons. By 1920 they were let to Messrs Attwood and Burwood, who were each paying £3.3d each per week, £16.18.00 per annum, and in the Everitt Sale of that year they were both bought by Mr Kemp for £330. They were described as 'containing Living Room, 2 bedrooms, Pantry, Wash-house with sink and copper, outside earth closet, and good Gardens ... Company's water is laid on.' No mention of electricity. In 1970 they were bought by Michael and Brigit Morton who rebuilt the cottages into the house it is today, naming it Downwood, and in 1982 added to the garden with 0.28 of an acre bought from the Albright estate.

* * * *

The next house along Dusthouse Lane is Appleshaw, which is quite different from any other building in the area. It was designed by Robert Furneaux Jordan very fashionably in the style of a Sussex barn. He designed the house in 1927 for his father John, who was a Birmingham gynaecologist of a then well-known family of medics, who was retiring there with his wife Mildred (née Player). John had been

Appleshaw in 1934. (BC)

surgeon to several hospitals and in particular the Birmingham and Midlands Hospital for Women, whose new buildings he was instrumental in building. He also had taken a leading share in the work of the new Maternity Hospital when it opened in Loveday Street in 1906. He believed in total abstinence from alcohol; he played lawn tennis and association football, and was a skilled gardener.[102] Robert, the architect of Appleshaw, was trained at Birmingham School of Art and the Architectural Association School of Architecture, London. Born in 1905 he was still studying when he designed the house. He didn't follow the creative architectural path but became a critic, journalist and broadcaster, remembered primarily as the architectural correspondent of The Observer. There is a story that he spent time when young drawing his plans in Appleshaw summer house where there was an interesting fireplace. He was author not only of books on architecture but also of detective novels under the name of Robert Player (his mother's maiden name). He was Principal of the national Architectural Association between 1949 and 1951 when its international profile as a progressive, modernist school was raised and cemented.

Appleshaw was, as the sale particulars of 1934 say, 'most artistically designed, well built of brick with a partly-tile-hung elevation and an old tile roof, and fitted throughout with all labour-saving devices. ... The house is lighted throughout by electric light, and there are power plugs in all the rooms. East Worcestershire Waterworks Co's water.' These notes show that even in 1934 electricity and water were not expected everywhere. The garage 'for two small cars' was built behind the house; there is now a double garage by the house.

When John Furneaux Jordan moved down to Devon, leaving the lovely garden he had created, with its 'flagged Walks, sunk Garden, Sundial, Pond and productive Vegetable Garden', the house was bought by E. Courtney Lord who was there until 1947, followed by E.V. Wynn. In about 1963 it was leased to David and Monica Parker, who succeeded in buying it from Miss Albright in 1972. David Parker was a Bromsgrove dentist, working from his wife's old home in College Road. He was a keen fly fisherman, very interested in wildlife, and, having a project to look after the young trees along Dusthouse Lane, he would tie coloured fabric to the hedge trees he thought should not be cut by the Council

Robert Furneaux Jordan, architect of Appleshaw, in 1949. (AA Archives)

---

102 John's father Thomas is chiefly remembered for his method of amputating at the hip-joint, though his operation is no longer performed very frequently; 'he was gifted by nature with a fine quality of brain and by fingers of extreme delicacy'. Thomas was also son of a Birmingham surgeon and father of three daughters and three sons, of which two were in the profession (*Royal College of Surgeons*).

machinery. A kind man and a good dentist, he was chatty with his patients though known by some of them as Hacker Parker!

* * * *

Next door to Appleshaw is Stonehouse Farm (earlier called Stoke Cross Farm), a Grade II Listed stone and timber framed building going back in part to the early 17th century, with mullioned windows, and a baffle-entry[103] against the chimney stack. A beautifully kept house nowadays, with various extensions, it was not until the 20th century that it became gentrified with a nice garden. The farm was worked by John Lilley, owned by John Ashmore, then Thomas Bourne and William Penn, after whom it was bought by Thomas Brettell. Robert Cordell farmed in the 1850s with his father, also Robert, in his eighties, who came up from Dusthouse and died in his 90th year in 1859. Their 120 acres were across the lane from the farmhouse, towards Finstall Hill. It seems that Francis Fetherstone together with his son John was working Combe Close and Combe Meadow, part of that Stonehouse farmland, which Fetherstone later bought to add to his small patch up by The Cross. Then John, his son, seems to have taken on the whole of Stonehouse Farm until his death in 1899 when it became part of the Albright estates.

Stonehouse farmyard in 1920. (BC)

Stonehouse Farmhouse, painted by Miss A. Aldham in 1870s. (WRO)

Sherwood Suffield farmed a smaller number of acres between 1901 and while there he began his successful milk round, selling but half a pint of milk on the first day. The round grew until 1952 when the family moved from Finstall Farm. Sherwood Suffield had come down from Cheshire, to become farm bailiff at the

---

103 The baffle-entry was when the front door led into a lobby, the far side of which was formed by the side of the chimney stack, and which usually had a staircase on the other side of the stack. Initially the chimney was placed off-centre in the house, but later came to occupy a central position, making it possible for the façade to be designed symmetrically round a central front door.

Reformatory at Stoke Farm, Ryefields, Stoke Prior – the Reformatory was opened in 1853 by the Quaker Sturge brothers. Stoke Cross Farm (Stonehouse Farm) had been advertised to let in 1900, with 31 acres, so Suffield left the Reformatory, with his wife Elizabeth and his family: John, Ann (known as Nancy), and Sherwood Thomas (known as Tom), and moved to Dusthouse Lane. The acreage had grown to 90 acres by 1912. One of his enthusiasms was keeping bees, and he displayed honeycombs and jars of honey at the Finstall Show. It wasn't long before he was attracted to work at Finstall Farm, renting it from Miss Catherine Albright,

Sherwood Suffield with his grandson John Humstone Suffield. (John Suffield)

finally leaving Stonehouse Farm in 1912 to live in Allotment Cottage on the Alcester Road. He died in 1921, leaving Elizabeth with John and Tom Suffield who continued farming.

Suffield was followed by Joseph and Mary Ann Stevens and family, Joseph working as farm bailiff for Mr Boultbee Brooks of Finstall Park. At about the time of their move their son 22 year old George had joined the 2nd Battalion Worcestershire Regiment and was serving in France as a runner for company officer Captain C. Pigg of C Company.

Stonehouse barns, now Willow Barn, alongside Stonehouse. (BC)

During the battle for High Wood, Longueval he was sent to deliver a message to the front line and he never returned. His name is on the Thiepval Memorial and the more personal Finstall memorial cross at Aston Fields.[104] And the poor family had to take two more deaths caused by the war: their son Daniel served with the Army Service Corps Transport Division in Greece and ended up dying of malaria and pneumonia on 14th November 1918 – three days after the end of the war; and another son John, serving as a driver with the East Lancashire regiment, died in 1920 of a war-related illness, an ear infection that led to mastoiditis, meningitis and facial paralysis.

---

104 The story of George Stevens comes from Alan Taylor's article in *The Village*, February 2015.

14. Dusthouse Lane: Finch End to the Dusthouse

1920 brought the big Everitt sale when one of the Goodman family bought Stonehouse. When the Stevens left, Robert Goodman took the opportunity to move in with Peggie, who apart from coping with seven children also became a founder member of Finstall W.I., was a marriage counsellor and a magistrate. She also was a vice-chairman of Hewell Grange Board of Visitors. When it was next sold the farmhouse had been brought up to date, with electricity, water and indoor lavatories replacing the outdoor earth closet. With the sale of its 25 acres the house became eminently attractive to the professional classes.

* * * *

Almost opposite Stonehouse Farm is the Withybrook bridlepath, one of the old roadways which doesn't actually go along the Withybrook but originally took farming folk up to Finstall Farm and onwards to the Hollow Tree Farm by Vigo, once owned by the same people. Sometimes known as Withybrook Lane it was known in my family as the Pig Track, because it used to lead to a small field, part of Stonehouse land, full of pigs. The Withybrook itself is named for the willow trees that grow along the damp side of the stream which when coppiced produced 'withies', used for tying, binding or basketwork.[105] The brook used to be the boundary between Finstall and Tardebigge.

Withybrook Cottage in 1956. (BC)

Withybrook Cottage is alongside the Withybrook, a now much enlarged cottage, which was sitting in ¼ acre when it was built. Records tell us that John and Mary Halliday and their five children lived in the small cottage in 1900 when it was owned by Mrs S. Butler of Edgbaston, with John Halliday as her tenant. John Cotton, the Bromsgrove architect, bought the cottage from Joseph and Sarah Butler in 1905 and very soon there were problems over access to the well that he was fortunate enough to have at the end of the property, legally shared with Lord Windsor's Dusthouse Cottage next door. Not that the well should then have been needed, since water had been laid on

---

105 The withy was once associated with mourning, for there is a traditional story about the child Jesus being beaten with withies by his mother Mary after he had unintentionally caused the death of three children. This is told at length by John Cotton under the title 'The With-ytwig Carol' in *Notes and Queries for Bromsgrove*, Vol I, pp.56-60, 1909.

along Dusthouse Lane and had been connected to the cottages. Piped water first came to Finstall in 1884, though it would have taken some time for the pipes to be laid in every road, and because of the cost of connection numerous poorer people did not want to spend two shillings and six pence (12½p) per quarter if they owned a bath, nor for a second water closet in the house which was charged at 1s 3d (6¼p). This was not cheap and many people preferred to continue using the wells, despite them sometimes drying up in the summer months. The Withybrook Cottage well was reached by the neighbours having to walk into the road and then across the garden, and this resulted in upsetting arguments between the two occupants.

In 1917 John Cotton sold Withybrook Cottage to Captain Edwin Goodman for £390 – and the next year Goodman sold it on to Mrs Madge Buckley for £400. She then sold it to Captain J.F.A. Ball, yet another Birmingham manufacturer, this time of newsprint paper, corrugated paper and containers made of paper. Captain Ball extended the property, buying some land from Dixons.[106] In July 2009 the oak framed double garage and loft space was given the Bromsgrove Society's Architectural Award for a new build; all the materials used in its construction were sourced locally, and it was Bromsgrove craftsmen who helped construct the building.

* * * *

One of the Dusthouse Cottages, Little Dusthouse in 1854, was lived in by Ann Pinfield, sister-in-law of James Green of Finstall who owned the property until his death, when his wife Mary in her will left the cottage to Sarah, her daughter, describing it as: 'A small Freehold Cottage with no upstairs room or Cellar situated in the Parish of Tardebigge, let on a yearly tenancy of £5.00, Saleable value £80.' Later the cottages near to Dusthouse Farm were owned by Lord Plymouth, until they were bought by the Dixons to add to their estates, and sold on to the Birds in 1970. One of the cottages was lived in by the Dixons' gamekeeper Bill Marshall, who bred pheasants in his garden for the Dixons' shoots, the birds let loose on those occasions into the London Lane Spinney and into Dusthouse Quarry. Another cottage had two bedrooms and a box room. When lived in by the Clarke family and their seven sons they hadn't much space, and had to sleep together, head to toe.

Earlier in this chapter is the story of Henry Swinson, who became 100 years old in 1899, as had Joseph Guise of Caspidge in 1895; the third of the Finstall trio was the widowed Mrs Anne Maria Perkins who had lived in one of the cottages in Dust House Lane before moving to Redditch in 1891. It seems that in the 1850s she was a laundress in a cottage at Stoke Cross. Having reached the splendid age of 100, she died in 1899. At this time average life expectancy for those born in 1800 was about 47 years.

---

106 *A Hundred Years in Tardebigge,* Revd. Alan White, Brewin Books, 2011, p211. This book tells much about the early lives of elderly people who had been brought up in the area.

The Dusthouse in 1897. (Jane & Terry Critchley)

* * * *

Dusthouse Farm, which is Listed Grade II, dates from at least 1513, sometimes known at that time as 'Alias Piplars'[107]; some of the fields nearby were still called Poplar Hill in 1785. It is, and always has been, in Tardebigge parish not Finstall. It is one of the most interesting houses in the area, and its history has been fully described by Rev. Alan White in a Tardebigge & Bentley Parish magazine.[108] Its Listing description describes the current house as being late 17th century, with mid 18th century and late 19th century alterations, with a 'baffle entry' through the central 19th century porch with Tudor arch and ledged and boarded door. The baffle entrance is similar to that of Stonehouse Farm, opening onto the wall of the chimney.

Ownership of the farm and its land belonged originally to Bordesley Abbey, prior to 1513 the Peyton family of Cattespoole holding various messuages and crofts in the manor of Tardebigge including Dusthouse. Among early inhabitants was William ffreeman who was there in 1604 and was a churchwarden. Approximately 1730 saw Thomas Mence at

---

107 Alias = otherwise.
108 *Tardebigge and Bentley Parish Magazine*, February 2015, an article which Rev. White thought of as a supplement to his *A Hundred Years in Tardebigge*, Brewin Books, 2011.

the Dusthouse when the Mence family were manorial tenants, and in 1786 Samuel Harris bought the 'Dusthouse, Puddles, Sandy Meadow, Sheep Meadow and the inmath and outmath of Puddles'[109]. Robert Cordell, churchwarden and Vicar's warden at Tardebigge Church, was at the Dusthouse in 1831, his wife Abigail dying in November 1842 aged 69.[110] Robert moved to join his son at Stonehouse Farm when he was about 80, and was followed at Dusthouse by the Partridge family, Isaac and son William, who in 1869 was elected Guardian for Tutnall & Cobley.

Simeon Round was at the farm between 1879 and 1895. There was an unfortunate incident in 1881 when Mr W.H. Kerr of Tutnall Mount was gored by one of his bulls, and in May 1882 there was a report in *Berrow's Journal* when Round summoned Francis Hill, his late wagoner, for leaving his service without notice and claimed £2.10s. damages. In reply Hill summoned Mr Round for assault. Mr Round stated he had remonstrated with Hill for cutting a young colt with a whip, when Hill became abusive and left his work. The magistrates dismissed the case of assault, and ordered Hill to pay £2 damages and nine shillings costs. A calmer piece in a newspaper was Round's 19th December 1882 advertisement offering 19 prime fat geese, presumably for Christmas.

John Taylor took on the farm after Simeon Round, followed in 1903 by his daughter, Miss Eleanor Taylor who also rented the 12 acres of Grimley Cottage and 6 acres of pasture land by the Withy Brook which were all sold in the Everitt sale of 1917. The sale included The Dust House as a 'Valuable Small Farm' of 72 acres, the House 'a picturesque old-fashioned building (suitable for a gentleman's residence)' with six bedrooms plus 3 attic rooms – but no bathroom nor lavatory mentioned, though there was a pump and a well. The farm buildings included 'two four-tie Cow-houses, a Bull-house, Stabling for 4 working horses and a Nag Stable, coach-house and Loose Box, etc, plus two convenient cottages with large gardens' – these are the Dusthouse Cottages.

The farm and farmhouse were bought for £2,400 by T&M Dixon[111] who were building up their 3,000 acre empire of fruit-growing (thought to be one of the largest in Britain), with extensive acreage mainly in Tardebigge and Tutnall of soft fruit, apples and pears. The apple trees – Cox's Orange Pippins, Laxton Superb and Worcester Pearmains as well as Conference and William pears – were planted on Dusthouse land. They also transported coal and other goods on the canal, lime production, and the keeping and marketing of cattle and their milk, poultry and eggs, pigs and sheep. In the 1960s there were some 50,000 fruit trees and 600 acres of orchards. The farm buildings are now converted into dwellings.

---

109 It is thought that Puddles was the area around the north entrance to Hewell Grange, the now demolished Lodge being known as Puddle Lodge.

110 See *A Thousand Years in Tardebigge*, Margaret Dickins, Cornish Brothers, 1931.

111 See Revd. Alan White's *A Hundred Years in Tardebigge*, 2011, and his *A Worcestershire Dynasty*, 1997 (a history of the Dixon family) for more information on the Dixon empire, both published by Brewin Books.

14. Dusthouse Lane: Finch End to the Dusthouse

After WWI many soft fruit pickers came from The Black Country, brought over by Dixons' steam lorry, who then stayed for about six weeks, enjoying the fresh air and countryside. During the First World War Italian and German prisoners who were working at this and other farms, and were housed in Dusthouse converted barn and lofts. They were put to work to clear out hedges in order to make huge fields for the orchards. Under Dixons' ownership the farmhouse was tenanted by their employees, the first farm manager being Tom Carpenter. When he moved on the Dusthouse was divided into two dwellings, continuing to house their employees.

One of the workers on the Dixon land for a short time was the student who would become a playwright, David Rudkin. His gripping play *Afore Night Come*, set in a Worcestershire orchard, was first performed in 1962 by the Royal Shakespeare Company.

After WWII the Dixons' organisation gradually changed and their orchard fruit growing, which had been a main part of their recent sales, had to compete with the French fruit which was coming over to England selling at a shilling a pound, whereas the best English apples were selling at 1s 6d per pound. This resulted in the grubbing up of orchards, the tree roots ending up in the Dusthouse quarry, and changing to arable farming of barley, wheat and linseed. In 1972 the Dusthouse farmhouse, farmland and cottages and other properties were sold, to be bought by John Bird who continued fruit farming for a while but then moved to arable. It was sad to lose the spectacular sight of blossom in spring in the huge field seen from the Alcester Road.

Chapter Fifteen
Slideslow and Caspidge Farms

Slideslow Farm is now the Bromsgrove Golf Centre, and Caspidge farm buildings are now known as Nostrebor[112]. Surprisingly, the word Slideslow is usually spelled correctly in old publications (though it has been printed in a directory as Slide Slow), while Caspidge has been Caspage, Casbridge, Caspidges and Castbridge – in this chapter the spelling of each quotation is used. One theory about the origins of the name of the latter is that it derives from 'a cress stream', from 'caersa baet' in a Saxon Charter from the 11th century – 'caerse' being cress. It also appears in a 1649 survey. Up until 1892 the two farms were usually owned and farmed by the same people and to make it more complicated the land of Hopgardens Farm[113] were often worked by Slideslow farmers, despite being so close and often owned by the Oakalls.

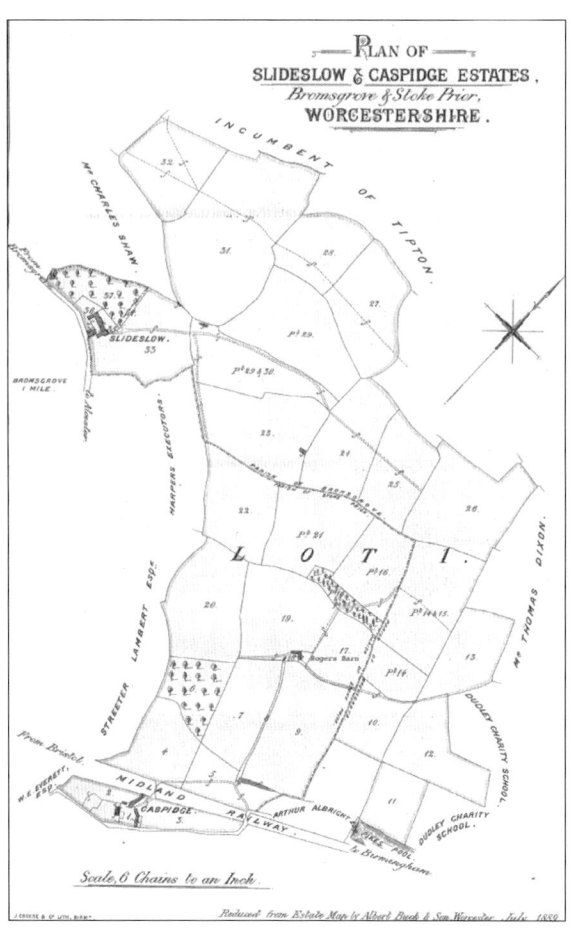

Sale plan of Slideslow and Caspidge Farms, sold as one Lot on 6th August 1889, for £6,386. (BC)

---

112 'Robertson' backwards; the Robertsons lived in Caspidge farm and had dog kennels; when Miss Robertson left the farm the barns and buildings were converted into dwellings.

113 See Chapter 9 on the Oakalls.

15. Slideslow and Caspidge Farms

It was in 1833 that 'A very compact and desirable FARM, called CASPIDGE in the occupation of Mr Rogers ... Also another FARM, called SLIDESLOW ... now also in the occupation of Mr. Rogers', were to be sold. Caspidge was 118a. 3r. 28p, and Slideslow was 88a. 2r. 11p. William Foley Rogers had been farming until his death in 1831, when the property was inherited by Thomas Rogers who put it up for sale. William Rogers had been a churchwarden at Stoke Prior church for thirty years, and his barn on the hill above Pikes Pool was noted on at least one recent OS map as 'Rogers Barn' – on some earlier maps it was down as Upper Barn.[114]

Because Slideslow land was often farmed by the person working Hopgardens as well as Caspidge, the farmhouses and cottages nearby might not have been farm workers, such as Edward Harris and Thomas Morden, both brickmakers, John Whieldon and his seven children who was a quarryman and James Wyatt, a gardener and his son Harry, an apprentice shoemaker, who were all at Slideslow in 1861. Others were employed there, such as Josiah Griffiths and *his* seven children, an agricultural labourer (1841, Casbridge) and also in 1861 at Slideslow, William Kempsey and Obedience his wife, when he was Farm Bailiff.

In 1868 the Slideslow Estate was sold in two lots, farmhouse and orchards 20 acres, and as Lot 2, 18 acres of land, sold to Mr R. Harper for £4,500, so much of the 88 acres of 1833 had already been sold separately. In 1870 there was a sale of 24 acres of 'building land', part of the Slideslow Estate, to be sold by private contract. However, in 1878 Thomas Wilson, Attorney of Law of Worcester (who was married to the third daughter of Joseph Guise of Caspidge – see below) left his four daughters tenancy of a 'Farm called Caspidge, 84a. 3r. 8p, in occupation of J.A. Partridge and Joseph Guise, yearly tenants, rent £190' and a 'Farm called Slideslow in occ. of William Brooke, rent £327'. Both the above were owned by John Joseph Wilson, a landowner of Crowle, Thomas Wilson being his tenant.

In 1886 40 acres were bought by Joseph Tilt, builder, of the Hop Pole Inn, Bromsgrove, for £2,575. Among his buildings were John Cotton's school in Stoke Road, Aston Fields, the Police Station in the Crescent, and the clothing factory in Carlyle Road, Aston Fields (now flats). After his purchase this builder then did as builders do, putting up for sale in 1887 four plots of land on the north side of the Alcester Road, offering them as 'A Capital residential BUILDING ESTATE ... in the occupation of Mr John Creswell ... This lot contains a bed of the well-known Bromsgrove building stone'. They were not sold, and there was no building there until Mr Fletcher's joinery workshop came in 1980, just after the Redditch Highway was built, and where the joinery stayed until 2003, when application was made for the blocks of flats that are there today.

It was during Mr Creswell's time that William Troth was charged with 'trespassing in pursuit of conies on Slideslow land. ... Witness Thomas Paddock saw the defendant shoot a rabbit on Sunday morning, the 5th, about 3.30. He ran away ... when P.C. Wainwright

---
114 This barn is thought by Worcestershire Archaeological Service to be 17th century.

searched the defendant he found a gun in two parts in his pocket. ... Defendant brought a rabbit to Mr Creswell, and wanted him to look over the offence; it was the first time, he said, and it should be the last. Mr Milward read out a list of seven or eight previous convictions ... Fined £2 and 10s costs, or a month's hard labour. Defendant said he would "pay it in ink".'

In March 1888 there was a sale of a 'Rick of First-class CLOVER ... containing about 23 Tons ... Rick of Prime New HAY, in the Rickyard of the Slideslow Farm and containing about 15 Tons ... Part Rick of Superior CLOVER in the Rickyard of the Slideslow Farm containing about 10 Tons'. Presumably Tilt's investment did not work out as he had hoped, for in 1889 the two farms (115 acres) were offered as 'ELIGIBLE INVESTMENTS', offered at 'the upset price of £6000', and were sold for £6,380 'exclusive of timber, valued at £198', to Mr E.G. Capon. Also in this sale were a meadow with a stone quarry, which is against the Alcester Road on the northern side. Mr Capon's stock then came on the market in November 1892, including '162 Pure-bred SHROPSHIRE SHEEP AND LAMBS, 7 Valuable CART and NAG HORSES ... SOW and 12 Pigs, 3 Fat Pigs ... a Herd of 29 Well-bred SHORTHORN CATTLE', plus all his agricultural implements, '14 tons of PRIME CLOVER and household furniture'. The same year Capon sold a portion of his new property to Francis C. Clayton, which two years later Clayton sold on to Arthur Albright of Finstall Farm. This must have been a difficult time for the tenants of both farms.

William Brooke had been farming Slideslow since 1870, though there was a Farm Bailiff, Frederick Archer, at Slideslow from 1870 until his accident. Mr Archer, then 68, had climbed a ladder to shake the fruit from a pear tree. 'The bough he was shaking broke, and he fell from about 20 rounds of the ladder to the ground, flat on his back. ... Mr Carey, surgeon, said ... there was no fracture of the spine but a lump on the back of the head. ... He thought a blood vessel at the back of the head was ruptured.' Which it had, and Mr Archer died. This was in July 1896; in September the same year Martin Ingram of Finstall had a similarly horrible accident when he fell from a ladder when painting the outside of a cottage at Slideslow. He fell on his face, and 'his left eye came in contact with a stick to which a rose tree was tied. This penetrated his eye. ... Dr. Ball sent him to hospital ... he became unconscious in a few hours and did not recover'. The inquest juries of both events returned verdicts of Accidental Death. Mrs Archer struggled on for a year, and unfortunately their son Frederick who was a boot and shoe maker could not carry on the farming work.

After this came the Wheelock family of farmers at both Slideslow and Caspidge until 1908, though from 1904 until 1912 Slideslow Farm was used as a nine hole golf course, measuring 2537 yards with a bogey of 38.[115] After the golf club moved to Breakback William Pearman farmed the land, as well as some at Crossbrook. William's son Henry,

---

115 For more on the history of the golf course see *Bromsgrove Society Newsletter*, Vol. 33, June 2013.

who had been a pupil at Bromsgrove School, also worked on the farm until he went into the 12th battalion of the Gloucestershire Regiment as a Lance Corporal in February 1916. He was severely wounded in action, and died in France in 1917.

It was in 1956 that the Morris family, who kept a dress shop in Bromsgrove High Street, bought the land to farm. A writer signing himself as R.B. wrote: 'I was a trainee agricultural worker [at Slideslow] in the mid 1960s. It was then a farm with a flock of around 100 ewes, a breeding herd of pigs, and roughly 120 acres of grassland and arable, growing barley and potatoes.'[116] The free range pigs were in a large field alongside the main Redditch road, with a mass of tin-roofed pigsties. Then in 1987 the Morris family changed tacks and opened Bromsgrove Golf Centre with a 41 bay floodlit driving range, followed soon after by the nine hole golf course and then, because it was so successful, extended the course in 1994 to 18 holes, also opening a restaurant which soon became popular for group events[117].

* * * *

The coming of the Birmingham to Gloucester railway, opened in 1840, made quite a difference to Caspidge Farm and Finstall. Not only had there been a thousand navvies moving up and down the railway site all day for months, but traditional roadways such as Turnpike Lane (Pikes Pool Lane) had to be realigned, stone bridges had to be built, and great embankments needed to be created to raise the line. The work took place from 1839, and by mid December 1840 the 2½ mile Lickey Incline, with its gradient of 1 in 37.7, was opened and the workmen went away. But even so, things weren't the same as before. Some nineteen times a day came the noise of the steam engines slowly moving up the incline, belching huge clouds of smoke and whistles as they went, and the bank engines then flying back down to the station depôt to prepare for the next journey. Also it brought railway workers to live in the village, many living as boarders. And for Caspidge the line divided the farmstead from the land. Even though a bridge was built to enable passage direct from the farmyard, it still meant that the farmers must have felt cut off from their fields.

A goods train climbing the incline.

---

116 Unfortunately I don't know where this quotation came from.

117 It was reported in the *Bromsgrove Standard* in October 2017 that application had been made by the owners of the golf club land to the District Council to release part of the land for housing.

There were also problems on the new lines when accidents happened, such as the one in October 1881 when at 'four o'clock in the morning a beer train (from Burton) coming down the incline broke its coupling to the engine, which went on down to the station. ... the guard applied his brake which reduced the speed of the train, but unfortunately he could not prevent a bank engine behind the train from running into the goods in front of him. There was a tremendous crash, throwing ten trucks onto the line. The wagons were all over the up-line, to the great detriment of an up beer train ... The line and adjacent fields for some distance were deluged with beer.'

* * * *

Caspidge Farm's history was tied up with that of Slideslow, as is shown above, but in 1849 came the tenant who was at the 90 acre farm for forty-six years, longer than any other. Joseph Guise was born at Park Gate, on the Kidderminster Road, on Lady Day, 1795. He was put to work in the Cotton Mill up the Kidderminster Road when he was eight years old, earning 3d a day, and also tried his hand

Caspidge Farmhouse in the 1890s. (JC Page)

Caspidge farmyard with members of the Page family and dog. (JC Page)

at nailmaking; by the time he was 20 he became a wagoner, then worked at the button factory in Bromsgrove. At 35 he was living at Finstall Heath with his wife Mary, daughters Mary and Sarah, and son George, taking over Caspidge in 1849.

Under the heading *Felony at Stoke Prior* in July 1853 *Berrow's Worcester Journal* reported:

> Fred Manning, 20, nailer, and Edwin Taylor, 22, nailer, were charged with having stolen on the 21st June last, at Stoke Prior parish, sixteen ducklings, the property of Joseph Guise. The prisoners declared themselves guilty, at the same time begging for mercy. They were sentenced to three months' imprisonment, with hard labour.

Six years later the poor man lost his right arm, crushed in a threshing machine, resulting in amputation at the shoulder joint. However he employed three labourers to work the farm, later relying on members of his family for support – in 1881, when he was 86, his labouring son Joseph was living at Caspidge, together with Mary, daughter Mary, daughter-in-law Emma who was a milliner, and grandsons George (aged 16, a clerk) and Joseph (aged 12).

In 1882 Guise showed he was a man with a temper, for it reached the Petty Session court that Guise charged

> Edwin Gittus, Stoke Works, with assaulting him at Stoke Heath. Complainant and defendant had a dispute about an account, and complainant alleged that defendant put his fist in his face and 'nunched' him in the breast. ... The magistrate said it was a trifling assault, and fined defendant 6d, and 8s costs.

Joseph Guise stayed on in Caspidge until he was 95, when he moved to Old Station Road in Bromsgrove. The quiet life there clearly suited him, for in 1895 he reached 100 years – and it must be remembered that the average life expectancy for those born in 1800 was about 47 years. Bromsgrove celebrated this event, holding an assembly in the Bromsgrove Institute and presenting him with 'a neatly framed photograph and an instalment of the sum of £25 which had been collected for him, and which will be paid to him in sums of £1 per month.' The Chairman mentioned that 'Mr Guise is in possession of all his faculties. As a test of his sight, he had asked him if he could read, and he replied that he never could read, but he could see to pull the hairs out of his head, and to count them.'

All this excitement sadly resulted in Joseph Guise's death a few months later and he was buried in the family's grave in Finstall churchyard. One wonders what happened to the remainder of that £25.

The land that Alderman F.C. Clayton had bought from Mr Capon was up the hill from Caspidge Farm, just beyond Rogers Barn. Here in 1892 he built a very attractive house, with views over to the Malvern Hills and the Clee hills. It was built of stone in the ground floor and was tile hung on the upper storey. It had just four bedrooms, a bathroom with hot and cold water and a lead safe under the bath, plus a kitchen with a Coalbrookdale range and hot, cold and soft water supplies. The large coach house

Joseph Guise standing outside Caspidge Farmhouse in the early 1890s. (JC Page)

had everything needed for horses and a loft used as billiard room. The boiler house had 'a 2½ h.p. engine, operating Pumps lifting water from well 130ft deep to tank over Boiler House, also Driving Dynamo for electric lighting'.

Francis Corder Clayton in 1889 was Lord Mayor of Birmingham, had served on the council as a Liberal for thirty years, and was on the Finance and Water Committees, especially involved in the great feat of building the 73-mile-long aqueduct between the Elan Valley reservoir and Birmingham. In 1912 he was made a Freeman of the City, awarded to those 'honoured and renowned for their tradition of generous public spirit'. An Essex man and a Quaker, he had come up to Birmingham to work at J & E Sturge in the chemical manufacturing industry, lived in Edgbaston, and probably used Caspidge House as a second home in the country.

By the time of the next sale in March 1916 on the instruction of John Glaisyer, solicitor, the whole of Caspidge House and farmland was owned by W.A. Albright, including the four fields that Mr Tilt had wanted to sell in 1886. Caspidge farmhouse and farm buildings, let to John J. Jeffery on a Lady Day tenancy at £188.5.00p.a., had been improved and was lucky enough to have mains water; there were two sitting rooms, an office, five bedrooms and a dressing room – making it sound more up-to-date than the posh house up the hill. There was no sale in March, but the property was sold in June to John Thomas Cocks of Moseley Road, Birmingham for £4,500.

This was the time of WWI, when many of the young men in the neighbourhood were called up or had volunteered. One was Victor Wheelock, 19 year old Private in 2nd Battalion Inniskilling Fusiliers, who was killed by shrapnel in 1918. His father, Walter, was at Caspage Farm at the turn of the century with Fanny his wife, and their other three children: Fanny, Gladys and Violet, and they later emigrated to Saskatchewan, Canada.

Francis Corder Clayton, JP. as Lord Mayor of Birmingham, 1889.

Another, Frederick Walduck, Lieut. Royal Field Artillery, died in a sanatorium in Llanbedr Hall, Ruthin, Wales. Frederick received a Military Cross 'for conspicuous gallantry. ... On a tunnel in which the personnel of the battery was sheltering being blown in, he volunteered to lead a party for 400 yards over a shell swept area to aid in extricating the buried men. ... he continued to dig in order to extricate the buried men until his task was completed. He displayed marked courage, determination and contempt of danger'. Fortunately Frederick's brother survived the conflict. His parents were Henry and Gertrude Walduck, Henry being Manager of an Engineering and Galvanising Works in Birmingham and a Quaker, who came to Caspage and remodelled the house using dressed sandstone from Finstall quarry. Outside the house were cottages built in converted stables, plus an Anderson Shelter. He employed Frank Stabbins who lived in the Caspage farmhouse as his farm bailiff.

Caspidge House and barn in 1916. (BC)

Caspidge House, 1955. (BC)

Between 1932 and 1951 Hugh and Cynthia Chance with their five children: Kathleen, Cecilia, William, Bridget and Hugh, were in Caspage House. The Chance family had a local interest, going back to Burcot in the 17th century, and had been involved in glass manufacture since the early 19th century, now having a large establishment in Smethwick. Hugh had served with the Worcestershire Regiment and the Royal Flying Corps during WWI. On the 17th September 1916 whilst on a bombing raid over Valenciennes, his plane was hit and had to make a crash landing in occupied France. He was captured and taken prisoner and spent the rest of the war in prisoner of war camps at Osnabruck and Clausthal. On return from the war he went back to Chance Brothers, becoming a director in 1924. During WWII he gained the rank of Honorary Colonel in the service of the Parachute Regiment (Territorial Army). Following a family tradition, for his father was Sheriff of Worcestershire in 1910, Hugh was 'pricked' by the King as Sheriff in 1936. An ancestor had been High Bailiff of Birmingham in 1830 and another, Mr John Chaunce, was Bailiff of Bromsgrove in 1529. Sir Hugh (for he was knighted in 1945) was Bailiff of Bromsgrove as well, was a County Councillor and awarded many other honours after

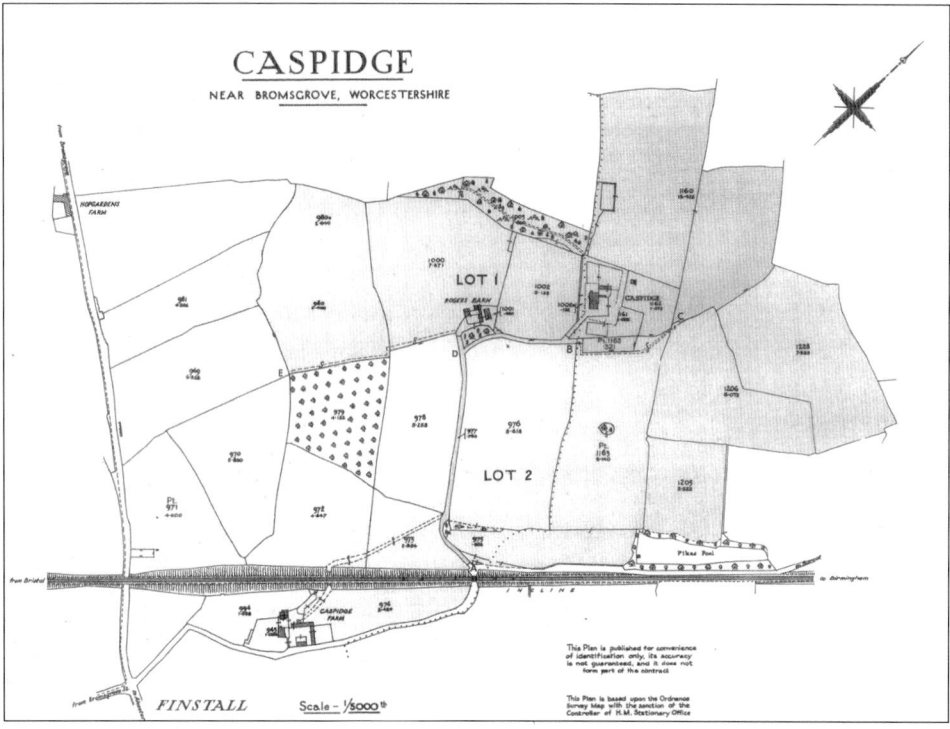

Sale plan of Caspidge, 1951.

moving from Finstall to Pershore. Before he left Finstall he gave a field in Stratford Road to St John's church for the upkeep of the Chance family tomb.

By the time they left, the house had expanded considerably, now with eight bedrooms, three bathrooms, an extension for a staff flat with three bedrooms, two living rooms and a bathroom. There was central heating and most important, a 'HEATED GARAGE FOR FOUR CARS'. Also important, and still regarded so today, he built a very elegant Peach House which had especially made Chance glass, curved to hold in the warmth, and with a steam powered boiler for winter warmth. Also of importance was how 'water had been taken from Pikes

Sir Adrian Boult, at Caspidge House in 1950s, drawing by Joy Finzi. (Finzi Trust)

15. Slideslow and Caspidge Farms

Pool conveyed by means of a petrol-driven pump, pipes and other works to storage tanks for use by the house'.

Sir Adrian Boult and his wife Ann came to live at Caspidge House for five years from 1950; described as being 'quintessentially British, his six-foot frame and military bearing as familiar as his walrus moustache' he must have been a noticeable addition to the area. He had previously been Musical Director of the City of Birmingham Orchestra for four years from 1924, since when his career had blossomed. But in 1950 he had been forcibly retired from his successful BBC position as Director of the BBC Symphony Orchestra (having made 1,536 broadcasts) so it is conceivable that he and his wife felt it important to have a bolt-hole in a country area far from the problems in London. Soon however he was invited to become Principal Conductor of the London Philharmonic Orchestra where he was able to continue his promotion of new English music by Vaughan Williams, Ireland, Parry and Walton – one of his most popular recordings was that of Holst's 'The Planets'. In 1953 Boult was in charge of the orchestral music at the coronation of Elizabeth II. So London called, and he put Caspidge House up for sale in 1955.

The Chance Brothers glasshouse at Caspidge House, after restoration in 2008. (Matt Gompertz)

Meanwhile at Caspidge Farm in the 1930s was John Blizard, and in the 1940s it was Michael McHale, who carried on farming with cows, pigs and potatoes, but also bought young ponies to train and then sell to young riders from Barnt Green and Edgbaston. Later the Robertson family took over and christened the farm Nostrebor. Their daughter ran a dog kennels for many years. When she sold the farm the old barns were converted into dwellings.

It was in 1979 that the Redditch Highway was built, cutting across the fields between the Vale House and Nostrebor, and the entrance to Pikes Pool Lane was diverted nearer to Elmwood. There was a narrow patch of land, just under an acre, between the new Highway and above the Alcester Road on the west of the Lickey Incline, which had previously been part of fields with the remains of quarries, and had had various owners, including Mr Ellins and Mr Everitt. Here Mr John Fletcher set up his joinery workshop and wood yard in 1981, selling it off in 2004 for the building of the flats, known as Maple Court.

Dr. Jim Swire, a Bromsgrove GP, his wife Jane and their three children had been living in Caspidge House for four years when tragedy hit them. On 20 December 1988 their

Caspidge Farmhouse (now Nostrebor) and farmyard, about 1950. The new house was built in front of the original farmhouse. There is a bridge under the Lickey Incline, allowing the farmer to reach his fields on the other side.

23 year old daughter Flora was on the transatlantic Pan Am Flight that crashed over the town of Lockerbie, Scotland, killing everyone on the plane – 270 people in all, including 11 on the ground. Dr. Swire became very involved in the aftermath of the crash, trying to discover who caused the explosion on board the aircraft. As a memorial to his daughter he planted 4,500 oak trees to the north of the house, which he named Flora's Wood. In 1991 he left Churchfields medical practice in order to devote his time to his investigation, and in 2001 Jane and he moved to the Cotswolds.

Chapter Sixteen

Finstall Vale: Fairways and Scotch House

The Vale was named for the dip of land lower than Finstall Heath, and it wasn't until the late 19th century that the Vale House took over that name. For many years there were only three buildings in Finstall Vale: the farmhouse Fairview (Fairways), probably not looking as grand as it did later; Scotch House (Vale House, the Vineyard) and a little timber framed farm cottage at the bottom of the field which was bounded by the turnpike to Alcester and a narrow lane to the Finstall chapel (now Heydon Road). A more restrictive boundary appeared in 1840 when the railway was built just behind Fairview, and behind Scotch House.

There is little early information about Fairways, a Listed house, which is described as having been built c.1800, with late 18th century and mid 19th century additions[118]; outbuildings have a part ashlar[119] wall from an earlier construction. The house is prominent when viewed from Finstall hill, with its white painted wooden porch across the front, and more recently for its pleached hedging along the entrance path.

By 1841 John Grosvenor was living at what was then known as Fairview and farming the nine acres belonging to it – he was listed in the directories as 'gentry'. In 1863 he died, his will leaving 19 guineas[120] to Queen's Hospital, Birmingham. His son Christopher took over, followed by his wife until 1876. The next resident was William Henry Avery, living with his sister and aunt Eliza Perkins. On the nine acres he held some cattle. He took part in local activities, was appointed one of the Overseers for the parish, and became a Poor-Law Guardian. When the new church at Aston Fields was built in 1884 he gave a brass eagle lectern, and was made a church warden. In 1886 he invested in five houses in Aston Fields from the estate of William Fisher, spending £630. In the mid 1890s he died, leaving his younger wife, Sarah, to continue organising the nine acres until 1901.

The smaller acreage of Fairview attracted William Quinney, a retired farmer at the age of 57, who had worked the much larger Finch End Farm, which he now left for his son, Edward. He and his wife lived at Fairview for four years before moving to the new up-to-the minute house, Elmwood, just up the road, now on the corner of Pikes Pool Lane. The Elmwood land had belonged to W.E. Everitt of Finstall House, who had bought it in

---

118 Worcestershire Archaeology Department.

119 A block of hewn stone with straight sculpted edges for use in building.

120 A guinea was one pound one shilling.

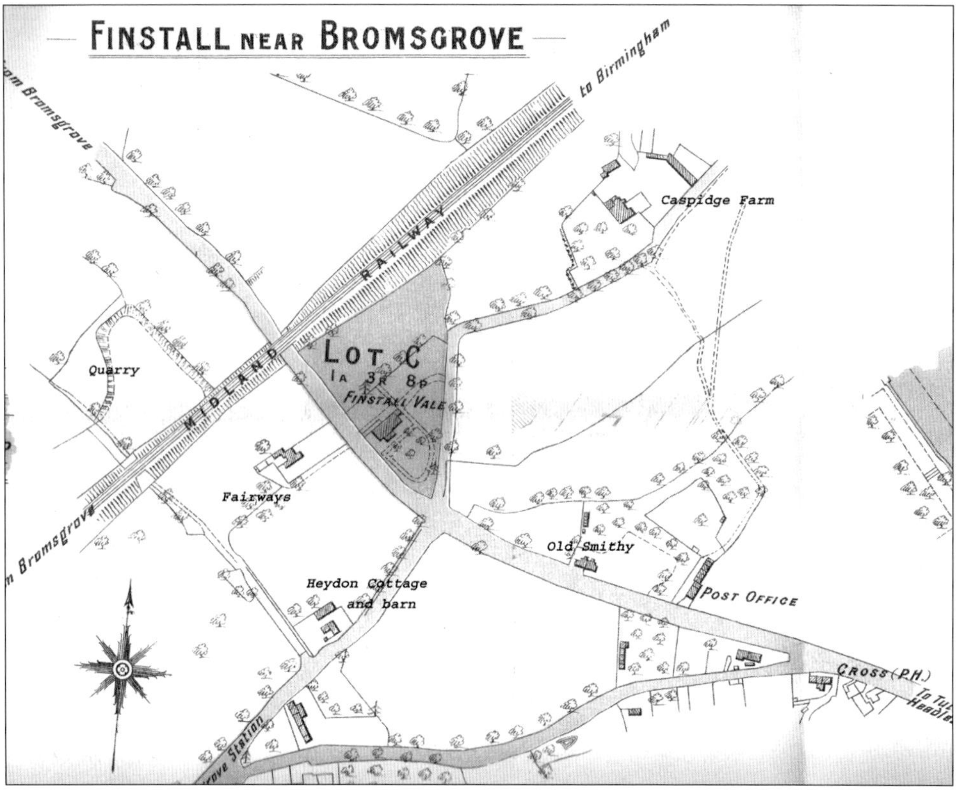

Sale plan showing the Vale as it was in 1903. Note the old way of Pikes Pool Lane which was moved when the Redditch Highway was built. (BC)

1875. William Quinney lived at Elmwood until his death in 1922, Mrs Quinney outliving him until 1940. The next two occupants of Fairview were Thomas Nock, another retired farmer, from 1901 to 1906, followed by George C. Spurgeon, who was a retired draper.

Dennis Darby Bayley and his wife were then at Fairview – now rechristened as Fairways – for many years between c.1936 and 1999. Bayley, a Quaker, worked in the Impey family's firm, Kalamazoo. On his retirement he was known to all Finstall people as the man who daily walked his dog down Finstall Road; over the years he had several dogs, all of them named Billy.

Fairways.

16. Finstall Vale: Fairways and Scotch House

Elmwood, an architect's drawing 1970s. (Messrs Hinsley)

* * * *

In 1843, when George Ellins of Rigby Hall became bankrupt, his property was put up for auction, including Lot 4, which had been known since 1810 as Scotch House,[121] together with just over four acres of arable land across the railway line from the house. It would be good to know why it was given that name. Scotch House was described as a 'well-arranged and substantially-built Dwelling House, with Offices and Garden attached, suitable for the residence of a respectable family and with Another Dwelling House, of the same character, immediately adjoining'. They were 'recently partly rebuilt and constitute a desirable investment', which Mr Everitt of Finstall House clearly agreed with, for he became their owner, including the two fields the other side of the railway. After this, until recently, the two dwellings were just one.

The Scotch House in the early 1880s was lived in for a few years by Mrs Barnett with her six children and step-daughter Ada Mary, to be followed in 1888 by George Page and family, who were happy to rent the house for £55. Described as an ironmaster, George Page, still in his twenties, had a works in Selly Oak which produced enamelled tin for advertising, known as the Birmingham Advertizing Tin Plate Coy. – the sort of advertising we used to see on shop walls and on railway stations. This family of four children – Millicent, Edmund and Dorothy who were twins, and Geoffrey – plus nurse, cook and housemaid, had an energetic mother, Agnes, who

> ... was a pioneer of the bicycle [wrote Edmund Page when an adult] and I can see her now, vividly, dressed in a pink blouse, short skirt and sailor hat. I do not think she ever sported a pair of what were called "bloomers". I believe she had an arrangement of elastic bands to keep her skirts down. Most of us learned to ride along the private road to Hewell Grange, "country house" of the Plymouths, who were friends of ours. It was important to find somewhere removed from the public gaze because in the early days the antics of any lady riding one of those "machines", as they were called, led as a rule to ribaldry.

---

121 A map on tissue paper dated 1810 of *Glebe Lands and Corn Tithes property of Dean and Chapter of Worcester*. This shows 'Lower Finstall House' where the Lodge is, and Finstall House in its proper place as are Rigby Hall, the Hopgardens and 'Casbridge'. The Vale House is named as Scotch House and the Oakalls is not named.

I remember being made humiliated by a formidable old lady, Mrs Smallwood of Rigby Hall, complaining to my Mother of the shocking bravado with which I had raised my cap to her when passing on my bicycle. They were 'dangerous' things, she said, and it was a pity for a nice boy to behave like a 'cad' on one. Poor old trout: she little knew that I was able to manoeuvre in most traffic without touching the handle-bars at all: and even able to stand on the seat if given the fairway.

This old lady in her black silk dress was one of my bêtes noire as a small boy. I am reputed in the catachism once to have replied to the question "who is your ghostly enemy"? – "Mrs Smallwood".[122]

Edmund Page. (JC Page)

George Page was a keen photographer, leaving albums filled with pictures of the Vale House, other local buildings and people, several of which are reprinted in this book. The boys went to Bromsgrove School, the girls to Alice Ottley in Worcester. Unfortunately the Selly Oak business did not do well and the family had to leave Vale House for Worcester. The house was sold by auction for W.E. Everitt in July 1903.

William and Jemima Cottam were next, originally having come down south from the north of England.

Making hay behind The Vale house. Note the row of young trees planted along the bottom of the incline, presumably to shield the house from the noise. This picture shows the pedestrian way under the bridge. (JC Page)

---

122 From Edmund Page's unpublished memoirs. On 24 April 1869 *The Messenger* had reported under the heading 'Velocipedes. Specimens of the new machines called "bicycles" have been seen in the town during the past week and we hear it is in contemplation to form a Velocipede Club here'.

16. Finstall Vale: Fairways and Scotch House

William taught at Inkberrow School for 31 years, where he had been a very conscientious headmaster, and retired to the Vale House in 1903. William and Jemima were heavily involved with the new church of St Godwald, he being a churchwarden. Their first four children – William Jr., Alice, Margaret, and Richard had already left home, but in 1910 their youngest daughter Ada married Frank T. Levens, son of Mr Philip Levens, estate agent and Clerk to the Local Board, of Thorndale, 80 New Road, Bromsgrove. William Snr. died suddenly in 1912 whilst working in the garden – 'succumbed within the hour' – and was buried in Finstall chapel burial ground, and Jemima, who had moved to College Road, Bromsgrove, followed him in 1921.

Herbert and Agnes Goodman were the second of that Birmingham family to come to Finstall[123], in their case moving here in about 1916 after a few years in Perry Hall, Bromsgrove[124]. Here they stayed with their two daughters Mary and Eliza Sylvia, and their son George. In 1926 the family were shocked by the death of Eliza Sylvia, who was found drowned in the River Thames three weeks after she had disappeared. This distressing unexplained event reached national newspapers – it was even reported in Australia. A friend, Miss Page, regarded her as a very gentle and sweet tempered girl, popular with other residents of the women's hostel in Rotherhithe and the students of the School of Arts and Crafts where she had been studying for six months; her father said that he had received a cheerful letter from her posted on the day she disappeared. The inquest recorded an open verdict. Herbert died the following year aged 70.[125]

Nit picking: Nurse working on the nits in Millicent's hair. Note cats drinking from a saucer. (JC Page)

---

123 See information about Walnut Lane.

124 Perry Hall was where the Housman family lived and A.E. Housman the poet grew up there. It is now owned by Bromsgrove School and is known as Housman Hall.

125 The Goodmans' son George Herbert served in WWII in the Royal Naval Volunteer Reserve as a Lieutenant Commander. Between January and March 1942 Goodman defused 14 parachute mines in the Suez Canal area and retrieved the first mechanism from a German C type mine to be recovered and examined. He also defused 2 torpedoes, 31 moored mines and the first 'Sammy' mine recovered in the Mediterranean. George was awarded an MBE, and the George Cross in 1942. He survived the war, just; he was killed in May 1945 when a booby-trap exploded as he entered a house in Rotterdam. He was buried in Westduin General Cemetery.

During WWII the Vale House was taken over by one of the Vineyard Schools, a group which offered education for boys and girls (in separate institutions) who had epilepsy and/or mental health conditions; one advertisement said 'Training, in addition to the ordinary school curriculum, is given in carpentry, handicrafts, rhythmic exercises, gardening, poultry keeping and farming'. The Vineyard Schools during this period were at Warwick (boys 6-16), Northfield (girls 14-19), and Finstall (boys 14-19). It is assumed that the reason for coming was to be in an area where there was no likelihood of bombing. It was not the only group that came to the Bromsgrove area in wartime. Bromsgrove School had to move to Wales while Government departments occupied their campus. A branch of Nonington College of Physical Education, based in Kent, was evacuated first to Avoncroft College and then to Grafton Manor in 1940, to allow their own buildings to be used to aid the war effort. This brought numerous students and staff to the town – all required to have a bicycle – many of whom were billeted at The Birches in New Road. Rigby Hall was also taken over by a Government department in 1943.

Finstall Bridge on Alcester Road in 1912.

Come the end of the war the Vale became a home again when Mr A Rupert Morcom, his wife Mary (née Carslake) and their live-in friend Miss Joan Durrant came and gave the house its old name of Scotch House. Mr Morcom was a Director of Bellis & Morcom, the makers of stationary steam engines, diesel engines, steam turbines, and compressors, with their works in Ledsam Street, Birmingham, and was the son of Reginald Morcom of the Clock House, Fockbury. The Morcoms took part in local affairs, Rupert being

The Vale House, c.1900. (Bob Richardson)

The Cottam family: William, Alice standing, Ada Jemima Levens, Jemima. (William Edward Cottam photo Collection)

a churchwarden at St Godwald's and becoming Bailiff of the Bromsgrove Court Leet in 1967.[126]

Two months after Jill Finden and family had moved to the Vale House in 1971, the scouts, who had bought Pikes Pool, decided to clean it out, which involved emptying it by taking down the dam at the Finstall end of the pool. This resulted in a huge swoosh of water sweeping across the field, down the lane, and down the drive into the Vale House gardens. It ended its journey by pouring into a shed and into two cellars of the house. The two lawns resembled lakes, and the Severn River Board thought that three million gallons had escaped Pikes Pool.

The new A448 was built in 1979 – Bromsgrove people think of it as the Redditch Highway; Redditch people think of it as the Bromsgrove Highway. The building of this meant that the Scotch House lost part of its land, and Pikes Pool Lane was diverted. In the past, the lane started opposite Heydon Road, but now that truncated old lane just goes to the Vale, which is now divided again, this time into three dwellings.

* * * *

Heydon Road was named by the Rural District Council as a compliment to Charles Heydon and the Heydon family who had been living in Finstall Vale since at least 1870 until the mid 1960s. They lived in the timber framed cottage alongside Heydon Road from which they helped farm the Fairways' nine acres but also worked as gardeners at Finstall Park. Thomas Heydon, born in 1828 in Tardebigge, was living in this cottage in 1871 with his wife Esther and six children. The cottage, built of timber and brick, was like many at the time, having a living area and an attached stable. The photograph was taken in 1965 after the Heydons had gone. It is possible that originally it was a hall house with the one chimney, and that the dormer windows were added later when an upstairs floor was built. It can be seen that the animal house has stone walling at ground level, which would have come from the nearby quarry, and the bricks probably were made by local brickmakers. Originally there was also a separate barn, between the cottage and the roadway. Nowadays the house is almost unrecognisable when compared with the decayed little cottage of the 1960s; it now has three reception rooms, four bedrooms and a double garage.

Thomas Heydon was a gardener, as was eldest son George at the age of 14. Thomas died aged 90 in 1918. Charles, who was the youngest, born in 1870, worked his way up in

---

126 Each year a new Bailiff is chosen by the members of the Court Leet and each year the Court processes down the High Street on Fair Day, wearing traditional robes, stopping to test the quality of meat, leather and ale on sale to make sure that they are of fit quality for the people of Bromsgrove. After these enjoyable tasks the Town Crier reads the charter, nowadays by the statue of A.E. Housman. The traditional ceremonies are a re-creation of the duties performed by the Jurors on the Court Leet since the 1199 Royal Charter of King John, who granted the Court jurisdiction over the town. Bromsgrove was given the right to hold a fair each year on the feast of John the Baptist, 24th June, another tradition that continues.

Heydon farmhouse in 1965 during restoration, but keeping its original chimney. The right hand end would be for a stable. Now much altered and enlarged. (BC)

the world by joining the *Bromsgrove Messenger*[127] offices as an errand boy when he left school at 15. He had applied for a job when there was no vacancy, and was turned away. But someone could clearly see possibilities, ran after him, and he was engaged. After his errand boy job he was promoted to becoming a compositor, setting up the type line by line. He then volunteered

Heydon Road showing the farm's barn, part of a stone cottage on the right, and newly built houses on the left. (Bromsgrove Messenger)

to become a reporter, taught himself shorthand, and ended up as chief reporter working under the then editor, Frank W. Harvey. When he retired aged 75 he was deputy editor *and* advertisement manager. Charlie, as he was known, had two daughters, Annie and Evelyn, who were described some years later as always wearing long black skirts and being very old fashioned. Retirement brought Charlie keen membership of Bromsgrove Rotary Club, ending, it is said, as the oldest Rotarian in the world when he died aged 98.

---

127 *The Messenger* is now called *The Bromsgrove Advertiser*.

Chapter Seventeen

Walnut Lane

Hollow Lane, Walnut Cottage Road, Brooks Lane, Walnut Lane – all the same narrow lane with a name that changed over the years.

At the start of Walnut Lane is the Lodge for Finstall House, which was probably built by Richard Brettell in the 1830s. Built of the same ashlar sandstone blocks as the surrounding wall of the property, the walls had decorative projecting quoins on alternate courses and there were decorative bargeboards and ridge finials. The sash windows had arched heads and with monolithic shaped stone lintels above. Built on a slope, there was an open undercroft to the Lodge, where in the early 20th century farm machinery was stored – this could be seen from Finstall Road. The Lodge was altered and extended several times during the second half of the 20th century, with most of these individual details now lost.[128] The early inhabitants of the Lodge were all employees of the owners of Finstall House, coachmen or gate keepers

As you walk up the lane the natural stone and the sandstone wall feel quite oppressive until the opposite side opens into several relatively new properties. The last of these is the earliest – Walnut Cottage.

Finstall Park wall along Walnut Lane. (Christopher Pancheri)

A carved stone used second-hand in Finstall Park Wall. (Christopher Pancheri)

---

128 The 1977 photograph and drawing of the Lodge (which can be seen in Chapter 4) were done by Christopher Pancheri (grandson of Celestino Pancheri of the Bromsgrove Guild, and son of Robert Pancheri the woodcarver and sculptor) when he was part of the Hereford & Worcester Architecture Record Group. I am grateful to him for use of his descriptions.

In 1855 the *Bromsgrove Gleaner* tells us of an 'Auction sale at The Dragoon Inn[129] near to Bromsgrove Station, Monday 7 May 1855 by Mr W. Cotton: A messuage or dwelling house with cow house, pig stye and other outbuildings and an excellent garden with 4 pieces of rich turf land or orcharding, 5 acres, at Finstall in the occupation of Mrs Griffin. Several large walnut trees as well as other timber and fruit trees.' Though the little farm might have been sold,

Birmingham architect PB Chatwin's proposal for Walnut Cottage. (Reproduced with permission of Library of Birmingham)

the widowed Elizabeth Griffin, cowkeeper, continued to live there, probably until she died in 1888. Also with her was a relative, Sarah Louisa, daughter of Henry Griffin of The Dragoon Inn. The Griffins could be found all around the area, all farming folk, at different times working at Tack Farm, Finch End Farm and Stoke Cross. Henry was at The Dragoon and its farmland for many years, but sadly died just before Sarah's wedding in 1869 to the architect Edmund Axten. This couple lived at Walnut Cottage for a few years before they moved away to Redditch to further his career. Little is known of his work, though he was responsible in 1871 for designing a £600 house in Greenhill, Blackwell, which was then not built to his plans, though the house when built proved to be far too similar. The owner, William Dugard, was later successfully prosecuted by Axten for stealing his work.[130] Better was his relationship with the congregation of Studley Wesleyan Methodists, for whom he designed their new chapel in 1872, but sadly by 1878 he was unsuccessfully working at his home city of Gloucester and became bankrupt, leaving the profession.

Walnut Cottage, with three elegant ladies. The woodwork is now removed.

William Everitt bought the property in 1887 – Walnut Cottage, with just 3 acres 3r.19p plus a small close of 3 roods next to the Hollow Lane, and in 1900 bought the copyhold

---

129 Now The Ladybird.

130 See *Victorian Greenhill*, Jennie McGregor-Smith, Coombe Cottage Books, p.21, now out of print.

for £1000. In 1892 he caused the old farmhouse to be rebuilt in the modern fashion for mock-timber framing. Among the architects he asked for ideas was the Birmingham P.B. Chatwin. His specification was to 'Take down the present house and re-use the materials. Stables and fowl pens are not to be interfered with'. Chatwin came up with a design which he called The White House, but when it was built it was similar but not as the architect had originally conceived.[131]

It was occupied by Everitt's son, Douglas, who was then managing director of the family copper works. And it was definitely now a gentleman's home, for in 1892 there was an advertisement in *Berrow's Journal*: 'Footman wanted who has had experience under a butler. Age 17-18. Apply by letter stating height, age, wages and last situation, to D.E., Walnut Cottage'. However, about 1903 Douglas moved into the exciting new world of motor car sales, had a wish for more grandeur and moved to Hill Court, Droitwich (now Dodderhill School).

After brief stays by Mrs Kearns, and then Sydney Fowler Wright, who called it Walnut House and who possibly was the science fiction writer, the next inhabitant and owner of Walnut Cottage was Sidney Wilkinson, yet another iron manufacturer, with his wife and two daughters. They were in the house until Sidney died, when Mrs Wilkinson moved to Drayton, in New Road (now demolished). The Rylands were next, from 1916, Mrs Muriel Ryland paying £4,000 in 1919, and they had quite an effect on the lane, for they not only created a nice house from their stables, but also built a new house across the road.

The family business was, and still is the manufacture of paints, varnishes, mastics and sealants in Balsall Heath, Birmingham. Llewellyn Madeley Ryland was a Captain in the Royal Welsh Fusiliers from 1914 to 1922. During WWII he was a Commander of C Company, part of 2nd Worcestershire (Bromsgrove) Battalion Home Guard[132]. He was President of the Finstall, Hewell and District British Legion (which met at Tardebigge Village Hall originally)[133], a Vice President of the Royal Cripples Hospital, Birmingham, and in 1944 was appointed a magistrate. A major gift he made to Bromsgrove in 1945 was what was first of all called the Bromsgrove Youth Organisation – now the Ryland Centre. The land and facilities, on part of Fordhouse Farm, on New Road, was bequeathed under covenant for the use of the young people of Bromsgrove, and when in 1952 he moved down to Devon, there was concern it would be wound up. Fortunately the County Council took it over, though it now is run by Sandwell Leisure Trust. It now holds a six lane running track, squash and badminton courts, has an enlarged building, and has facilities for netball and hockey, and is used by many organisations and schools.

---

131 Library of Birmingham Archives, MS 891/74.

132 See chapter 21.

133 Formed locally in 1930 by Rev. P. Scott Warren of St Godwald's for the benefit of ex-servicemen. After WWII the British Legion met at The Cross, then amalgamated with the Aston Fields group in 1955 which met at the Working Men's Club.

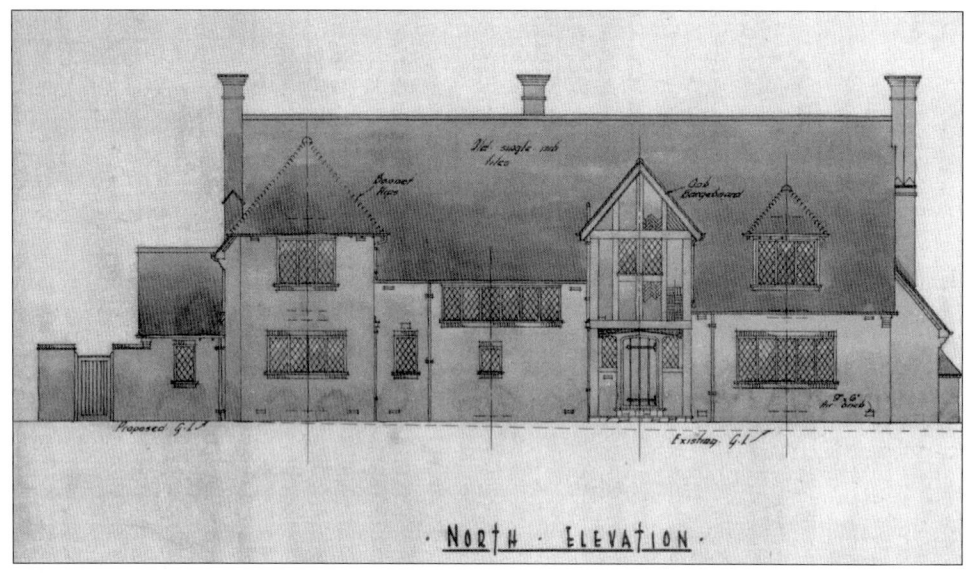

Littlehall front, drawing by the architect HB Archer of Coventry in 1933.

Littlehall garden front in 1996.

In 1953 Mrs Ryland sold Walnut Cottage to Denis Morris (gentleman) and his wife Catherine, for £7,900, who were moving from the Manor House, Studley. The 3 acres 3r 19p were included as well as field No.884 for £100, though they were required to put up a fence between that and field No.885. The Morris's sold the house to Enid Croft Impey, of the Quaker Kalamazoo family.

Use was made of the redundant stables with their wrought iron divisions in 1973, when first plans were made for a conversion. Final alterations were made in 1984, resulting in the mahogany panelled tack room becoming the sitting room of High Barn another attractive home and garden in Walnut Lane.

High Barn, originally stables. Drawing by Frances Rogers.

During the 1930s there was a small addition to the property, known as the Maisonette, where an elderly gardener James Tremlett and his wife lived. Also living with the Tremletts, was Gladys Corbett, an eighteen year old unemployed factory hand, who was volunteering at an HRP First Aid Post at the beginning of WWII.

In 1933 Mrs Ryland had asked H.B. Archer, an architect from Coventry, to plan a country house to be built across the lane from Walnut Cottage. It was said that it was in Mr Archer's brief to model parts of the house on some favourite aspects of the Rylands' former ancient timbered home in Rowington, and the result was an appealing English vernacular building. Even the windows were leaded lattice style (now removed), and the interior has exposed ceiling beams and a traditional panelled inglenook fireplace. A small three bedroomed lodge house was built adjoining the garage. This delightful property was for the Rylands' son, Llewellin Winter Ryland and Nancy his wife, and in 1942 Nancy was advertising in *The Times*: 'Experienced nurse wanted, for first baby. Ryland, Littlehall'. This Ryland family stayed in Littlehall until 1996.

Chapter Eighteen
Finstall Hill

Although in the past Finstall Hill reached from The Vale, for the purposes of this book we shall take it from Finstall Croft, leaving the lower part as Finstall Heath. Finstall Heath was the early name for that area, and it was not until the 18th century that houses and cottages were built up the hill. In the 18th century the north side of the road was bounded by Mr Albright's Finstall Farm fields, Carthorse Meadow with its pond, and Finstall Meadow after the track to the farm, and on the south side by John Featherstone's Finstall Farm, quarry and fields with appropriate names – Combe Close and Combe Meadow, 'combe' meaning a steep, narrow valley or large hollow on the side of a hill.

* * * *

The two major engineering feats that cut across Finstall in the 19th century were the canal and the railway. But the building of the Redditch Highway in the late 1970s also had a great effect. The idea was to take pressure off the Alcester Road and other roads in Redditch, which was expanding greatly. The highway cut across numerous fields, and roads in Finstall and Tardebigge had to be changed, especially Pikes Pool

Preparation for the building of the Redditch Highway (A448) in the late 1970s. (J & J Wilson)

Lane, Tutnall Lane and up at Tardebigge around Hewell. Finstall Farm suffered, with the Finstall Meadow by The Vale, and Carthorse Meadow being cut in two, with the pond in the latter field almost disappearing. The effect of that was that house martins, with no fresh mud that they needed to build their nests, flew off to find another more welcoming site.

* * * *

Finstall Croft on the south side of Alcester Road is described by archaeologists as being 18th century, built from stone and with slate roof tiles. Looking at the life and properties of John Featherstone – see chapter on Finstall Heath – it would seem logical that he lived here, in

18. Finstall Hill

a house rather bigger than other Finstall cottages, with a drive sweeping up from the road through its front garden – maybe he updated it for his retirement. After his death in 1898 it was given the name Stonehurst, and appears to have been divided into two dwellings, lived in by both retired farmer Thomas Nock and by Arthur Rame[134] and his family – both well off enough to afford a servant. A Mr Bishop followed in 1905, and then a young Birmingham stockbroker, Reginald Gower Wootton, his wife Ethel and son Anthony Gower who came in 1907. They christened the house Finstall Croft, the name it still known by today.

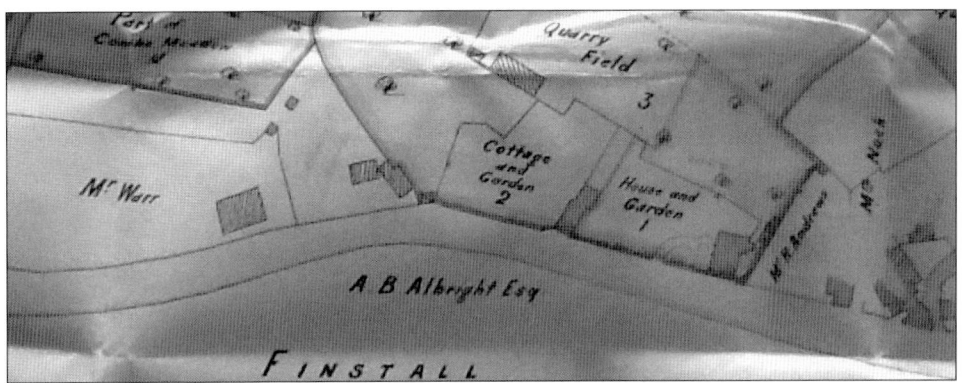

Featherstone sale plan showing the Cross on the far right, 'House and Garden' being Finstall Croft with a sweeping drive to the house; 'Cottage and Garden' is No.44 Alcester Road.

Wilfred and Pauline Brooks came to Finstall Croft in 1911, after their glamorous London wedding the previous year. By this time the house and the land surrounding it had been bought by John Boultbee Brooks of Finstall House, and no doubt the Croft was refurbished again for his son and new wife. Wilfred was works manager at the family leather business, and was responsible for the design and production of leather satchels, knapsacks and shoulder bags by the Brooks firm, which are still on sale today, even on the continent. Sadly, Wilfred succumbed to the dreaded influenza and died aged 34 in 1919. His wife and several children must have moved elsewhere quite soon, when Mr Herbert E. Judge came to live at the Croft with his wife, Olivette (née Eadie) who had lived at Rigby Hall for a few years.

Mr Joseph St Ludger and his wife came next to The Croft, with their son Thomas (known as Buster) and a daughter. Sadly Buster died in a motorcycling accident in 1938. Mr St Ludger travelled each day to Birmingham, catching the bus down to the station. He was described as wearing 'a bowler hat and having a rolled umbrella, being a proper businessman'. 'He was a great one for telling the bus men about being late (or early). "My watch is right by BBC time" he would say.'[135] Topsy Hobbs described Joseph St Ludger

---

134 This man's name is impossible to read in the 1901 census.
135 From *Memories of Bygone Finstall*, Ann Thompson. Unpublished.

as 'a man who drank, and who lost his leg on the railways'. Maybe we can understand him drinking, when reading what happened to him and his son, but maybe he would have cheered up when his daughter Valerie married Group Captain B.K. Burnett, DFC, AFC, RAF in 1944, who in 1958 was appointed an Air Vice-Marshall, and on retirement became Chairman of the All England Lawn Tennis Club at Wimbledon.

John Adams, FRSA, ARPS, of Finstall Croft, in his favourite position as a photographer.

One of the couples who lived at Finstall Croft much later were John and Kay Adams. Kay was an artist, and John was an enthusiastic train man, involved in saving and restoring the Talyllyn Railway in Wales. He and Patrick Whitehouse broadcast a popular children's series about railways called *Railway Roundabout*; they made 100 films and there were 52 programmes between 1958 and 1962. John was a keen photographer, and also made a film about Finstall. In 1981, finding the Croft too large for them, they built a semi-bungalow in their garden, with garages facing the road.

* * * *

Almost opposite Finstall Croft was Finstall Mount. After Arthur Albright bought Finstall Farm in 1874 he could have begun house building along Alcester Road, though this did not happen until The Mount was built in about 1884. The first inhabitant was Charles Robert Sayer, who came, possibly with some relief, from his uncle Samuel Ainge's house in Harborne, Birmingham. Sayer, in his thirties, had been working in his uncle's business as a coal merchant until Samuel Ainge was found guilty of embezzlement of £2,000, probably stolen from the Smethwick and District Building Society, of which he was Secretary. He had been arrested as he tried to join a ship sailing to America. His punishment was five years' penal servitude. It is a strange story, for until then Ainge had been involved in charitable work for the Midland Counties' Electoral Union, aiming for the repeal of the Contagious Diseases Acts by which women suspected of having a sexually transmitted disease could be arrested, detained in locked hospitals and then forcibly inspected for signs of venereal disease (VD). These Acts were brought about as a result of concern over increasing levels of VD in members of the armed forces, but were the subject of attack by campaigners for women's rights, libertarians and other socially-concerned groups. In 1873, when Charles Sayer was living with him, Samuel Ainge himself published an anti-Act pamphlet entitled *Christians, Moral Reformers, and Politicians: Wickedness and Vice Ought not to be Regulated, Fostered, and Made Easy and Healthy by Government*.

It is not known whether Charles Sayer or Arthur Albright built The Mount, which was typical of the time as a red brick building with steep roofs, but Sayer had it as his home, rented from Albright from 1893, leased for 30 years at £54 per annum. Included in

18. Finstall Hill

the lease was Coombe Cottage, a small house across the road, previously known as The Boot alehouse, presumably wanted for an employee. Sayer must have loved fishing, for he also, in 1897, rented Pikes Pool, its boat house and grounds from Albright, for seven years, paying £6.00 per annum.

In 1888 there was an advertisement in the *Birmingham Daily Post* offering 'A Country House, well furnished, to be let for 4 years at a nominal rental. ... No children. Sayer, Finstall'. This was because Sayer was up in Barton upon Irwell in Lancashire working as an insurance manager – maybe learning his future trade – leaving Elisabeth Chatwin as caretaker of The Mount. By 1901 he was home again, managing an insurance company, with his sister Caroline (who was unmarried, as was Sayer), his niece Ethel aged 22, and a nephew who was working with him as an insurance clerk. He did take part in local activities, becoming a JP, and there was a garden meeting in 1910 in connection with the British Women's Temperance Association. 'He had a motor car, the only person in the village to own one then and I recall Miss Sayer used to sit beside him with a scarf tied round her hat to keep it on. It was an open car.'[136] His 30 years' tenancy was up in 1923, but a Henry Eveson was at The Mount in 1916, and in 1921 relations of the Albrights, Alan S. Giles and his wife (who became Lord and Lady Mayoress of Birmingham in 1945/46) were there, followed in the 1930s by Paymaster Lieutenant-Commander Geoffrey Jennings Rapkin, RN, who had been Secretary to the Divisional Naval Transport Officer, Murmansk naval base. This was another big family, including governess and cook. In the 1940s the Hillcoats lived at The Mount, moving from Augustus Road in Edgbaston; sadly in 1941 their son Flight Lieutenant Harry Hillcoat, RAF, AAF, was killed in action aged 26.

Moving onwards to the 1980s, planning permission was given for building a small guest house and a new Christian Life Conference Centre, with a widened entrance to make it safer. People in Finstall still remember their horror on 30th May 1985 when despite a tree preservation order being put on a beautiful towering copper beech above the road, workmen began to chop the tree down; despite desperate phone calls to the Council the tree was felled. And the Christian Life Centre never happened.

Following many years of The Mount being a bed & breakfast establishment and a hotel, in 2016 the building was demolished and a group of bungalows were built by 2018.

* * * *

Opposite The Mount are several brick cottages. Two were part of John Featherstone's Finstall Farm and were left in his will to Featherstone's daughter Sarah Warr, though always noted on maps as belonging to *Mr* Warr. The rest of the cottages up the hill would have been built for farm workers by landowners or tenant farmers. Information about the cottagers along this stretch in the 1920s is beautifully told by Rene Brake (née Frisby) in Chapter 22 of this book. The land behind the cottages drops considerably; an application to

---

136 From Rene Frisby's recollections, Chapter 22.

The three cottages in 2018.

fill the depression in 1970 was refused on grounds of road safety. The fields behind the cottages are mainly pasture and orchards, with no buildings allowed. However after No. 44 is the entrance to Finstall Gardens, which for most of the 20th century was a market garden. To begin with it was the Hall family who worked there, Douglas coming down each day from Rockville to work with James Hall, later Norman Hall. After the Halls came the Empsons, George Empson also being the energetic postman for the village, while the Blizards took over at the beginning of the 1950s, buying the land from Boultbee Brooks' estate.

Harold Blizard's land included a right of way at the side of The Cross Inn and a track and footpath along Combe Meadow, which led down to Dusthouse Lane. Also part of the old quarry, six cottages along Alcester Road and the fields known as Quarry Field, Barn Piece, Pear Tree Piece, The Earl and Quarry Bank, Combe Close and part of Combe Meadow and Fern Hill. The Blizards gradually sold off lands behind these cottages and some in Finstall Road, and finally sold Finstall Gardens in 1989. Permission was given for the stone barn to be converted into a house, now called the Cider Mill.

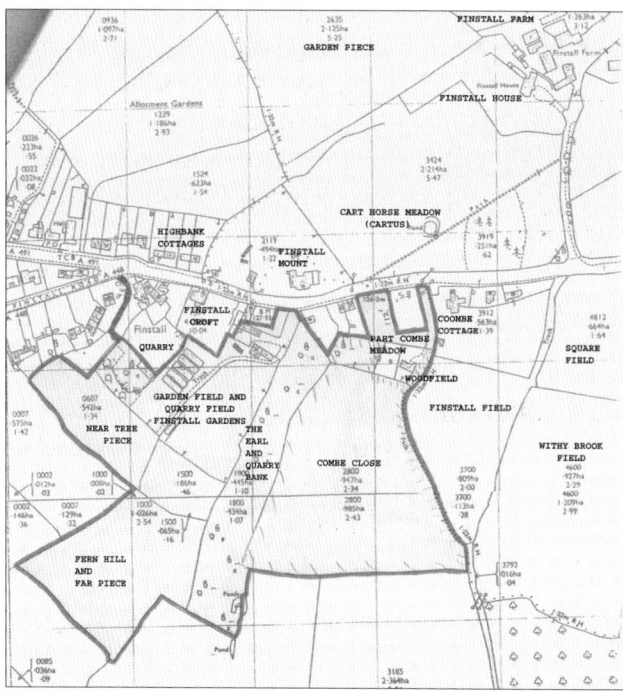
Sale plan, 1989. Area for sale has line round it. (BC)

There is one fairly modern house, Woodfield, which was allowed to be built in the late 1950s in the field named Combe Close. John Kirkwood, who was a VAT Inspector, living at the time at No.6 Marlborough Avenue, also used a caravan sited in part of Combe Meadow.

18. Finstall Hill

The barn in Finstall Gardens, now converted into a house named Cider Mill.

No. 44, Alcester Road, once part of Finstall Gardens.

The story is that he persuaded the planners that he lived in the caravan, and his application to build a house on the green belt was allowed. In 1971 John Kirkwood bought some 568 square yards of field from Harold Blizard, and in 1993 he bought the drive from Alcester Road and a car parking area, as well as the rest of the field below and beside his house.

Woodfield, when for sale in 1995.

John's wife Pauline was very friendly with Mrs Cove who was then living in Coombe Cottage, and they made a path through the dividing hedge so they could visit one another more easily than walking down to the road.

Woodfield was a small house, built by the side of a beautiful oak tree, with a wonderful view across to the Malverns. More recent owners have enlarged the house, and Combe Close now has a ménage and stables used for horses. The public right of way down the side of Combe Close is an ancient track giving access for the farm workers who lived in the cottages on Alcester Road needing to get to Stonehouse Farm – or, of course, for those living in Dusthouse Lane to come to the Boot beerhouse.

* * * *

The first known name attached to Coombe Cottage was when it was The Boot alehouse, an appropriate name since George Harford was a boot and shoemaker. The Harford family had been in Finstall Heath at least since 1840, when the menfolk were agricultural labourers or quarrymen, and the women were charladies. By 1870 George was running

Coombe Cottage, with Finstall House in the distance, in 1969, drawing by Noel Sinclair.

The Boot, with his wife Mary, a dressmaker, five children and a lodger. In 1872 at the Petty Sessions, before Captain Bourne of Grafton, Robert Smallwood Esq. of Rigby Hall, and Arthur Ryland Esq., permission was given for the beerhouse to be transferred to J. Thomas Price. The Price family only stayed for a few years, as Thomas took over the running of The Cross in 1876, following publican Fred Townsend's bankruptcy which caused him to leave the inn.

At some point before 1895 Coombe Cottage[137] was bought by W.A. Albright to add to that family's properties, and a strange family briefly stayed in 1897 – a Mr Robert Francis Spaull, a shipping and insurance broker of 14 Temple Street, Birmingham, who had seven children, and who became bankrupt the year he lived at Coombe Cottage.

In 1898 Coombe Cottage was leased from W.A. Albright by Charles Sayer of Finstall Mount, and in 1903 Mr Albright bought from the Ecclesiastical Commissioners the rights for both Caspidge Farm and 'all that cottage or tenement called Coombe Cottage with the outbuildings and garden, 841 square yards ... unoccupied and in lease to Chas R. Sayer'.

The Boot was a small cottage near the road, with entrance facing uphill, opening onto a yard with a pump, and was probably built at the beginning of the 19th century. Gradually it was extended to become Coombe Cottage, at first as two cottages, the front entrance of the later cottage facing down hill, reached from the road by a path along the side of the house, and gradually the two cottages became one house, suitable for the

---

137 Although it seems a modern name, Coombe Cottage was known by that name in the 1890s.

gentlefolk who were to live there. Also the small garden began to become larger as it encroached into what the Albrights called Finstall Field.

Between 1908 and 1932 it was Thomas Horton of the Bromsgrove solicitor family who lived at Coombe Cottage with his wife Claribel (née Goodman), and their children Christopher (nicknamed Scud), Lucie (known as Goop), and John (rather more boringly known as Johnnie). Johnnie and Lucy walked to Hollow Tree Farm, near Vigo, for lessons with the Dixon family, before he became a pupil at Finstall Park School. During their time the Hortons made many changes to the expanding garden, planting a magnolia, near to the road, which still blooms today. They made a grass tennis court, for the Goodman family was very sports minded and would have encouraged family tennis parties. It was possibly through Clara and Thomas visiting Hewell Grange for women's suffrage meetings that they had the idea of creating a set of grass steps, a rather smaller version of those that climb up to Hewell's water tower. Clara briefly had been secretary of the Bromsgrove Women's Suffrage Society, which was firmly 'non-political and non-militant'. They had held their first 'Drawing Room Meeting' at Coombe Cottage, which led to a large public meeting in the Assembly Rooms in Bromsgrove. The President was Mrs Hugh Dixon of Tutnall, the Treasurer was Miss Green, 27 year old daughter of John Green of Whitford Hall, and the new secretary was Mrs Marston of The Lilies, Stourbridge Road – a group of well-off and middle-class women who wanted to be involved in the fight for suffrage, and notably it was doctors and clergymen who supported them.

Clara Horton, who was a women's suffrage campaigner. (Matthew Horton)

Thomas Horton was in the habit of walking to the office in Church Street, which he had built in 1911, the land costing £128 – much to the consternation of the Goodmans, who thought it an extravagance to build and own one's place of business. Thomas, having worked in the office for part of the morning, was in the habit of meeting fellow professionals at De Greys in the High Street for coffee, to discuss and transact business. He would then walk the 1½ miles home to Finstall for lunch, walk back to the office, and frequent De Greys again for afternoon tea with his managing clerk. He believed in moving with the times, and bought an early typewriter

Thomas Horton, Bromsgrove solicitor, at Coombe Cottage between 1908 and 1932. (Matthew Horton)

for their correspondence, to the horror of fellow solicitor J.Y. Holt, who hated 'these newfan-dangled contraptions'.

From 1935 Major Philip H.P. Gunton was living in Coombe Cottage and also was renting Allotment Cottage next door. During WWI he was in the Middlesex Regiment as a Captain, and at the end of WWII he was at the War Office as a Major from the Royal Warwickshire Regiment. After the death of Miss Albright in 1945, Gunton bought Coombe Cottage, and then sold it in 1947 to Henry Lewis Cranmore, a retired motor engineer, who sold it on to the Austin Motor Company in 1952. They off-loaded it in 1956 to Brigadier Bendyshe Brome Walton CBE (known as Ben, from a long established military family) who later was appointed Honorary Colonel in the 7th Battalion of the Royal Warwickshire Fusiliers.

The grass steps up to the Hewell Grange water tower.

Gradually the garden became bigger, taking over land which had been used for allotments, behind the two cottages above them, and then, when Godfrey Ashwin sold Tutnall Hall in 1971 the opportunity was taken to buy the whole of Finstall Field.

* * * *

Above Coombe Cottage are two cottages, both on land owned by John Moore of Tutnall Farm in the 1880s. Both cottages were built against a promentary of rock, the reason for their small gardens. The earlier cottage, thought to be 18th century, is one like many lower down in the village which were built with bricks on layers of stone, and was surrounded by stone walls. Like most of the cottages in the road it had a deep well. It was once known as Daylesford, but now just No. 60.

Grass steps at Coombe Cottage, copied from those at Hewell Grange.

It was not until 1904 that Allotment Cottage next door was built, named because the field behind – Finstall Field – was at the time being used for allotments, probably because Miss Albright was keen to encourage villagers to grow their own vegetables. When Sherwood Suffield moved over from Stonehouse Farm to Finstall Farm he

18. Finstall Hill

lived in Allotment Cottage for a while until the new farmhouse was built. It was when Topsy and Bill Hobbs moved in that the house was renamed Lynwood, and they lived there until she died.

Topsy's energies outside of her work were very beneficial to the community. It was she who started the Youth Club in the village, one that was extremely successful, drawing members from well outside the area; she also was a major force in the creation of the children's playground at the top of Penmanor, and she and her husband, both born in Finstall, donated the Topsy and Bill Hobbs Challenge Cup to the Flower Show. Her nickname came from one of her older brothers, who said 'when she was a baby she grow'd like Topsy'.[138]

Lynwood, which was not a particularly exciting house, was demolished in 2012 and the new one built shortly after. An interesting find in the garden during the building, in a spot between Lynwood and Coombe Cottage, was a well, which no-one knew existed. Unfortunately this is now full of builder's rubble and is lost again.

The early stone & brick cottage, Daylesford (left), and Allotment Cottage, renamed Lynwood, recently demolished and a new house built. (aerial photo 1977)

---

138 A phrase that tickled the public's fancy and grew like Topsy all round the world; it was a quotation from Harriet Beecher Stowe's book *Uncle Tom's Cabin*, 1852.

Chapter Nineteen
Back Lane or Finstall Road

Finstall Road was earlier known to the villagers as Back Lane – Front Lane being the Alcester Road from The Vale to The Cross. As is described in Chapter 7, early on there was no building on Finstall Heath field, apart from the old Post Office and the row of three stone cottages at the bottom. However, after the Village Hall was built John Boultbee Brooks built the corner shop, which was attached to the old Post Office, probably designed by Philip Green who was architect of the Village Hall. The two buildings then complemented each other and very much added to the looks of the village.

Mr Holmes and his grand-daughter Ann feeding his flock of hens in the field between Finstall Road and Heydon Road, showing two pairs of newly built houses, either side of Finstall Road. (Ann Thompson)

The corner shop was built on land previously owned by the Price family of The Cross, and before that by William Hedges who owned most of the Finstall Heath triangle. The Holmes family ran The Stores in the 1920s, Stanley Holmes being the son of the Stud Groom. It was a general stores, as was normal then, with groceries and butchery on one side of the shop, with tools, hardware, animal feed and other useful goods on the other. Not only running the shop with his wife, Stanley bred poultry, keeping some 2,000 hens on the field behind The Cross and down Finstall Heath field.

Earlier in the 20th century, below the terrace cottages, a rather more superior pair of three storey houses was built against the roadway, quite different from the cottages. The first half was occupied by Mr and Mrs Avery and Frank. Mr Avery, known for his chrysanthemums, was Head Gardener at Finstall Park, Frank working with him. Opposite them in the early 1930s was built another pair of houses, white rendered as was the fashion of the time, bought from John Boultbee Brooks' estate. Eldon was lived in by the Crees family, and the other by Mr David, a schoolmaster. A bit later was built Ashdene, up on the rise, built for Mr Deague for his retirement from The Cross.

19. Back Lane or Finstall Road

Pair of houses built circa 1903.

Ashdene, into which Mr Deague of The Cross moved when he retired.

Bungalows on the corner of Heydon Road, typical of those all along Finstall Road, which, with a few houses, reach down to the cemetery. In the background are the railway, Fairways and The Vale. (Chris Milton)

And in the Stud Farm Sale of 1920 Mr Deague of The Cross bought Lots 5 (for £270) and 6 for (£290) in order to have land to build a house for his retirement. These were two fields behind the stone cottages. There was a bit of trouble with the Council over Deague's wishes, for they insisted that there should be no more building in that stretch of the road. What Councillors didn't realise, of course, was that there was a great need for housing at the time, and a huge surge of building, so they then found they had to give permission for the long row of mainly bungalows in the field between the road and the railway and, later, upwards to the Alcester Road, using Deague's land.[139] 'Homes fit for Heroes' was the popular cry after WWI, and though these weren't council houses, there was a great deal of house building all over the country and a lot of the ribbon development which is so unpopular nowadays.

Park Stores opened in 1930, built by R.E. Griffin for Emily Poole to run. Emily had previously been in service at Packwood House in Knowle, and later at Buckingham Palace. It was a two storey house, now No.127, opposite Walnut Lane, which cost £1000 to build plus £25 for a verandah behind, for growing tomatoes. Her husband Harold worked at the Austin,[140] and every day travelled by one of Mr Perrygrove's motor coaches[141] with a suitcase full of groceries and cigarettes which he sold to other workers. This made more money than the shop did. The stock of the shop was mainly groceries, cigarettes and sweets for the children. Bacon and ham was hung from the ceiling covered with white pillowcases to stop flies touching the meat, while butter, margarine and

---

139 The idea of bungalows was brought to England from India by the East India Company, though they weren't built in quantity here until after WWI, when large numbers were built.

140 It was usual to speak of the Austin Motor Company as 'the Austin'.

141 Mr Perrygrove lived at No. 151 on Finstall Road.

The Gospel Hall, 2014, before alterations to make a dwelling.

John and Mollie Suffield on their milk round, opposite to Eldon on Finstall Road. Note churn of milk. (John Suffield)

Finstall Cottage, previously the first school in Finstall, built on land owned by the church; later lived in by Mrs Jessie Cotton.

cheese were kept on a pine table in the middle of the shop, covered with a damp muslin cloth dampened with vinegar. One side of the shop was selling useful hardware – nails and screws, buckets, paraffin, etc. Milk came from Mr Pugh Jones of Crossbrook Farm and Mr Suffield of Finstall Farm, whose milk was particularly creamy, coming from Jersey cows. It was sold in jugs, taken from the milk churns on their vans.

Behind the shop, down a path at the side, was Mr Higgins' bungalow, almost under the railway bank. No more bungalows were built there because the field tended to flood.

Lower down the road, amongst the newly built bungalows, was a neat little Gospel Hall, built in September 1939. Having changed to become a New Life Centre, this closed in 2004, and was altered to make a home in 2015. Opposite the cemetery, just before the skew bridge, is the house that was Finstall's first school. This was built on land belonging to the church, and opened in 1848. It was set up under the auspices of the National Society for the Education of the Poor. Starting off with one classroom and one teacher, as the area expanded it became too small (about 56 children in the 3-5 age group, and 160 in the 5 plus – and the school leaving age was only 13 until 1902). So John Cotton's school in Stoke Road was built in 1881. In 1861 there was a complimentary item in *The Messenger*, but it ends 'Its contiguity to the Bromsgrove Station makes it of especial benefit to the families of the workpeople belonging to the Midland Railway Company who live at the Works; but we regret to hear that certain "scruples of conscience" do not permit the Directors of that flourishing Company to tender any assistance towards its maintenance.' There were many poor children attending Finstall school – in 1870 there was a need for a 'clothing club'.

Finstall children either went down the hill to this school, or walked up from Finstall to Tardebigge School by the church. In 1916 *The Messenger* reported that despite Bromsgrove's reputation for high attendance rates, there was worry that since the outbreak of war and the number of farmworkers who had signed up, children were needed more and more to help in agricultural work; they were invaluable in gathering in crops, including the potato harvest and fruit picking. When the little school closed, the building was bought by Mr Everitt of Finstall Park, altered, and became known as Finstall Cottage. It was described as a 'Brick and Tile Freehold Bijou Residence', but did not sell in the 1920 Sale. Mrs Cotton lived there for many years, and with extensions it is still a pretty house today.

Bromsgrove Rugby Football team, 1912-13 before the move to Finstall Park.

Opposite the row of bungalows is the beautiful half mile long stone wall which was built bordering Finstall Park fields. The wall now suffers from salt spray in the winter, which has worn away many of the lower stones, though the worst of these have been restored. The Rugby Club bought their first land from Mr Thomas, a silversmith who kept The Dragoon pub (now The Ladybird). Miss Jocelyn Albright had bought the rest of the land, and eventually agreed to sell enough for the second pitch. After her death in 1982 the Rugby Club bought extra land from her executors. She had made a covenant with the National Trust that the land should never be built on, apart from by the Rugby Club, which even now protects the land when parts are sold. Long may this continue.

Chapter Twenty
The Tutnall and Vigo Connections

Tutnall, with its four big Georgian houses, also attracted the Albrights, though the connection of Tutnall Hall Farm with Finstall Farm and High Barn Farm at Vigo goes back much further than the Albright time.

There are differing views by experts on the age of Tutnall Hall, which was listed Grade II in 1952. The listing says it is 'early 18th century, partly rebuilt early 19th century'. The early 18th century owner was probably Thomas Bell, vicar of Tardebigge (see Chapter 3), a wealthy man who owned Finstall Farm and Hollow Tree Farm at Vigo, and could have built the back part of the present day house. It is very unlikely that anyone would have built a house with as many as twenty windows in the front of the building while the Window Tax was in operation! They say that the term 'daylight robbery' came from this tax, which charged two shillings per house rising to 8 shillings for those with the most windows, which would have included Tutnall Hall. It was repealed in 1851, after campaigners called it 'a tax on light and air'. The then owner, Wm Farmer Parkes of Astwood in Dodderhill, leased the farm in 1849 to John Cullwick who lived at High Barn Farm, Vigo, and must have then taken the opportunity to rebuild the front of the building in this grand manner. A celebration of the repeal of the Window Tax indeed. The front of the house makes a bold statement, but as it is only one room deep it was clearly built for show. It has, however, a beautiful early 19th century staircase which you can sometimes see through the central windows. There are now of course many additions to the original house, which currently is a care home.

Tutnall Hall Farm, before 1971, when the Ashwins were farming. (Rosemary Ashwin)

Twenty years after John Cullwick came to the farm the land was taken over by Thomas Smith, and then in 1875 it was being farmed in conjunction with Finstall Farm by Thomas

20. THE TUTNALL AND VIGO CONNECTIONS

Gardner (see Chapters 3 and 6). And it was in 1881 that Arthur Albright bought Tutnall Hall Farm for £10,400 including timber, and also bought Hollow Tree Farm, Old Hill Farm, and Vigo Close. Gardner continued working Finstall Farm, lived in Tutnall Hall and needed to employ several men. By 1888 Gardner was 77, and Albright was advertising a:

> Cheap Country Residence near Bromsgrove, Tutnall Hall £30 p.a. Two large parlours, small office room, six full-sized bedrooms, two dressing rooms. Apply to owner Arthur Albright, Mariemount, Edgbaston and Finstall Farm nearly adjoining Tutnall.

There was no mention of farming, so Albright was clearly expecting that his two farms would continue to be run together.

The next long term farmer of Tutnall Hall land and that of Finstall, was George James. He took out a ten year lease on both farms for £225.3.0 annual rent in 1895, though the house was lived in, often rented for only a year or so, by non-farmers, one of them being William Lester Smith, a hardware manufacturer, and his wife Naomi. When George James gave up farming, the two properties were split, with Mr Mebb taking on Finstall Farm. Leonard Jeffrey took on Tutnall, followed in 1933 by Edward and Nancy Ashwin (née Suffield), with their son Godfrey.[142] After the death of Miss Albright, Edward Ashwin bought the farm and the house for £6000, including part of High Barn Farm, and so ended the Albright connection with Tutnall. In 1971 Godfrey Ashwin sold the farm.

Worcestershire Hunt meeting in 1900 outside the toll house on the corner of Tutnall Lane and the old Alcester Road. (BC)

With its garden attached to Tutnall Hall land was the little toll house, projecting into the road, with its gate across the Alcester Road, ready to catch those going to Tardebigge church and Hewell Grange and Alcester, as well as those turning into the lane, which hundreds of years before had been cut through the stone to go to Alvechurch. 'The United Trust of the Alcester Roads in the Counties of Warwick and Worcester' had in 1872 expired, and Thomas Farmer Parkes bought the toll house with its garden, outside earth closet and other outbuildings for £45. The sunburst gate, of a style introduced by Thomas Telford, ended up at the Tardebigge Vicarage, now the Old Vicarage, where it is today. The house continued to be lived in, until in 1936 the cottage was demolished, not surprisingly, on safety grounds, and its little piece of land absorbed into Tutnall Hall's front garden.

Between Tutnall and Finstall, built on the Albright's Square Meadow, part of Tutnall Hall farm, just by the Finstall sign, is The Ridgeway. Bought in 1935 by Albert John Bott,

---

142 Alan White in his book *A Hundred Years in Tardebigge*, Brewin Books, 2011, tells the story of the Ashwins and later time at Tutnall, pp.152-154.

he built a typically 1930s three bedroomed house, which has now been extended. The Botts were there for many years, to be followed by the Mumbersons, with their son Ian who was a collector of old lorries and cars, working on them in the garden of The Ridgeway.

Next to Tutnall Hall is the first Tutnall Mount (later Whitegates), a good house which has recently been restored, though sadly has lost its full-width porch at the front. In 1960 it was sold by Lt.Col. W.H. Kerr who had been living there, and also had gradually been buying up Finstall Farm, including Finstall House. Tutnall Mount was described as having four reception rooms, three bedrooms and a nursery suite with day and night nurseries. Drainage was mentioned: 'a collecting tank which is emptied periodically by the Bromsgrove Rural District Council, with overflow on to land on the opposite side of the main road'. The Water Rate was £3.13s.8d per half year, including use of garden hose.[143]

The other four large 18th and 19th century Tutnall houses have no connection with Finstall, but help to make a very attractive corner of Worcestershire. Across the lane is Tutnall House (previously Tutnall Farm), a mid 18th century house, with a converted timber-framed barn on a sandstone plinth, thought to be part 17th century, both of which are Listed Grade II. Next door to Tutnall House is the second Tutnall Mount, of similar age and with good outbuildings, and across the road is what is now known as Tutnall Farm (originally The

The Tutnall toll house, opposite Tutnall House. (Jane & Terry Critchley)

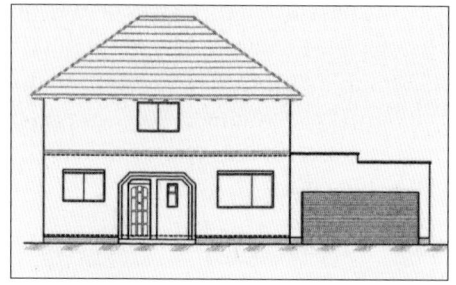

A drawing of the front of The Ridgeway before its recent additions.

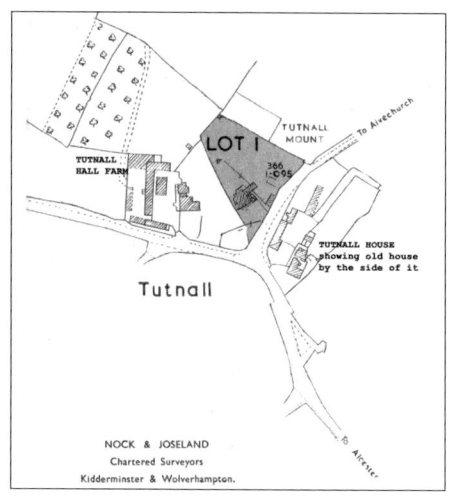

Sale plan for Tutnall Mount (White Gates), in 1960. To the right of Tutnall House is the second Tutnall Mount, and what is now known as Tutnall Farm is opposite Tutnall House. (BC)

---

143 More about the Tutnall houses in *A Hundred Years in Tardebigge*, Alan White, Brewin Books.

20. The Tutnall and Vigo Connections

Cottage) with its converted 19C barn designed by Bromsgrove architect John Cotton. All these houses are very close together and could be the important features of a Tutnall Conservation Area.

Tutnall House built beside the old farmhouse, which was demolished after 1900. (Jane & Terry Critchley)

* * * *

In October 1825, Benjamin Ashmore of Finstall Farm and his brother John of Bromsgrove, bought The Maltshovel Inn at Vigo from Thos. Sanders. Benjamin, bachelor son of the important Bromsgrove Ashmore carrier family, already owned house, land and buildings at Hollow Tree – a 17th century farmhouse, now Listed Grade II, down the lane from Vigo. Buying The Maltshovel meant that with the land behind it the Ashmore land reached all the way from Finstall to Hollow Tree. He died in 1837, when his estate was kept

Whitegates, previously Tutnall Mount, the white lines showing where originally there was a porch.

One of John Moore's barns, c.1900, now converted to a dwelling.

The present day Tutnall Farm and barn with JM in the brickwork for John Moore, in 2000.

The second Tutnall Mount in 1978. (BC)

The Maltshovel and cottages at Vigo. (Zilla Wildridge)

in the family, leaving Finstall Farm to his brother John. The land opposite Vigo, the land behind The Maltshovel, and High Barn Farm beside it, he left to a relative, John Bonnaker, who was a maltster in Evesham[144]. They sold High Barn Farm to Wm Farmer Parkes in 1841 for £3,310. So the connection with the owner of Finstall Farm might have disappeared had not Arthur Albright bought it in 1874, and Thomas Gardner, his tenant, rented the 23 acres of Hollow Tree Farm, Old Hill's 8 acres 3r 15p and the 3 acres of Vigo Close.

In 1883 Arthur Albright also bought The Maltshovel and its land from the new owners, Warwick Hall Estate, once again joining it up with the Finstall Farm lands.

Albright & Wilson's factory was in Oldbury in The Black Country. Most of their workers lived very near the factories, which were belching smoke and chemical gases, and this caused massive health problems. The workers often suffered from breathing difficulties

---

144 While the railway was being built in 1840 The Maltshovel Alehouse was very popular with the many navvies doing heavy work on the sandstone to build bridges and embankments. After a night of drinking in The Maltshovel in 1841, a massive escape of steam from the engine of a locomotive on the nearby railway killed William Creuze, the chief engineer at Aston Fields Wagon Works. This is fully described in *The Wrangler who went to the Railway: The Story of the Life and Death of William Creuze BA*, Neville Billington & Warwick Sheffield, Came Hundred Publishing, 2010.

and asthma, the working conditions with their lack of fresh air causing stunted growth and rickets. Aware of these problems the Albrights decided to build a small 'holiday bungalow' in the narrow field opposite The Maltshovel, to which they could send some of their workers to recuperate from illnesses. It was laid out as dormitories with toilets and washrooms outside. A nice idea, but not very many could benefit from it! However it continued until 1937 when the field was sold to Boultbee Brooks of Blackwell Court for £100. It has now been converted into a modern bungalow.

It was not only The Black Country that was risky. In September 1870:

> a loaded waggon of straw ... passed under the railway bridge in Burcot Lane. As an up train passed over the bridge a spark or live cinder fell upon the straw and set it on fire. All that could be done was to remove the horse from the shafts; the straw and waggon were entirely destroyed, and the hedge on either side were alight.

The Holiday Bungalow opposite The Maltshovel.

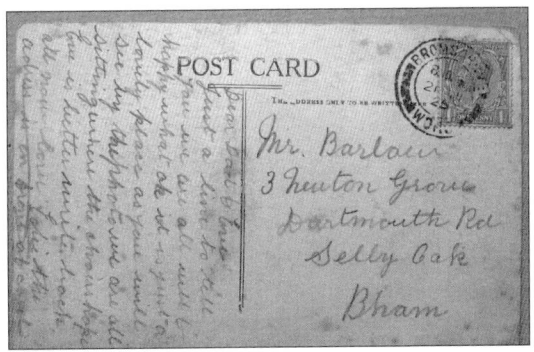

The reverse of the Holiday Bungalow card: "Dear Dad & Eve. Just a line to tell you we are all well and happy [....] it is just a lovely place as you will see by the photo we are all sitting where the chairs [are] hope Eve is better write back. all now. love Edie".

After the death of Arthur Albright's son William in 1942, Miss Catherine Albright inherited, amongst other things, Finstall Farm, Tutnall Hall Farm, Malvern View (the estate house near to Tutnall Hall), High Barn Farm and Pikes Pool, 3 Vigo cottages (which had housed The Maltshovel) and Finstall Parish Allotments.

Chapter Twenty One
Wartime in Finstall

We began this book thinking about the Civil War. We end it by looking at how Finstall was affected by war in the 20th century.

The Crimean War was between 1853 and 1856, after which the government embarked on a much-needed reform of the British army, for it had been clear that the army had serious shortcomings. Rupert Smallwood of Rigby Hall took part in the Boer Wars, 1899-1902, which involved two battalions of the Worcestershire Regiment but also relied on volunteers who were sent out to join the regulars. So it was clear that the need for trained officers was important, and the government encouraged schools and universities to form Officer Training Corps. Also, based in Bromsgrove was the volunteer Bromsgrove Cavalry, formed by Captain John Adams of Perry Hall. Their uniform was very smart,

Troops marching through Tutnall, c.1880. (Jane & Terry Critchley)

blue jacket with yellow facings and white breeches; officers added gold lace. This later became the Second Worcestershire Volunteer Rifles. Lord Windsor, commanding the Queen's Own Worcestershire Hussars when they left for South Africa in February 1901, said he believed that every single man in the company went on active service with a full sense of the gravity of the work before him. The conduct of all in barracks had been exemplary, and he was convinced the country would be proud of them.

Bromsgrove School OTC in 1911. Nearly 100 boys in uniform from a school of but 120. (Bromsgrove School)

Finstall villagers were very used to seeing soldiers en masse. Nearly every year there were summer camps for Worcestershire Volunteers or the Worcestershire Regiment in either Finstall Park or at Hewell Grange, which also included the cadet corps from schools. Ernest Montague Everitt, JP, Worcestershire Hussars Yeomanry, living at Sillins, Tardebigge took part between 1881 and 1895.

Records of Finstall participants in the Boer War are difficult to find, but we know that Mrs Everitt offered to help raise money for the Association for Giving Relief to the Sick and Wounded in the Boer War. There is slightly more information about those who served in WWI. From those who fought, at least 14 young men who lived in Finstall were killed. Not too far away, in Tardebigge, the third son of the Earl of Plymouth, Archer Windsor-Clive, died in 1914 defending the village of Landrecies, two days after the Battle of Mons. Closer to home, Lieut. Leslie Brooks, 4th battalion W. Yorks Regiment, son of John Boultbee Brooks of Finstall Park, was killed in action aged 23. He lost his life in the battle of Loos in 1915, and his mother donated £50 for a bed for the Imperial Yeomanry Hospital Fund to be known as the 'Finstall Bed'. In 1917, among the more ordinary folk, were Private Charles Brooks, dairyman, killed in action; Lieut. Herbert Cutler of the Oakalls (aged 26) who enlisted into the Royal Flying Corps, to be killed in France after only a few weeks

Officers of the Worcestershire Imperial Yeomanry with Lord Windsor (seated).

William Moore of Tutnall in his Boer War uniform in 1900. (Jane & Terry Critchley)

of flying. Private Reginald Cund joined up in 1916, and a year later was admitted to hospital with wounds to his leg and died; Private William Tustin, of Broad Green, a poultryman with two children, died of bronchial pneumonia following measles; Private William Walton, a 'happy lad and always cheerful', was bombed in a trench, aged 19. Three workers for the Brooks family lost their lives: Private George Colley who died from pneumonia aged 23 in 1916, Corporal Harry Merget died at the front in 1918, and Corporal Harry Powell, groom gardener for Wilfred Brooks of Finstall Croft, died of malaria in 1918. Lance Corporal Henry Pearman, the elder son

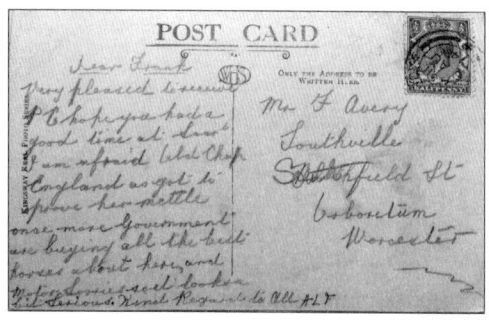

A postcard written in expectation of war: "... I am afraid Old Chap England [h]as got to prove her mettle once more Government are buying all the best horses about here, and Motor Lorries so it looks a bit Serious. ... "

of William Pearman, farmer of Slideslow, died in 1917 aged 23. 2nd Lieutenant Robert Cotton, son of Jessie Cotton of Finstall Cottage and the late Ernest Cotton, auctioneer, was awarded an MC for his leadership of a raiding party in 1918, but was wounded a month later and died from complications, aged 20. His two brothers, Leslie and Maurice survived after giving distinguished service. Captain Harvey Carter also received an MC after being wounded in the leg by a bomb and, in spite of a severe loss of blood, crawling a long distance to posts to issue orders. He was later killed in action aged 22.

Bromsgrove's Women's Volunteer Reserve, 1916.

The next year, 1918, Lieut. Frederick Walduck, whose parents lived at Slideslow, died in a sanatorium in Wales. Frederick received a Military Cross 'for conspicuous gallantry.' When a tunnel in which the personnel of the battery were sheltering was blown in, 'he volunteered to lead a party for 400 yards over a shell swept area to aid in extricating the buried men. ... he continued to dig in order to extricate the buried men until his task was completed. He displayed marked courage, determination and contempt of danger'. His brother, Cyril, survived.

Private William Walton of the Sherwood Foresters, youngest of three sons of Mr and Mrs Edward Walton, who all served in the forces, died aged 19. Private Victor Wheelock, whose family were at Caspidge before going to Saskatchewan, died that May also aged 19. The three Stevens brothers of Stonehouse Farm all died: Private Daniel who died of disease aged 26 three days after the end of the war (he caught malaria in Salonika), George aged 22, who was killed during the battle for High Wood on the Somme, and John, who served as a driver with the East Lancashire regiment, who died in 1920 of an ear infection that led to mastoiditis, meningitis and facial paralysis. Also in 1918 Douglas Hall was killed in action and his brother Roland

Soldiers marching past The Dragoon at Aston Fields. Note that the houses have yet to be built opposite the pub.

Tardebigge and Finstall women who made cheese as their war effort. (John Suffield)

died of disease the same year, after losing his right arm and his right leg. They were sons of James and Emma Hall, who had eight children, six of whom served in the war. Three were wounded and two, Douglas and Roland, died.

The following are a few of the many others who fought in WWI but returned: Edmund Page of The Vale was at Ypres and Arras on the Somme as a Captain in the King's Royal Rifle Corps, aged 26, having been in the OTC at Bromsgrove School and at Keble College, Oxford. Hugh Chance, who came to live at The Vale after the war, served with the Worcestershire Regiment and the Royal Flying Corps. On the 17th September 1916 whilst on a bombing raid over Valenciennes, his plane was hit and had to make a crash landing in occupied France. He was captured and taken prisoner and spent the rest of the war in prisoner of war camps at Osnabruck and Clausthal. During WWII he was given the rank of Honorary Colonel in the service of the Parachute

Edmund Page in uniform as a Captain in the King's Royal Rifle Corps. (JC Page)

21. Wartime in Finstall

Lieut. W.H.S. Chance, 1915.

Finstall War Memorial at Aston Fields, designed by Philip Green, with The Dragoon, built 1905 (now The Ladybird), and the old railway buildings at the bottom of Station Approach.

Regiment (Territorial Army). P.H.P. Gunton who came to Coombe Cottage, was a Captain in the Middlesex Regiment, and at the end of WWII served at the War Office as a Major from the Royal Warwickshire Regiment. Godfrey Winn, who stayed at the Oakalls, served as an Able Seaman in the Royal Navy on HMS Ganges, to be discharged because of injury. Paymaster Lieutenant-Commander G.J. Rapkin, OBE, RN, who came to Finstall Mount, had been Secretary to the Divisional Naval Transport Officer, Murmansk naval base. Llewellyn M. Ryland of Walnut Lane was a Captain in the Royal Welsh Fusiliers from 1914 to 1922; during WWII he was a Commander of C Company, part of the 2nd Worcestershire (Bromsgrove) Battalion Home Guard.[145]

* * * *

Thankfully, WWII did not lose so many Finstall men, though this is an example of seven. Sergeant Samuel Packer of High Bank Cottages, died in Egypt in 1942 aged 28; Horace

---

145 The Home Guard was formed from volunteers who responded originally to a request broadcast on 14 May 1940 by Anthony Eden, Minister for War. In operation until 1944 it was composed of 1½ million people otherwise ineligible for military service. The nickname Dad's Army was due to the average age of local volunteers who were too old – or too young. Despite the great fun of the TV programme *Dad's Army* they should be remembered for guarding factories and explosive stores in the case of invasion, but also the distressing job of supporting the fire services when air raids on residential areas took place.

Finstall's Home Guard, No.10 Platoon. The central seated figure is Lieut. L.T. Oldaker. (Rob Oldaker)

Quinney, in the Royal Artillery, a farmer's son, was killed; Bert Loxton, a Flight Sergeant from The Cottage, Penmanor, died in a flying accident; Oliver Goodman, a Leading Airman on HMS Daedalus of the Royal Navy, was killed in 1941 when he was 23; Harry G Ryland of the South Lancashire Regiment died in 1945; in 1941 Flight Lieutenant Harry Hillcoat, RAF, AAF was killed in action aged 26; and 2nd Lieut. John Farrar, who was a very successful and popular teacher at Finstall Park School, who ran the cub group in the village, went to France in January 1940 and died aged 27 in May the same year.

Those in Finstall who joined the Home Guard (previously known as Local Defence Volunteers, LDV) had to use Tardebigge School as their post, though later they moved to Finstall Village Hall, and were part of the 2nd Worcestershire (Bromsgrove) Battalion. Its HQ was the Wagon Works, Aston Fields. On the Bromsgrove Battalion roll there were 1,234 officers and men. At Finstall and Tardebigge the rather smaller squad of men were on duty 5.00 pm to 8.00 am in the winter months, 6.00 pm to 6.00 am in summer. As well as the Home Guard there were Air Raid Wardens who ensured blackout was observed and issued and checked gas masks.

Life became very different in WWII, affecting food, clothing and the number of available men to work, particularly in the fields.[146] This is the time when Land Girls came to take the place of the men at war, and they showed their worth in running farms when the farmers were away. Sometimes German prisoners were sent to work in the fields, an

---

146 I am indebted to Charlie Poole, who grew up in Finstall, for his helpful memories of wartime.

offer that Pugh Jones took advantage of. Not all Germans in Bromsgrove were prisoners; from May 1939 Oakley House (a Bromsgrove School property) in New Road became a hostel for refugees from Czechoslovakia, Austria and Germany. This was a scheme initiated by the Quaker trustees of Avoncroft College. Thirty young men, all single, were to be accommodated at Oakley; none were Jewish, and all had been persecuted by the Nazi state. They were trained in agriculture, with the hope that after a year's training they would be able to emigrate.

Probably, apart from members of families suddenly going off to war, the thing that affected people most was rationing, even in the country. Almost all foods apart from vegetables and bread were rationed by August 1942. In 1941 weekly rations were 3 pints of milk, 55 grams of tea, meat costing up to one shilling, 225 grams of sugar, 30 grams of cheese, 225 grams of jam per month, 170 grams of butter, 55 grams of cooking fat and 115 grams of bacon. We were allowed one egg per week, or one packet of egg powder per month. Everyone had a ration book, and you had to register at a particular shop. The shops themselves had to register with Bromsgrove Rural District Council, handing over all the coupons they received, then the shop was allocated credit notes to purchase more goods. The worst thing for children was that rationing of sweets continued as late as 1953.

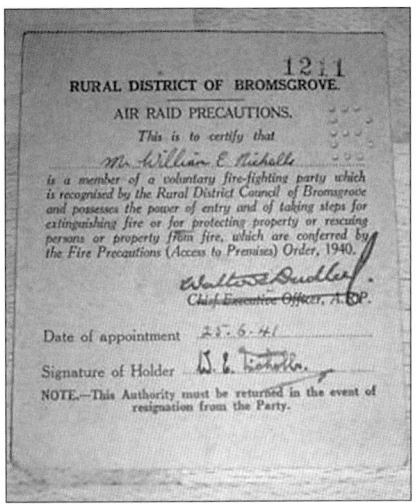

1941 Certificate giving right of entry to private property for a voluntary fire-fighter after an air raid. Fortunately there proved to be little need for this in the Finstall area.

People were encouraged to keep hens, though hen food too was rationed and bought from Weaver & Guest in Bromsgrove. It was definitely worthwhile doing this, for, with six birds, it boosted the household ration by about 20 eggs per week. And after a year of laying, the birds would be used to provide a nice Sunday lunch, and numbers were kept up with pullets from Blizard's market garden. Pigs, which happily ate household waste, were also kept in fields, like that behind the Park Stores, and people were allowed to keep two. The Pooles and Mr Higgins agreed that when one was killed they would divide it between the two households. There was one family that had a spare half pig, and they swapped it for an Austin 7 Tourer.

Clothing was rationed as well, so people were well used to using old curtains for dresses, and late in the war bought black market silk from used parachutes, often the only way to buy enough fabric for a wedding dress. The normal silk stockings became almost unobtainable, so for women the most popular item brought over to England by

An Anderson Shelter, named after Sir John Anderson, the man responsible for preparing Britain to withstand German air raids.

A Morrison Shelter, named after Herbert Morrison, the Minister of Home Security.

the Americans was nylons. Without the real thing girls would stroke their legs with cold tea, or if they could afford it, Max Factor's Pan Stick, and then run eyeliner up the back of the leg to denote the seam, for all stockings then had seams.

American soldiers did come to Finstall, sometimes with nylons and sweets in their pockets. Blackwell Convalescent Home was not far, so convalescent men came along the railway line to The Cross in the evening. There were also lorries with equipment passing through the village, and on the trains going up the incline. Apparently the train drivers would toss lumps of coal from the engine into the fields, trying to hit the rabbits. Then the local children ran into the field with buckets to bring the coal back home; they would be lucky to find a rabbit, though the local chimney sweep regularly cycled round the village with rabbits hanging from his crossbar.

When air raids happened people kept indoors, hid under the stairs or slept in a Morrison shelter indoors (a metal table large enough for the whole family; I always worried because my father's feet stuck out at the bottom), or in an Anderson shelter in the garden (metal sides and top, dug into the earth and with a covering of earth above, to take six people). Anderson shelters were issued free to all householders earning less than £250 a year – probably quite a number in Finstall. The boys at Finstall Park School slept in the cellar, and were quite safe even though at least one German plane dropped high explosives and incendiary bombs in the grounds and at Grimley Hall. It is thought that this happened because there was a searchlight and an AA battery between the school and the station. Finstall was lucky; Birmingham was bombed 77 times, and Finstall was both near to the BBC radio mast at Wychbold, and the Austin Motor Company which was producing trucks and aircraft, including Avro Lancaster bombers. One shell fell on Alcester Road and bullets onto Stoke Road during an air fight overhead, with damage at Burcot. There was one bomb which caused laughter as well as anger, for it landed in a potato field and potatoes flew everywhere – ripe for the picking.

Chapter Twenty Two

"Our Village in the 1920s"

This vividly written story by Irene Brake née Frisby was first published, after her death, in the Bromsgrove Society Rousler *2007 and 2008. This is an edited version, concentrating on Finstall village and those who lived there.*

Irene Brake as an elderly lady.

In the 1920s Finstall was just a hamlet although it was known as Finstall village. It consisted of what we called the Front Hill and at the bottom of the hill was the Vale, lived in then by the Goodmans, a large but seemingly dark house with trees in front and not very inviting. The back entrance opened into Pikes Pool Lane, a narrow lovely lane leading to Burcot. Further up the hill was the house where Mr and Mrs Quinney lived, Elmwood with its beautiful lawns and gardens.

Mr Quinney was a retired farmer [Finch End Farm] and had the house built to his own specifications, very grand it seemed to me. A long lawn running along the road the length of the house, in spring festooned with daisies and we were free to gather them and make daisy chains. There was a huge laburnum hanging over the posh double gates and all sorts of ornamental shrubs along the edge of the lawn underneath the fence. Sometimes we would reach up on our way to school and pinch some of the 'golden chain' and flowers from a lovely flowering laurel. However sometimes Mr Quinney would be waiting by the gate or perhaps mowing the lawn and then we would try to slink by as if we had not seen him. But unsuccessfully – he would call us back and in those days you always obeyed your elders; and then he would proceed to ask us our names, where we lived and even where our fathers worked (my mother later forbade me to tell him any of our business). However he was a kind man really and would often reach in his pocket and give us a few shrivelled apples which at that time in our childhood was quite a treat.

Next to that was an old smithy with a very large barn at the side.[147] I remember a big steam roller was housed in it at the time. The man who lived there, Mr Davis, used to work for the Council. It was no longer a smithy but there was an old forge still at the side of it.

---

147 This must have been the earliest building in Finstall hamlet.

Further up the hill was a row of cottages going back from the road, only one tap between the three of them, [each with] only one living room and two bedrooms. Very pleasant, a long path in front leading down to what we called the 'Big Meadow' with a brook running through it and where we spent many happy hours during our school holidays. The lads would stop the brook up with clods of earth till it was deep enough to bathe in, much to the annoyance of John Suffield who rented the field. We girls would paddle and then run up and down to get our feet dry (no towels). Sometimes we took our tea down – a bottle of tea and some bread and whatever; that was how we spent our days, little pleasures, and no longings for seaside holidays, our parents just couldn't afford them.

Our pair of houses, Orchard Cottages [where Irene lived], were next up the hill with large windows and a long garden, at the bottom of which was a huge tall elm tree. We had three damson trees down there, apples and plums, and it edged on to the Pleck, the path leading to the meadow and we could get through a gap and run down to the stile without having to go out through the front gate. There were eight steps up to the back door and thirteen steps up the stairs to the first floor and another twelve steps up to the attic where Bert, Ron and Sam slept. It was a very roomy pleasant attic with a window to the south-west through which streamed all the afternoon sun and on a clear day you could see all over Bromsgrove and as far as the Malvern Hills. There was also a skylight in

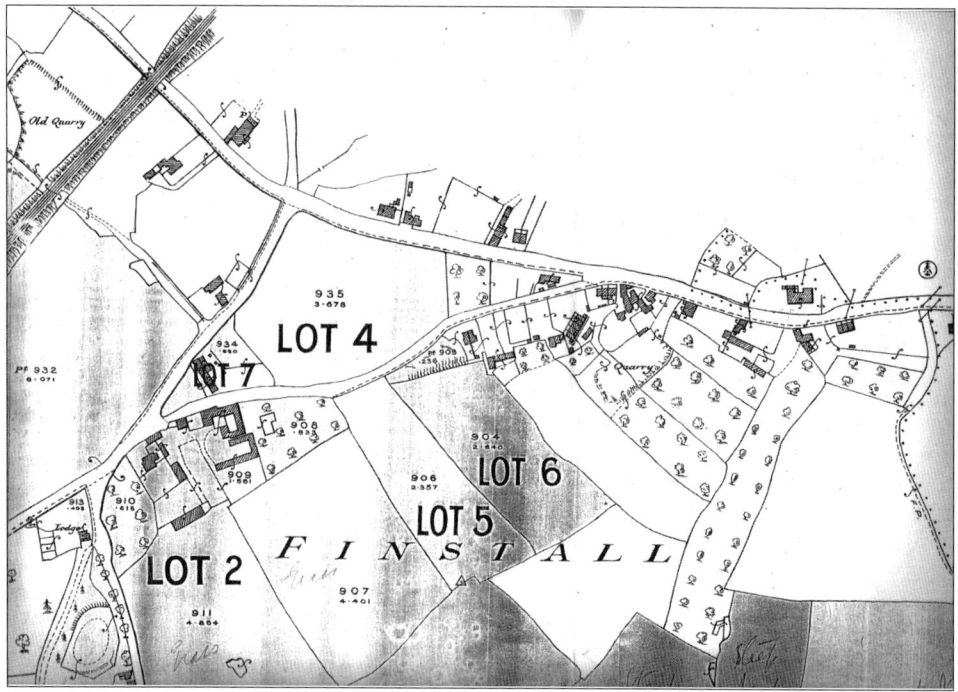

A slightly earlier than 1920 map of the village. (BC)

22. "Our Village in the 1920s"

John Humstone Suffield driving past Carthorse Meadow – see gate in hedge, and behind the tree, the swings. (John Suffield)

the roof through which we used sometimes to shout to friends passing by and they would look around puzzled as to where the voices were coming from. The adjoining house was occupied by the Websters, Donald and Jack and later Peggy.

The next was the Post Office and General Stores run by various members of the Cond family and we used to spend our pocket money at the weekend, first gazing in the window deciding how to make best use of the 2d. or 3d. we were given usually on a Friday evening when our Dad came home from work. Should it be Lucky Turnovers containing some tawdry trinket, Liquorice strips, Sherbert suckers, Gobstoppers, all laid out to tempt us? I think I usually had some straightforward bottled sweets, they lasted longer. Sometimes they stuck to the bottle and Alice Cond got a little hammer to knock them out. She was in a wheelchair and was a bit skinny, never giving us more than the exact weight. We used to get about 5 Bluebird toffees for a penny, 4d. a quarter [lb], bottled sweets 2d. a quarter.

Above the Post Office was the Village Hall built by Miss Albright where dances used to take place and we invariably had a children's Christmas Party there when we were school children, and were each given a small present and an apple and an orange.

There were no more working class houses on that side of the road. The next house up was occupied by Mr and Miss Sayer. It was called Finstall Mount. He had a motor car, the only person in the village to own one then and I recall Miss Sayer used to sit beside him with a scarf tied round her hat to keep it on. It was an open car. I can't remember whether it had a hood or not.

Next to Sayer's garden, which extended quite some distance further up the road, there was a meadow called the Cart Horse Meadow but we always called it the 'Cartus'. It was designated to be a play field for the village children by the owner, Miss Albright, and there were a couple of swings and some parallel bars and we used to gather there in summer evenings and play.[148] It was a very interesting field with a couple of spinneys and we used to climb the trees and had all sorts of fun, and the top spinney, just at the entrance to the drive to the farm, was particularly interesting. It had a cherry tree.

At the top of 'Cartus' John Suffield had a poultry run and there was a particularly fierce gander, and we used to go up as near as we dare and the gander would come flying after us with wings outspread and we would run to get back to the stile.

Although John Suffield was the farmer, the land really belonged to the Albrights, and Miss Catherine Albright lived in the house and it was always called Finstall Farm and John lived in a smaller house nearby [Allotment Cottage]. Later she had another house built for him nearer to the farmyard. Miss Albright (Katy we used to call her, behind her back of course), was a very dominant figure in the village and many of the people living there were her tenants, ourselves included, and my mother paid seven shillings a week, but in her later years bought it as a sitting tenant for about £500 to £600, I forget the exact amount. Anyway we all had great respect for Katy, she was a Quaker, very plain in her dress, and used to ride a bike at that time to and from Bromsgrove and we all had a good laugh one day when we saw her pushing her bike up the hill with one leg of her combs[149] hanging down. She would throw a party for us children, sometimes in the big kitchen at the Farm and sometimes in the Village Hall, generally around Christmas time.

Sometimes on Sunday evenings she would have a little service in what she called the Granary[150]. It was a long low ceilinged room, once upon a time a grain store, I guess. A lovely room it was with padded seats around the wall and little chairs for children left from their childhood days. My first remembrance of the Farm was when she had a Mrs Maynard living there as a housekeeper and sometimes she would take us on rambles as far as Spion Kop, organise some games for us and I remembered once she scattered ripe gooseberries for us to collect up and eat. She also had a little sewing class for the girls and it was from her I first learned how to make 'pom-poms'. There was another interesting character, Harry Newbold, who was the handyman, a bachelor, who could not pronounce his s's but who could talk a lot nevertheless. He used to come round and collect the rents

---

148 There was also a pond, which dried up when the Redditch Highway was built, cutting the field in half.
149 Combinations, long legged knickers.
150 This was a Quaker meeting.

22. "Our Village in the 1920s"

every Monday and would generally, when he called on us, sit down and have a 'cank'[151]. A very popular figure in the village.[152] When he had his 'cank' to my mother he would say well 'I shall go Mittes' meaning 'I shall have to go to missus'. Every Friday afternoon he could be seen driving Katy's pony and trap to Bromsgrove for her groceries and sometimes he would give us a lift. The pony was a bit wayward and once I remember the pony tried to follow Harry into a shop (there were no cars on the road then). I laughed and Harry told me not to as the horse did not like being laughed at!

The Farm was the end of Finstall village, a long lovely walk up the drive with bushes on either side. Among the visitors who came for an occasional weekend with Katy was a Miss Rose. A group of us children including Lil Holland, Mary and Fred Dobbs, spotted her one evening sitting in the field next to the Big Meadow, a field at the bottom of a grassy slope full of primroses and bluebells in spring, and she was apparently reading a book. We crept up curiously to her and she looked up and invited us to come near and struck up a conversation with us asking us our names and ages, etc. When I told her my name was Irene, that was the first time I knew it was the Greek word for 'Peace'. We commenced a very pleasant friendship with her and ever after she called me 'Peace Child', not a very apt name I must admit at times!

Playing in the snow at Finstall Farm: Janet Holmes, Margaret Ryland, Ann Holmes, and Marian Suffield with dog. (John Suffield)

However after that whenever she did come down to the farm for weekends, she would invariably invite Lil, Mary, Fred and myself to a little tea party. We made such a fuss of her too and when she went back I remember we loaded her with flowers from our gardens and Harry Newbold would run her down to the Railway Station in the pony-cart. I still have several Postcards she sent to me back in the 1920s commencing 'Dear Peace Child', one of them thanking us for the 'lovely flowers'.

The long rambles over Hogg Hill and down over High Barn Farm occupied then by the Waldrons, a lovely country walk. We had to go through the farmyard (a right of way)

---

151 Midlands dialect meaning chat or gossip.
152 Harry Newbold died in 1962, aged 99, as Finstall's oldest inhabitant. While he was still at school Harry 'used to push his crippled father in a wheelbarrow from Burcot to Lickey, where the old man would sit and break stones for the roads until Harry collected him after school.' He said he did try to find a wife. He courted a maiden for 65 years, but ended the romance by pushing her into a bed of stinging nettles. From *The Bromsgrove Messenger*, September 1961.

and disturbed all the chickens and ducks as we went through. One could see for miles over Clent and the Malverns and Bromsgrove of course, and we were very proud to show her all the interesting landmarks. This was during the First World War and there were many wounded soldiers at the Blackwell Sanatorium situated high up at the top of the 'Cinder Path' leading to Blackwell Station. Groups of them we would sometimes meet going for walks and they would sometimes get as far as the Cartus Playfield and I quite innocently said to Miss Rose one day 'Lets give them the glad eye'. I wondered why she was so amused. I know now!

I have named all the houses on the left starting at the bottom of the hill, but of course now there are quite a few more built and the old ones modernised, some beyond recognition almost. Starting at the bottom of the hill there were no houses at that time on the right till one got opposite our house. There was a rough field belonging to the Brooks who lived at Finstall Park and sometime there were big stud horses in the field. Just above and opposite to Orchard Cottages were two cottages, the first one occupied by Mr and Mrs Crees and their daughter Mary and son Harold. In the next lived Mr and Mrs Holmes, their son Stanley and two daughters Hilda and Molly. An extension was built on to the end of the other cottage and the Holmes opened a General Stores including sweets. They didn't do very well as the sweets were always dearer than those sold by the Conds at the Post Office Stores.

The Holmes's corner shop, with the wall the children gathered on, signpost and rough edges to the footpaths.

There was a garden in front of Holmes' shop surrounded by an ornamental wall. It was right on the crossroads, one going down Finstall Hill and the other going down the Back Lane. All the kids used to congregate here and sit on Holmes' wall which didn't please them very much, and also I suppose we made a bit of a din with our playing about till eventually Stanley Holmes tarred the wall to stop us sitting on it and henceforth he was nick named 'Stanley Tar Pot Holmes'.

We used to play at the top of the hill because the road was only tarmac down as far as Holmes' shop. Further down it was only a very rough stony road and you could not spin a top or make hopscotch beds, so we all used to flock to the top. There was very little traffic but about six o'clock dozens of people came back from work in Redditch on their bikes and we all had to retreat to the path while they went by. There were lots of factories in Redditch then to provide work for many Bromsgrovians.[153]

---

153 Rene doesn't mention the 332 bus which ran from Redditch to Bromsgrove via Hewell from 1920, half hourly during peak times.

22. "Our Village in the 1920s"

Just beyond the crossroads, where incidentally there was a wooden signpost on a triangle of grass pointing 1¼ miles to Bromsgrove, 1 mile down the Back Lane [Finstall Road] to Bromsgrove Station, and 4¾ miles pointing to Redditch, there was The Cross Inn occupied by Josiah Deague, his name clearly written on the sign hanging outside. This pub was also a focus point in the village especially on Sunday evenings and I have seen many a one staggering out after just a little too much. When the strawberry pickers descended on the Tardebigge Dixons' strawberry fields and were lodged in barns for several weeks during fruiting time, they used to come to The Cross Inn for a drink and things got very lively at times and gave us quite a lot of entertainment with their singing and various other antics.

Next to the pub was a brickyard with three cottages, one occupied by Mr and Mrs Gately, the top one facing the road by the Mitchells and the other facing downhill by Mr and Mrs Garfield and their daughter Lizzie who lived on there till she died. A very independent spinster who worked as a domestic help and kept herself very respectable.

Next up the road was a very large house called The Croft and here lived Mr Wilfred Brooks and his family, a son of Mr Brooks who lived at Finstall Park, quite a wealthy family having a well known firm in those days in Birmingham, Brooks' Saddle Company. Mr Holmes from the shop was at one time a groom and was well in with Wilfred Brooks who built the shop and stocked it up. I am going back to November 1918 or 19 when Wilfred Brooks organised a bonfire party in one of their fields and burnt an effigy of the Kaiser. I remember it vividly, seeing him light the fireworks, and he had his two young daughters with him. Alas some weeks later he caught the dreadful flu which was raging through the country and killing hundreds, and he sadly died in his early thirties, a great shock to all the villagers – all stood around talking in whispers about it. His riches could not save him, yet we much poorer ones came safely through and I don't think anyone else in the village died from it.

Next to the Croft was a smallholding called Finstall Gardens run by Norman Hall from whom we bought milk and I used to go up with a can to fetch it; for a ha'penny we could get a quart tin full of skimmed milk and they had a dog called Spot who always came to meet you when you went through the gate. They were a large family, all boys, Bill, Norman, George, Lionel (called Bart), Roland, Hereward, Oliver and Douglas. Doug was killed in the war and Roland died from wounds, Bill emigrated.

Next came another pair of cottages occupied by Mrs Halfyear and her husband and daughters and her daughter's daughter, Lilian who was my childhood friend through all our schooldays. Her father was a bit of a mystery but we didn't wonder in those days why he had never been around. Lil used to spend a lot of her time at our house. Their cottage was very poor habitation, no water in the house and an old earth closet at the bottom of the garden shared by the two cottages, the other occupied first by an old man called Brookes, no relation to the other Brooks, and later by the Collins family. How they all got in I don't know, a mixed family and only two small bedrooms, and yet they all survived and did well in later life. Lil my friend grew up and quite good looking, married Harry Langley, a teacher.

Next down a small slope and some few hundred yards further on was a row of three cottages, first occupied by Miss Perkins and a Mr Gend and they sold pop. Next was Mrs Walton and Mr Walton, their big family had all grown up and left. Mr Walton had no education and could not even read. She learned to read after she grew up and liked a little 'tale book' to read as she called them. She made home made pop and sold it 2d a bottle, large pint bottles and I used to be sent up for three bottles at weekends and she always used to give me a small bottle extra – 'one for the fetcher' she used to say.

The end cottage was occupied by Mr Langston and his daughter Amy, a somewhat half soaked sort of girl but harmless, although after her father died she had quite a few men callers. These cottages had long gardens extending up the road as far as the Fordrough.

Then came a larger dwelling called Coombe Cottage where lived Mr and Mrs Horton, a Solicitor and his family, John, Lucy and Christopher. Quite a posh family and the children had a governess, they did not mix with the village children.

The last house up the road was occupied first by the Hintons and Dolly and Albert. Dolly worked at Whitfields & Parry's in Bromsgrove. A very superior girl who could be seen walking to Bromsgrove every morning between 8 and 9 and if we wanted anything urgent or a note left at the doctor's she would always oblige.

At the bottom of the road [Finstall Hill, Alcester Road] turn left, and there was a picturesque little road, a brook running alongside with willow trees, some of them quite hollow from age, hanging over the footpath.

Finstall Hill down to the Vale in 1911, showing the decorative lamp over the gate to the Village Hall, and the rough edges to the footpaths. (J.H.)

Halfway along was a beautiful half-timbered cottage where lived Fanny Heydon with her Dad. A long garden ran parallel to the lane with fruit trees in abundance. 'Old man Heydon' as we then called him, was very old and nearly blind. Anyway he stored his apples in a big barn sort of place which was joined on to the end of the cottage and there they were, lying all over the floor, and we passed by there every day on our way to school and in apple time we would call in and ask for apples. Sometimes he would be at the gate and call us in and give us some. However, one day when we called in he evidently did not hear us coming, for there he was relieving himself (his back to us) in the barn where the apples lay on the floor. Needless to say we did not call for any more apples!

22. "Our Village in the 1920s"

Later the lane was built up and became Heydon Road. The old man had died, but Fanny lived on there alone and eventually became confused in her mind and used to beat the washing on the line and tell it to 'hurry up and dry you so and so's'. Oh, the march of time, it is no longer the lovely lane I remember in my schooldays.

The Back Lane [Finstall Road] started below the Pub with three cottages situated high up on the bank, about half a dozen steps leading up to the doors. The first was occupied by Harry Newbold, Miss Albright's handyman of whom I spoke earlier; the second one housed the Swinbourne family, Edna the eldest, who was my lifelong friend, and Ted a very clever lad with his pencil and paint brush. I think he could have been an artist but with lack of money he didn't have the chance of an art education. Kitty the youngest at that time, was also quite clever, especially at making up poetry, but she too had to go into domestic service when she really was quite an intellectual. Mr Swinbourne had been married before and these were children by his first wife. Later another daughter arrived and was called Ethel Jane and I am afraid she got rather spoiled. However, Mrs Swinbourne was a good stepmother as far as her means would let her. She was kind to me too; on Saturday mornings when there was no school I'd go up the road and wait for them to come out 'to play'. If it was very cold Mrs Swinbourne would call me in and we would play in their shed. Although they were poor they had some good aunts and uncles and they had some nice books and knowing how I liked reading Mrs Swinbourne would lend me one by one her books which she had received as Prizes when she went to school.

I always remember the cups of cocoa she used to give us, very strong, not much milk but plenty of sugar and very warming. She had been a cook at Blackwell Court. As a treat for Sunday she would bake them a plain cake and they would eat it hot from the oven and of course I had a piece, very indigestible. Edna my friend, just a few months older than me, also had to go into domestic service at a house in Pikes Pool Lane with the Potters; I remember she was paid the handsome sum of five shillings per week, one half day a week and every other Sunday off.

Next to the Swinbournes on the last of those three cottages lived an old lady named Mrs Griffiths. We used to call her Mrs Griff; she was a stern old lady and would help anybody out. She came and looked after us kids when our Sam was born and in her rough way would feed us and wash us and keep the place tidy for a sixpence, with which she would then go and buy a 'pint' from the pub, and she also liked a pinch of snuff.

A short space further on from her was another row of five cottages called The Terrace. These were situated up high too and you had to go up quite a long flight of steps. Just small cottages, two bedrooms and one room and a back kitchen, no mod cons. Mrs Jones lived in the first with her son-in-law Mr Prentice (who was a widower) and had four children, Harry, Ethel, John and Emmy and they all grew up healthy. Later Mrs Jones took in another granddaughter, Doris, and brought her up when her mother died, so she did her bit!

Then there were the Darleys with their children, Fred[154] and Margaret, but they soon moved to a better house, one of a pair Miss Albright had built later on [Highbank Cottages]. Next there were the Woodwards with Harry, Bert, Ernie and Joyce, all now departed bar Joyce. Then came the Laytons, George, Nelly and Jack. Mrs Layton died in childbirth after Jack was born and later Mr Layton married Min Collins, a woman of dubious character, and then innumerable children came along whose paternity was somewhat uncertain.

Next to the terrace after a short gap came two more cottages approached by a flight of steps and a long path up to the door. In the first lived a Miss Bell who was a professional gardener and worked for Miss Albright, bossed poor Harry about a bit. In the second lived a brother and sister, the Harris's who kept turkeys and had a long productive garden with raspberries, gooseberries, etc., and we could get over the wall and sneak a few.

Another gap and another cottage up a long path. The Masters lived there with their sons, Tom, Steve and Joe. Next came two slightly bigger cottages, one of which was occupied by the Empsons and their large family, Bertha, Sid, Edna, Raymond, Tom, Leslie and Doug. Bertha was a special friend and Edna. They were very poor and had their tea out of jam jars, had no cups – I suppose they had broken them all.

Next came two more semi-detached houses of more superior appearance. The first one occupied by Mr and Mrs Avery and their only offspring, Frank. Mr Avery and Frank worked in the gardens and greenhouses at Finstall Park and became quite well off but never moved. The other house was occupied by a Mr and Mrs Gibson and two sons, Jimmy and Wilfred who for some reason was called Cali Gibson. When they left Levi Davies and his family came to live there and stayed there for many years.

On the other side the road opposite were two more decent sized houses where lived the schoolmaster Mr Davis, a Welshman who walked to Linthurst School night and morning. When he retired and went back to Wales the Crees took up residence there. There were no more houses at that time actually in the Back Lane but a row of stone cottages facing towards Aston Fields. Since that time the Back Lane has become Finstall Road and lots of new houses have been built but this is a description of Finstall in the 1920s.

We had about 1½ miles to walk to our school [Stoke Road, Aston Fields], a winding road in those days along Heydon Road, past Finstall Park, which was surrounded by a high wall along the top of which the more daring of us would walk coming home, we were in too much of a hurry when going to school. Past Finstall Churchyard and the little church in the churchyard where funeral services were then held and many a cortege we have followed up the path leading to it and watched with awe the coffins lowered into the

---

154 Not all these local children became agricultural labourers or worked on the railway. Fred Darley was awarded a scholarship to the County High School, continued to further education and became Head Pharmacist of the Bromsgrove General Hospital and other linked bodies, running a large department. His sister became Matron in a London hospital.

graves and the scent of the flowers so pungent and tied up with ribbon, purple or white. The churchyard is now derelict and the little church pulled down. I remember the figure of the Sexton or Verger in a long black robe, Jimmy Evans they called him, and sometimes he would take some of the kids down the crypt.

Just past the Stud Farm was a lane on the left which for the want of any other name we called Brooks Lane [Walnut Lane]. Just inside the lane was a long drive on the right leading up to Finstall Park House occupied by the Brooks family. A very grand house, they had a valet, a butler and various other servants. Sometimes we would venture up to sing a carol at Christmas time. Sometimes we were lucky but generally we were shooed off by one of the menservants. A long lane ran alongside the drive with high banks either side, the home of many wild birds, robins, tits, etc. who used to build their nests there high up and we would sometimes clamber up to see the eggs if ever we saw a bird fly out of the bank.

Further along on the left was a little house called Walnut Lodge approached by a flight of steps, it was quite a pretty house, a long path up to the door surrounded by flower beds either side. Here lived the Larcombe family, Mr and Mrs and Annie, the eldest, then came Billy, Reg and later Marjorie. Annie was my school friend for many years and won a free place to the Secondary School the same time as I did. She was a very bright girl and no doubt would have done well but her father became an invalid and they could not afford to keep her at school and they moved on and I lost touch with her.

The house where Mr Larcombe worked as gardener, chauffeur, etc., was a little further down the lane. It was called Walnut Cottage and a Mr Ryland lived there at that time, a large black and white house with its side to the lane.

On we go a few more bends and twists in the lane past the Park Stile and a long path, a short cut to Aston Fields for folks in the lane. Then we come to the crossroads, one leading to Tardebigge, one down the Tack Lane to the Station and straight on to Grimley House, again occupied by a branch of the Albright family.

Just inside this lane were a pair of cottages known as Crossbrook Cottages and in the first one lived the Lewis's, Tom and Betty and their Mother and Dad, who worked for the Albrights at Grimley and they were not too well off at that time. Their grandad, a Mr Wilson, lived with them. He was very old then, about 90. I became very friendly with Betty when she started at the Secondary School. They were both paid for and I used to keep her company a lot during the long summer vacation. I had a ramshackle old bike I borrowed from another member of the family and I taught Betty to ride up and down the Tack Lane. Tom was a bit of a wild one and would sometimes snatch the old bike off us and ride all over the place up and down the banks much to my dismay. I was afraid he would puncture the tyres and Betty would be shouting 'Tommy, Tommy, I'll tell Mother'.

In the summer of 1925 Tommy suddenly took ill. He was an ardent cricketer and I was told that a knock from a ball had suddenly caused his leg to go tubercular, but I don't know if that is true. He was in hospital for many months at Bromsgrove and, eventually died at the age of 15. Meanwhile while his father and mother were so busy looking after and visiting him I guess they didn't notice Betty too much. Anyway before Tommy died she was away from school for a few weeks with a very bad cold and when she came back with her mother to see the Head Teacher she came to the cloakroom and told us she had to go for a holiday to Weston. I remember her words so well. 'I don't know what's the matter with me but Mother does'. Later her Mother told me that she, Betty, had had a very bad time. That was the last I saw of her, she grew gradually worse and was sent home from Weston the week after Tommy died and in another week she was dead too and there were two funerals within a fortnight. She was only 14. That was sixty years ago and I never forgot them.

My grandfather, Samuel Frisby, was a brick and pottery manufacturer who lived at Tardebigge a couple of miles from us. Sadly he died before I was born and thereafter the once prosperous business declined, mainly due to bad debts of builders who had the bricks and then didn't pay up.

[Rene and her siblings usually visited their grandmother on Sundays, who was still living near the brickworks, by the canal.] Up Finstall Hill we would go to what we called the Foredrough, over the stile in Norman Hall's field, full of cows I was rather scared to pass, over another stile to the Withybrook [Lane], a long winding path whose banks in summer were filled with foxgloves, etc., and my father with his walking stick sometimes had to push back the brambles and nettles. There were rabbit holes by the score and rabbits scurrying back to them at the sound of our approach – it was beautiful on a sunny morning.

Irene Frisby and her brother Sam. (Andy Frisby)

Eventually we came out into Dusthouse Lane, the occupiers in their gardens would call out 'Good Morning' to us. In one of the cottages lived a gamekeeper who hung all the animals he had killed, stoats, weasels, etc., onto a tree in the garden to dry and rot in the sun. Horrible thoughts I have of them. A long trek then past Dusthouse Farm, Fanny Taylor feeding her chickens; the old man was blind and walked around with his stick.

Then we came into London Lane and an uphill walk till we finally came to the entrance to the Brickyard along a cart track, to a second gate where there were cocks and hens running about and a big turkey cock would come strutting towards us with all his feathers stuck out and was I scared of him, I dared not go past him by myself. In spring I could walk along the path round the clay pit to a little bit of pasture at the end and gather bluebells and cowslips, my favourite wild flowers. In summer towards the end, there were blackberries growing in glorious profusion all along the canal bank. In autumn we could collect nuts from the little coppice adjoining London Lane.

Appendix

Abstract of Title

of Miss M.C. Albright (deceased)
to land at Finstall at 27 May 1945

Ordnance Map No.	Stoke Prior Parish	Tenure	Tenant	Acreage
61a	Finstall Meadow, pasture	Copyhold	George James	7.9
66a	Finstall Piece, arable	Copyhold	George James	8.7
66a	Orchard Cottages	Copyhold		.350
67a	Blacksmith's shop	Copyhold	Mrs I Edwards	
	2 cottages and garden	Copyhold	Ruth Rolley & Mrs Worgin	1.157
115a	House & Garden (Finstall Mount)	Freehold	Charles R Sayer	.353
2301	Field adjoining	Freehold	Charles R Sayer	1.073
2301	Part of garden	Freehold	Charles R Sayer	.092
2302	Coombe Cottage & garden	Copyhold	Charles R Sayer	.169
	Bromsgrove Parish			
2248	Plantation	Freehold	George James	.150
2250	Vigo Meadow and shed, pasture	Freehold	George James	3.289
2251	Vigo Meadow, pasture	Freehold	George James	5.198
2251	Garden	Freehold	George James	.050
2252	Maltshovel Inn (now 3 cottages)	Freehold	Mrs Woodward & others	.411
2257	Plantation	Freehold	George James	
2261	Pleck building & cottage (High Barn?)	Freehold	George James	.375
2262	Pleck, pasture	Freehold	George James	1.041

2263	End Pit Meadow, pasture	Freehold	George James	8.030
2264	Longlands, arable	Freehold	George James	6.011
2265	Hanging Hill, pasture	Freehold	George James	6.699
2266	Old Hill, arable	Freehold	George James	9.873
Part 2267	Upper Pipes and Lower part, arable	Freehold	George James	5.146
Part 2267	Upper Pipes & Lower part, pasture	Freehold	George James	4.725
2268	Yew Tree Hill, pasture	Freehold	George James	8.289
2272	Embankment	Freehold	Charles Robert Sayers	.487
2273	Pikes Pool	Freehold	Charles Robert Sayers	1.113
2278	New meadow, pasture	Freehold	George James	6.219
2279	Railway Piece, arable	Freehold	George James	3.983
2281	Sheep Walk & part Pit Close, arable	Freehold	George James	9.160
2281	Sheep Walk & part Pit Close, pasture	Freehold	George James	3.767
2282	Calves Close, pasture	Freehold	George James	4.642
2283	Pool and Plantation	Freehold	George James	.110
2284	Hogg Hill, pasture	Freehold	George James	7.766
2285	The Seven Acres/Pool Piece, arable	Freehold	George James	13.626
2287	Spring Hill, pasture	Freehold	George James	5.175
2288	Garden, garden	Freehold	Miss Albright	.290
2289	Arable	Freehold	George James	5.536
2290	House Ground, pasture	Freehold	George James	1.028
2291	Finstall Meadow, pasture	Freehold	George James	4.351
2292	Roads		Miss Albright has easement	
2293	Garden	Freehold	George James	.575
2294	Finstall Farm buildings & yard	?Homestead	George James	.664
2295	Rickyard Field, arable	Freehold	George James	1.256
2296	Siden Meadow, pasture	Freehold	George James	4.638

2297	Quarry, pasture	Freehold	George James	4.653
2298	Finstall Piece, arable	Freehold	George James	2.993
2299	Garden Piece, arable	Freehold	George James	6.676
2300	The Green, garden	Freehold	Miss Albright	.612
2301	Carthorse Field, pasture	Freehold	George James	5.245
2302	Allotment Cottage & garden	Freehold	George James	.112
2303	Square Meadow, pasture	Freehold	George James	4.160
2305	Long Meadow, meadow	Freehold	George James	4.507
2306	Finstall Field, arable	Freehold	George James	3.307
2307	Withybrook Field, arable Tutnall	Freehold	George James	5.284
343	Burcot Holloway		Not known	6.072
344	Little End Pit, pasture			4.458
345	Top Ground, pasture			3.835
346/351	The Four Acres, The Six Acres, arable			11.161
347	The Top Piece, pasture			2.104
348	Orchard Field, arable			1.617
349	Orchard Field, arable			.674
350	Orchard, pasture			1.617
365	House & premises			1.464
367	House Ground, pasture			4.051
368	Long Meadow, meadow			1.810

Birmingham Archives, BA 10787/25/ii

Bibliography

Much detail and background has been drawn from the following:

Birmingham Library, Wolfson Centre for Archival Research

British Library Newspapers online

Bromsgrove Society Journals, *The Rousler*

Bromsgrove, Redditch and Droitwich Weekly Messenger, 1860 onwards, online

Brotherton Collection, for house sale prospectuses and photographs, private collection in Bromsgrove

Census Returns, online

Ordnance Survey maps, pre 1965

Palmer's and Kelly's Directories, Bromsgrove Library

Worcestershire Archive and Archaeology Service, The Hive

Publications

Banner, David J., *Piano Row: Childhood Memories 1940s-1950s in Aston Fields & Finstall*, privately published, 1996

Billington, Neville, *Flint and Steel: The Story of the Founding of the Institution of Mechanical Engineers*, Came Hundred Publishing, 2010

Billington, Neville & Sheffield, Warwick, *The Wrangler who went to the Railway: The Story of the Life and Death of William Creuze BA*, Came Hundred Publishing, 2010

Bowen, Philip, *Bromsgrove School at War 1914-19*, Bromsgrove School, 2014

Brooks, Alan and Nikolaus Pevsner, *Worcestershire: The Buildings of England*, Yale University Press, 2007

Cox, Thomas, *Worcestershire*, T. Cox, London, 1720

Dickens, Margaret, *A Thousand Years in Tardebigge*, Cornish Brothers, 1931

Dyer, Christopher, *Bromsgrove: a small town in Worcestershire in the Middle Ages*, Worcestershire Historical Society, 2000

Ekwall, E., *Concise Oxford Dictionary of Place Names*, OUP, 1936

Foster, John (Ed), *Bygone Bromsgrove*, Bromsgrove Society, 1981

Fowler, Rae, *Burcot Millennium, 2000 AD*, Burcot Village Hall Committee, 2000

Gaut, R.C., *A History of Worcestershire Agriculture and Rural Evolution*, Littlebury & Co Ltd, 1939

Grierson, Janet, *St Godwald's: A Parish and its People*, St Godwald's PCC, 1984

Henderson, Simon, *Fairly Mounted on a Hill: Bromsgrove's Church and its People*, Kissed Off Publications, 2015

Hurst, Derek et al, *Dodderhill Through the Ages*, Dodderhill Parish Survey Project, 2011

Icely, H.E.M., *Bromsgrove School through Four Centuries*, Blackwell, 1953

Leadbetter, William G., *The Story of Bromsgrove*, 1946

McGregor-Smith, Jennie, *From Bromsgrove to Aston Fields: a story of Victorian expansion*, Brewin Books, 2008

Middlemass, Barbara, *John Corbett, Pillar of Salt, 1817-1901*, Revised Edition, 2017

Nokes, BCG, *Finstall Parish Handbook*, Friends of St Godwald, 1958

Notes & Queries for Bromsgrove and the district of Central Worcestershire, Volumes I, II, III, IV, Bromsgrove Messenger Office, 1909-1914

Pugh, John, *The Bromsgrove that I knew: a personal memoir*, Daily Mail Publication by Central Services, 2005

Scaplehorn, Alan & Swann, Connie, *Worcestershire Turnpike Trusts and Tollhouses*, Milestone Society, 2009

Stubbs, Pamela, *Finstall War Memorial*, privately published, 1988

White, Revd. Alan, *A Hundred Years in Tardebigge: The Parish in the Twentieth Century*, Brewin Books, 2011

Wilks, Mick, *Chronicles of Worcestershire Home Guard*, Logaston Press, 2014

Unpublished

Fredrick, Serena, *Place Names in Northeast Worcestershire: The Impact of Feckenham Forest and the Lickey Watershed*

Page, Edmund, *Memoirs*

Thompson, Ann, *Memories of Bygone Finstall*

Index

A

A448 (see Highway)
Adams, Captain John, 64, 156
Adams, John and Kay, 138
Ainge, Samuel, 138
Albright & Wilson, 154-155
Albright, Arthur, 42, 84, 151, 154
Albright, Alfred Beaumont and Mabel (May), 71, 72, 101
Albright, Maria Catherine, 32-38, 106, 155, 168
Albright, Dinah, 72
Albright family, 28-40, 72
Albright, Jocelyn, 39, 40, 60, 71-75, 87, 101
Albright, Rachel Patience, 31, 72
Albright, William Arthur, 71, 118, 142, 155
Alcester Road (turnpike), 163
Aldham, A, 90, 97, 99, 105
Allbutt, E, 66
Allbutt, W, 11
Allotment Cottage, 37-39, 74, 106, 144, 168
Allotments, 39, 45, 73, 144
Ansell, Edward, 93
Ansells Brewery, 93
Appleshaw, 103
Archer, H.B., architect, 135
Architects:
  Archer, H.B., 135
  Axten, Edmund, 132
  Chatwin, P.B., 132-133
  Cotton, John, 53, 58, 60, 64, 107, 148, 153
  Edge, Charles, 88, 90
  Gadd, G.H., 57

Green, Philip, 32, 146
  Jordan, Robert Furneaux, 103-104
Ardenvale Schools, Ltd., 60
Ashdene, 37, 146-147
Ashmore family, 12, 13, 82, 105
Ashmore, Benjamin, 153
Ashwin family, 151
Avery family, 59, 123, 146, 174
Axten, Edmund, 132

B

Ball, Captain J.F.A., 108
Barrow, James and Dorothy, 66, 71, 100
Bayley, Dennis Darby, 124
Beilby, Dr. Julius Henry, 56
Bell, Thomas, 11, 12, 150
Bell, William, 8, 11, 12
Bevan, William and Susannah, 44
Bird, John, 111
Blackford family, 23, 25
Blacksmith, 12, 38-39, 41, 42, 165
Blackwell Adventure: see Scouts
Blackwell Court, 57, 173
Blake, Harold, 36
Blizard family, 121, 140
Boot Inn, The – see Coombe Cottage
Bott, Albert John, 151
Boulders, 99
Boult, Sir Adrian and Ann, 121
Boy Scout Association – see Scouts
Brazier, J & A, builders, 59, 93
Brettell, Ananias, 17, 71
Brettell family, 16, 21-22, 51
Brettell, Joseph, 97

Brettell, Mary 21-22
Brettell, Richard, 17, 41
Brettell, Thomas, 13, 70, 71, 97, 105
Brockencote, 18
Bromsgrove Cavalry, 157
Bromsgrove Golf Centre, 115
Bromsgrove Highway, see Highway
Brooks, Boultbee, 57, 87, 155
Brooks, John Boultbee, 44, 49, 50, 55-58, 76, 78, 137, 140
Brooks, Wilfred and Pauline, 137, 171
Brotherton, Tim (R.B.), 74
Butler, A.W. Cadbury, 79

C
Cadbury, Barrow, 79
Cadbury, William Adlington, 79
Caspidge House, 14, 84, 117
Chance, Hugh and family, 50, 119, 160
Chapel-of-Ease, Finstall, 18-19, 174
Chatwin, P.B., architect, 132-133
Chetle, Thomas, 8-9, 11
Clayton, Alderman Francis Corder, 30, 85, 117-118
Clovelly Cottage/House – see Stud Farm
Collett, Dr, 63
Cond family (see Cund)
Connard family, 13
Conscientious objectors, 36
Coombe Cottage (Boot Inn), 36, 38, 47, 139, 141-142, 144, 172
Corbett, John, 89-90, 92
Cordell family, 105, 110
Cottam, William and Jemima, 126
Cotton, John, 53, 58, 60, 64, 107, 148, 153
Cotton, Jessie and family, 159
Crops:
  Flax, 23-24, 61
  Hemp, 23, 61-62
  Hops, 62
  Linen, 23-24
  Oakum, 62
  Potatoes, 61, 64, 164
  Watercress, 83, 84
Cross Inn, The, 46-48, 171
Crossbrook cottages, 58, 103, 175
Crossbrook House (Cottage), 102
Cullwick, John, 150
Cund/Cond family, 43-44, 158, 167
Cutler, A. Charles and family, 67-68, 157

D
Daylesford, 144
Deague, Josiah, 48, 58, 146-7, 171
Dixon, T & M, 108, 110, 171
Downwood, 103
Dugard, Benjamin and family, 20, 70
Dugard, Henry, 63, 70
Dugard, William 63
Dusthouse, The, 105, 110
Dusthouse Cottages, 108, 110

E
Eadie, Albert, 93-94
Edge, Charles, (see Architects)
Edwards, William, 16
Ellins family, 23-27, 41, 20, 13, 49, 62, 63, 95, 125
Eldon, 146
Elmwood, 98, 123, 165
Empson, George, postman and family, 140
Everitt family, 98
Everitt, Douglas, 133
Everitt, Ernest Montague, JP, 58, 157
Everitt, racehorses (see Stud Farm)
Everitt, William, 49, 50, 53-54, 71, 76-77, 98, 123, 125-126, 132, 149

F
Fairview (Fairways), 98, 123
Farms:
   Caspidge, 13, 30, 86, 112 for Chapter 15, 116
   Crossbrook, 19, 65-66, 100, 110
   Dusthouse, 19, 58, 98, 105, 109
   Finch End, 14, 19, 58, 73, 97-99
   Finstall, 15, 13, 28, 37, 40, 48, 105, 168
   Gambolds, 19, 58, 98
   High Barn, 39, 135, 151
   Hill Farm, 19
   Hollow Tree, 11, 13, 30, 107
   Hopgardens, 61, 68-69, 71, 112
   Old Hill, 30
   Slideslow, 112
   Stoke Cross, 20, 105-106
   Stonehouse, 19, 37, 58, 103, 105-106
   Tack (Finstall Park Farm), 19-20, 53, 59, 71, 100
   Tutnall House, 12, 144, 152
   Tutnall Hall, 12, 30, 39, 86
Featherstone, Francis, 46, 105
Featherstone, John and family, 18, 48, 105, 136, 139
Fidkin, John, 17-18
Finch End Farm (see Farms)
Finstall Cottage (school), 59, 148
Finstall Cottage (see Stud Farm)
Finstall Croft, 49, 93, 135-138, 171
Finstall Farm (see Farms)
Finstall Gardens, 67, 140, 171
Finstall House (ex. Finstall Farm), 11, 16, 21, 40, 48, 152
Finstall Mount, 138-139, 167
Finstall Park/House, 58, 174-175
Finstall Park Preparatory School, 59, 143, 164
Finstall Terrace, 32, 42, 72, 173

Flax – see Crops
Fletcher, John and Joinery, 113, 121
Foot and Mouth, 65-66, 100
Foxlydiate House, 14
Frisby, Samuel, 176
Frisby, Irene (Brake), 139, Chapter 22

G
Gadd, G.H., 57
Gambolds, see Farms
Gardner, John, 97
Gardner, Thomas, 12, 14-15, 30, 83, 154
Golf, 115
Goodman, Robert and Peggie, 107
Goodman, Captain Edwin and Muriel, 58, 103, 108
Goodman family, 162, 165
Goodman, Herbert and Agnes, 127
Gospel Hall, 148
Green, Philip (see Architects)
Griffin family, 97, 100, 132
Grimley Hall (House), 19, 21, 32, 66, 71
Guise, Joseph and family, 113, 116-117,
Gunton, Major Philip, 144, 161
Grosvenor family, 123

H
Halfyear family, 171
Hall family, 67, 140, 159-160, 171, 176
Harford, George, 47, 141
Harper, Philip, 99
Harvey family, 24, 100-101
Hedges, William and family, 43, 146
Hemp, see Crops
Henzey family, 16
Hewell & District Nursing Association, 72
Heydon family, 129, 130, 172
Heydon Road, 129, 147
High Barn (see Farms)

Index

Highbank Cottages, 45
Highway, Redditch/Bromsgrove, 40, 113, 121, 136
Hill Farm, see Farms
Hillcoat family, 139
Hobbs, Topsy and Bill, 33-34, 81, 145
Holiday bungalow, Vigo, 154
Hollowtree Farm (see Farms)
Holmes, Stanley and family, 146, 170
Holyoake, James, 88, 91
Holyoak, John (Bromsgrove), 65
Holyoak, John (Droitwich), 67
Hopgarden Farm (see Farms)
Horton, Thomas and family, 36, 74, 143
Housman, Rev. Thomas and Mrs., 21-22, 71

I
Impey, Enid Croft, 135
Impey, Frank, 67, 94

J
James, George, 151
James, John, 86
Jeptha, William, 100
Johnson, Richard William and Sarah, 13, 14, 84
Jones, Ernest R., 94
Jones, Newton and Margaret, 67
Jordan, John, 103-104
Jordan, Robert Furneaux, 103-104
Judge, Herbert E. and Olivette, 137

K
Keeper's Cottage (Park Cottage), 58
Kerr, Colonel William Harcourt, 37, 40, 110, 152
Kinder, Thos. William, 89
Kirkwood, John, 140-141
Knight, Francis, 11

L
Littlehall, 134-135
Lodge, Finstall Park, 60, 21, 131
Lord, E. Courtney, 104
Lynwood (see Allotment Cottage)

M
Mackmillan, James, 17, 41
Maltshovel, Vigo, 13, 153
Malvern View, 39, 155
Mariemont, 31
Marsland, E.C., 69
Martino, Edward B, 68
Mebb, G, 35, 37, 151
Moore, William, 62, 144
Morcom, A. Rupert and Mary, 128
Morris family, 115
Mumberson, Ian, 152

N
National Trust, The, 35, 40, 60, 72, 75, 149
Newbold, Harry, 168-169, 173
Nostrebor (see Farms, Caspidge)

O
Oakalls, The, 6, Chapter 9, 69, 71
Old Hill Farm, later Tutnall Hall Farm (see Farms)
Old Smithy (see Blacksmith)
Orchard Cottages, 35, 45, 166

P
Page family, 56, 125-126, 160
Palmer, William, 52-53
Pancheri Robert, 33
Park Cottage (Keeper's Cottage) 58
Park Stores, 101, 147
Parker, David and Monica, 104
Parkes, Thomas Farmer, 12, 30, 150-151, 154

Pearman family, 68, 101, 158
Penmanor, 80-81
Perkins, Anne Maria, 108
Perkins, Edward, 65
Pikes Pool, 13, 30, 39, 82, 139
Pikes Pool Lane (Turnpike Lane), 11, 82, 173
Plymouth, Lord (Rt. Hon. Lord Windsor), 12, 107-108, 157
Post Office, 35, 44, 72, 167, 170
Price, Joseph, 48, 141
Priestman, Bertram: painting, 34
Pugh Jones, farmer, 101, 148

Q
Quakers, 28, 38-40, 67, 118-119, 135, 163, 168
Quarries, 4, 49, 96, 111, 140
Quinney family, 97-98, 100, 123, 162, 165

R
Racehorses (see Stud Farm)
Railway
  Birmingham & Gloucester Railway Company, 22, 12, 115
  Bromsgrove Railway Carriage & Wagon Company, 14
  Midland Railway Company, 85
Rapkin, G.J., 139, 161
Redditch Highway (see Highway)
Ridgeway, The, 151-152
Rigby Hall, 20, 23-24, 41, 63, 88 (Chapter 9)
Robertson family, 121
Robson, William, 63
Rockville, 67
Rogers family, 113
Rose & Crown, Lickey, 8, 188
Miss Rose, 169

Miss M. Rose, 44
Round, Simeon, 110
Routh, Ivy, 44
Rugby Club, 60, 149
Rutherford, Joseph, 25
Ryland Centre, 133
Ryland family, 133, 161-162

S
Salt, 27
Sanders family, 13, 63
Sayer, Charles R., 85, 138, 142, 167
Scarfe, Thomas, 25
School (see Finstall Cottage)
Scotch House (The Vale House) 87, 123, 125-129
Scott, Dr. E. Jebb and Kate, 55
Scouts, 59, 87, 129
Shaw, James, 52, 91
Sheldon family, 6-7, 11
Sheldon, Captain William, 6-9, 11, 15
Simon, Bombardier Raoul de Paravicini, 68
Slideslow Farm (see Farms)
Smallwood, Robert and family, 52, 85, 91-93, 95, 126
Smallwood, Rupert, 156
Society of Friends (see Quakers)
St Ludger, Joseph and family, 137-138
Stevens, Joseph and Mary Ann and family, 106, 159
Stoke Cross Farm (see Farms)
Stoke Grange, 90
Stone Cottages, 49, 72, 174
Stonehouse Farm/House (see Farms)
Stonehurst (see Finstall Croft), 138
Stud Farm, 54, 58, 76 Chapter 11, 78, 80
Suffield, Sherwood and family, 37, 39, 59, 105, 144, 148, 166, 167
Suffrage, Women's, 35, 143

Swinson, Dr. Henry, 102
Swire, Dr. Jim and Jane, 121-122

T
Tack Farm (Finstall Park Farm), (see Farms)
Taylor, Charles, 88
Taylor, John and Eleanor, 110
Tennant, A., 55
Thomas, Lou and Jessie, 60
Tilt, Frederick and Eliza, 101
Tilt, Joseph, builder, 44, 113, 118
Townsend, Alfred, 48
Turnpike Lane (see Pikes Pool Lane)
Turnpike Road, 163
Tutnall Hall Farm (see Farms)
Tutnall House, 153
Tutnall Mount, 152
Tutnall Mount (Whitegates), 152
The Vale (see Scotch House)

V
Vaughan, Major Douglas J., 68
Vernon, Thomas William, 89
Vigo Close, 151
Village Hall, 32, 167-168
Vineyard Schools, 128

W
Wagon Works (see Railway)
Walduck, Henry and Gertrude and family, 119, 159
Waller, Gerald Lee (Gerry) and Mabel (Bunny), 59
Walnut Cottage, 131-132, 175
Walnut Lane, Chapter 17, 131
Walnut Lodge, 175
Walton, Brigadier Bendyshe Brome (Ben), 144

War
  Boer Wars, 157
  Civil War, The, Chapter 2, 6
  WWI: deaths of Finstall men, 106, 157
  WWII: deaths of Finstall men
    Home Guard, 162
    life in the village, 128, 163
Ward, Thomas Hanbury, 102
Warr, James and Sarah née Featherstone, 139
Warrington, Rev. Percy Ewart and Miss Lilian, 79-80
Warwickshire Monthly Meeting, see Quakers
Water, 82, Chapter 12, 84, 108
Wheatfields, see Finch End Farm under Farms
Wheelock family, 114, 118, 159
Whitegates, see Tutnall Mount
Wilde, John and Mary, 97
Wilkes, John, 11
Wilson, John Joseph, 113
Windsor, Rt. Hon. Lord, see Plymouth
Winn, Godfrey and his mother, 68, 161
Withybrook bridlepath, 107, 176
Withybrook Cottage, 107
Women's Suffrage Society, 36, 143,
Women's Institute, 33-34, 59
Woodfield, 140-141
Wright, Sydney Fowler, 133
Wynn, E.V., 103

By the same author:

*Victorian Greenhill, Burcot to Blackwell:
The Development of a Worcestershire Lane*,
Coombe Cottage Books, 2000

*John Cotton: The Life of a
Midlands Architect 1844-1934*,
Coombe Cottage Books, 2002

*From Bromsgrove to Aston Fields:
A Story of Victorian Expansion*,
Brewin Books, 2008